# Records of Girlhood

# Records of Girlhood

## An anthology of nineteenth-century women's childhoods

*Edited by*
Valerie Sanders

## Ashgate

Aldershot • Burlington USA • Singapore • Sydney

Published by

Ashgate Publishing Ltd
Gower House, Croft Road,
Aldershot, Hampshire GU11 3HR
England

Ashgate Publishing Company
131 Main Street
Burlington, Vermont 05401
USA

Ashgate website: http://www.ashgate.com

ISBN  0 7546 0148 X


**British Library Cataloguing-in-Publication Data**
   Records of Girlhood: an anthology of nineteenth-century women's childhoods. —
      (The nineteenth century series)
      1. Autobiography — Woman authors — History and criticism.
      2. Girls — Great Britain — Social conditions. 3. Childhood in literature.
      4. Great Britain — Social conditions — 19th century.
      I. Sanders, Valerie
      820.9'354


**US Library of Congress Cataloging-in-Publication Data**
   Records of Girlhood: an anthology of nineteenth-century women's childhoods /
   edited by Valerie Sanders.
         p.  cm. — (The nineteenth century)
      Contents: Amelia Opie — Dorothea Herbert — Mary Martha Sherwood —
      Mary Somerville — Lady Caroline Lamb — Charlotte Elizabeth — Anna Jameson
      — Mary Howitt — Sara Coleridge — Fanny Kemble — Elizabeth Sewell —
      Frances Power Cobbe — Charlotte M. Yonge — Annie Besant
      (alk. paper)
      1. Girls—Biography. 2. Autobiographies—Women authors. 3. Women authors,
      English—Biography. 4. Biography—19th century. I. Sanders, Valerie.
      II. Nineteenth century (Aldershot, England)
      CT3205 .R43 2000
      941.081'0835'2—dc21


This volume is printed on acid-free paper.

Printed and bound in Great Britain by MPG Books Ltd, Bodmin, Cornwall

# Contents

# The Nineteenth Century General Editors' Preface

The aim of this series is to reflect, develop and extend the great burgeoning of interest in the nineteenth century that has been an inevitable feature of recent decades, as that former epoch has come more sharply into focus as a locus for our understanding not only of the past, but also of the contours of our modernity. Though it is dedicated principally to the publication of original monographs and symposia in literature, history, cultural analysis, and associated fields, there will be a salient role for reprints of significant texts from, or about, the period. This, we believe, distinguishes our project from comparable ones, and means, for example, that in relevant areas of scholarship we both recognize and cut innovatively across such parameters as those suggested by the designations 'Romantic' and 'Victorian'. We welcome new ideas, while valuing tradition. It is hoped that the world which predates yet so forcibly predicts and engages our own will emerge in parts, as a whole, and in the lively currents of debate and change that are so manifest an aspect of its intellectual, artistic and social landscape.

Vincent Newey
Joanne Shattock
University of Leicester

# Acknowledgements

I am grateful to Professor Joanne Shattock for her encouragement of this project, and to the members of the Graduate Studies seminar at the University of Leicester for their constructive response to an earlier version of the Introduction given as a paper for discussion. For permission to quote from Sara Coleridge's *Autobiography*, thanks are due to the Harry Ransom Humanities Research Center, the University of Texas at Austin, and the Coleridge Estate. I am also grateful to the Theosophical Publishing House, Adyar, Chennai 600 020, India, for permission to reproduce passages from Annie Besant's *Autobiography*. Every attempt has been made to trace other copyright permissions. I apologize if there are any outstanding.

# 1

# Introduction

> I had led a very unhappy life as a child – had no scope for my very
> violent feelings of affection – had no brothers and sisters to live with –
> never had had a father – from my unfortunate circumstances was not on
> a comfortable footing with my mother ... – much as I love her now – and
> did not know what a happy domestic life was![1]

These are not the reminiscences of a deprived twentieth-century child from a broken home, but Queen Victoria confiding in her eldest daughter, the Princess Royal, whose childhood, she hoped, had been happier than her mother's. Although the upbringing of a queen is unlikely to be representative of her generation, Victoria's extract shares one characteristic with those in this anthology: a sense of unsatisfied emotion, the 'very violent feelings of affection', which seem to have been the hallmark of nineteenth-century autobiographers, men as well as women, writing about their childhood.

According to Simone de Beauvoir, 'women more than men cling to childhood memories'. They recall childhood, she argues, as a time of freedom and independence, with the future open before them, whereas as adults their horizons dwindle: 'once they were to conquer the world, now they are reduced to generality: one housewife and housekeeper among millions of others'.[2] Childhood gives them individuality and ambition, which absorption into the adult world subsequently removes. Nonetheless, all the best-known nineteenth-century autobiographical accounts of childhood – outside fiction – are by men. The enduring images are of William Wordsworth consumed with guilt over the boat-stealing episode in *The Prelude*, John Stuart Mill learning Greek at three, Anthony Trollope being tormented by fellow Harrovians, Charles Dickens in the blacking warehouse, appalled that he could so easily have been cast away, and John Ruskin, denied toys, studying patterns in the carpet, and being allowed, as a special treat, to eat his father's left-over custard. Judging by the absence of Victorian women's autobiographies in print today (Margaret Oliphant's and Harriet Martineau's are the only ones recently reprinted, and Sara Coleridge's appears at the back of Bradford Keyes Mudge's biography),[3] it would be easy to assume that none were written – or that their childhood memories were channelled into fiction, such as

*Jane Eyre* and *The Mill on the Floss*. Critics of autobiography, with a few exceptions, are still reluctant to stray away from the established canon, stretching from St Augustine to Henry James, and on the whole, the recovery of women's autobiography has been uphill work, performed by women critics focusing specifically on an alternative female canon.[4] The primary object of this anthology is to correct the impression that Romantic and Victorian women had little to say about themselves in autobiography, and to suggest that far from being silent, they were writing some of the best material on childhood of the century. The reasons why their work has been overlooked for so long are many and complex, inextricably tied to the history of canon formation.

The nineteenth century was the great age of autobiography; yet most of the works excerpted in this collection have been out of print for many years. At the time, however, women's autobiographies were widely reviewed and applauded. No less a critic than Henry James claimed that Fanny Kemble's was 'one of the most animated autobiographies in the language',[5] and Harriet Martineau's quickly became one of the most controversial, with its outspoken attack on her undemonstrative mother, and spirited defence of a literary single life. Nor were these isolated productions. Actresses, novelists, scientists, Quakers, philanthropists and reformers all rushed to record their first stirrings of success, their difficulties and triumphs, their hopes for the future, and criticisms of the past. Daughters put together their mothers' unfinished memoirs; friends supplied reminiscences; reviewers made comparisons between women's accounts of their lives; women themselves read each other's works, and, in some cases, were conscious of doing something different from their male contemporaries. 'I have been reading the life of Mr Symonds,' wrote Margaret Oliphant in the middle of her *Autobiography* (1899), 'and it makes me almost laugh (though little laughing is in my heart) to think of the strange difference between this prosaic little narrative, all about the facts of a life so simple as mine, and his elaborate self-discussions.'[6]

Oliphant recognized that women were outsiders when it came to writing autobiography. Their lives were meant to be private and hidden, not emblazoned for all to read. As Laura Marcus has shown, the Victorians had clear ideas as to who was meant to write autobiography and who not: 'Autobiography proper is perceived to be the right of very few individuals: those whose lives encompassed an aspect or image of the age suitable for transmission to posterity.'[7] Women clearly fell outside this category, as being in no sense representative of the age. They took no part in politics or business, they invented nothing, they failed to exhibit anything important at the Royal Academy, they contributed little to public debate. Those who did write justified their entry into a male arena on the grounds that they were passing their experiences on to their children, or teaching the public something useful about childcare and household management. 'The life of a woman entirely devoted to her family duties and to scientific pursuits affords little scope for a biography', Mary Somerville's daughter Martha prefaces her mother's *Personal Reminiscences* (1873), apparently unaware of any disjunction between the housewifely life and the 'scientific pursuits', though this, of course, was exactly what made women controversial.[8] Mrs Somerville largely got away with it by playing up her ordinary homeliness, but even in 1873, her daughter took a defensive stance. Women were traditionally the 'Other', not the centre of attention. As Linda Anderson has argued, autobiography 'enacts an active appropriation of identity – the laying claim to both a life and a text'.[9] In the nineteenth century, therefore, women were doubly transgressive in writing about themselves, and claiming a place in the history of their times.

Yet women's autobiography, however hidden, has always been there, shadowing men's. One of the paradoxes of nineteenth-century literary history is that whatever was said publicly about autobiography being inappropriate for women, women themselves were busy writing it. Interest in the fictional female *Bildungsroman* was keen, as was evident from the excited reception of *Jane Eyre* (announced, on its title page, as 'An Autobiography') and the controversies over Maggie's fate in *The Mill on the Floss*. The most popular Victorian novels traced the evolution of female, rather than male lives – as novels have largely done before and since – and novelists focused intently on the childhood of their heroines, their emotional needs, and progress towards married life. If the first twenty years of their lives had a rich appeal to novelists, autobiographers were likely to benefit from the stimulus of example. Setting aside, for a moment, the vexed question of definition, which has plagued autobiography criticism without reaching a satisfactory resolution, what we might broadly call 'self-writing' by women has existed since at least the days of Margery Kempe and Julian of Norwich; it flourished in the seventeenth century with Margaret Cavendish, Lucy Hutchinson and Lady Halkett; dipped into scurrility in the eighteenth, with Con Phillips and Charlotte Charke; resurfaced more respectably in the nineteenth, and is still going strong in the twentieth, with Simone de Beauvoir and Kathleen Raine at one extreme, and the Duchess of York at the other. But writing about the self is not the same as writing autobiography. 'The genuine autobiographic effort', according to Karl J. Weintraub, 'is guided by a desire to discern and to assign meaning to a life'.[10] Partly because it fails to meet the more austere criteria established by (male) critics of autobiography, such as Weintraub, Philippe Lejeune and Georges Gusdorf, women's autobiography has often been seen as a sub-genre: too closely related to memoirs and reminiscences and other biographical ephemera to match the inflexible entry qualifications of a strictly demarcated canon. Too often, it fails to present a unified image of a developing persona examining the evolution of a successful life, and interpreting its philosophical significance. It seems to be more than a matter of semantic convenience that the first serious theorists of autobiography as a genre used the pronoun 'he' when defining the typical autobiographer and his work. Leslie Stephen felt it was actually imperative on men to write about themselves: 'As every sensible man is exhorted to make his will, he should also be bound to leave his descendants some account of his experience of life.' Stephen's essay on 'Autobiography' (1881) employs a consistently virile vocabulary to evoke the right mood of energy and struggle which he sees as being essential to the autobiographer's art.[11] While Stephen stresses the autobiographer's vanity and willing exposure of his follies and vices (failings women could not afford to indulge), Georges Gusdorf argues that 'autobiography appeases the more or less anguished uneasiness of an aging man who wonders if his life has not been lived in vain, frittered away haphazardly, ending now in simple failure' – an uneasiness more likely, perhaps, to depress the average woman.[12] Either way, autobiography is seen essentially as a masculine activity, with a strong public dimension, and those Victorians who discussed autobiography as a historical genre rarely mentioned any women practitioners of it. 'Perhaps', argues Roy Pascal, 'one might say that it involves the philosophical assumption that the self comes into being only through interplay with the outer world.'[13] Though women went on publishing autobiography, pronouncements of this kind ensured that it remained unacknowledged, and consequently undiscussed, for many years.

Partly, too, the problem is that the women themselves are no longer famous. Although they were household names in their own time, few people have now heard of Elizabeth Sewell, Sara Coleridge, Mary Somerville or Fanny Kemble, though they probably know something about Wordsworth, John Stuart Mill, Trollope, Ruskin, Darwin, Newman, and all the other celebrated male autobiographers of the last century. The Victorian women everyone knows – the Brontës, George Eliot, Elizabeth Gaskell, Florence Nightingale – wrote autobiographically, but did not write autobiography. Nevertheless, all the women in this selection lived more or less extraordinary lives, broke with convention, and established themselves in careers of their own choosing. Their childhoods are vividly remembered, and treated more seriously than the childhoods of many Victorian men anxious to hurry over their earliest years and reach the period of intellectual development and success. In several cases, such as Sara Coleridge's and Charlotte M. Yonge's, their childhood was the only section that did get written. Women either died, or lost interest in their autobiographical writing before they could complete the story of their adult lives. It was as if childhood was the most emotionally intense period of their existence, and the most vividly remembered – as for Catherine Earnshaw in *Wuthering Heights*. Yet it was rarely the happiest. The struggle for recognition by many nineteenth-century women becomes all the more remarkable in the light of their often unpropitious beginnings.

Why childhood? Why did women write about this period of their lives with so much energy and curiosity? Traditionally, of course, women have a closer relationship with childhood than men do; as mothers, nurses, governesses or elder sisters, they have historically been responsible for raising children and writing about them. It is hard to imagine any woman autobiographer writing, as T.H. Huxley did in his brief autobiography, 'I have next to nothing to say about my childhood'; or, like David Hume, writing only one page about his; or, like Mark

Pattison, deciding to omit his altogether, so as to hurry on to his time at Oxford.[14] Nineteenth-century women, by contrast, keenly examined their earliest years, writing at length and in detail about their first visual memories, their first long journeys, their fears and embarrassments. Childhood can easily be made entertaining and impersonal, and with so many subjects regarded as taboo for women writers, it was one of relatively few areas freely available to them, a legitimate domestic theme with distinct educational potential. Childhood is both intensely individual and entirely commonplace. Although children are egotists, and the childhood section of autobiography asks the reader to be interested in apparently trivial incidents, quirkiness of character can be made endearing and acceptable in children – a source of amusing anecdotes – whereas in adult women it becomes an embarrassment, something to be concealed, rather than written about. Women who wanted to celebrate their individuality stood a better chance of doing so without criticism if they wrote about themselves as precocious or mischievous children, and there was ample precedent in fiction. Yet however great the variation in detail, or the apparent eccentricity of the family under scrutiny, readers could be counted on to identify with the shared emotional experience of being young, frustrated, and powerless. As Ethel Smyth has argued, the early section of an autobiography is like a 'Diary of a Nobody': 'the daily life described in the first part of these chronicles might be that of any English family in analogous circumstances, and my own confessions the autobiography of any child'.[15]

At the same time, women writers have always been concerned with the hidden emotions of very specific and individual children. Seeing their lives as exemplary in some way, they offer their experiences as a means of understanding more about childhood, and improving the care of growing minds and bodies. This was certainly Anna Jameson's aim in her essay, 'A Revelation of Childhood' (1854), which puts the case for a far deeper understanding of the child's world of 'instincts, perceptions, experiences, pleasures, and pains, lying there without self-consciousness' (p. 77 of this anthology). By investigating her own emotional landmarks as a child, going back to babyhood, when she was disturbed by the sound of music, Jameson hopes to throw some light on the 'the under current, the hidden, the unmanaged or unmanageable' (p. 79) of childhood experience. The primary achievement of nineteenth-century women autobiographers is this very determination to articulate the fleeting but deeply complex web of impressions received by themselves as children, and to find new forms of language to represent them.

The women included in this anthology were all born between 1769 and 1847, and though their autobiographies are technically Victorian, roughly half lived through the Romantic period, the era of introspection and special attention to childhood experience. It was a congenial context for self-writing, as Anne K. Mellor has pointed out: 'Central to the construction of both masculine and feminine Romanticism is the conception and linguistic representation of the self.'[16] On the other hand, this 'linguistic representation of the self' was fraught with problems, for men as well as women. Even Wordsworth acknowledged it was 'a thing unprecedented in literary history that a man should talk so much about himself' in devoting a thirteen-book epic to an account of his own spiritual evolution.[17] For reasons which are still being examined by scholars recovering the lost ground of female Romanticism, the male self-image of the period – heroic, solitary, moody, communing with nature and detesting society – was distinctly problematic for women writers, poets or otherwise, who were contemporary with the 'six male poets' synonymous with English Romanticism. Many women simply had no choice but to participate in society, to marry, have children, and run households. Moodiness in women was too often confounded with hysteria or instability to be worth cultivating as an aesthetic stance. Two key Romantic women, Dorothy Wordsworth and Mary Shelley, repeatedly present themselves as subservient, apologetic figures on the edges of an illustrious male circle. 'I did not make myself the heroine of my tales,' confesses Mary Shelley in the 1831 preface to *Frankenstein*:

> Life appeared to me too common-place an affair as regarded myself. I could not figure to myself that romantic woes or wonderful events would ever be my lot; but I was not confined to my own identity, and I could people the hours with creations far more interesting to me at that age than my own sensations.[18]

Both Meena Alexander and Anne Mellor suggest that women Romantics turn more than men to their own physicality:[19] Dorothy Wordsworth often mentions her headaches and illnesses; she is always interested in the material details of how people survive, while Mary Shelley stresses the radically different conception of human existence held by women who have given birth. The most compelling parts of *Frankenstein* have traditionally been the 'birth' of the Creature, and his struggle for survival; the details of what he eats and how he keeps warm, which were also what Dorothy Wordsworth observed in the Leech-gatherer. Women's ego boundaries, seen by theorists such as Nancy Chodorow[20] as being more permeable than men's, dissolve in Romantic women's writing as they forget their own troubles for a while and enter the anxious psyches of outcasts: hence the hidden nature of Romantic women's autobiography, which is to be found in prefaces, letters and appendices; fragments of memoirs inserted into the lives of others, or brought in by biographers writing posthumously. Coleridge's daughter Sara was one of few women directly connected with the best-known male Romantics who began writing an autobiography, and even she died before she had completed her childhood memories. Although a sense of her own inferiority to her brothers and inadequate relationship with her father pervades what she does write, embedded in her memories are mini-biographies of her mother's spinster sisters, Martha and Elizabeth Fricker, who maintained themselves with little aid from others, and 'laid by a comfortable competency for their old age' (p. 107). Mary Howitt, who completed a full-length autobiography, has to stop herself from telling her sister Anna's thoughts instead of her own.

A consistent theme in Romantic women's autobiographical writing is relationship with the community. Either the author is anxious about her ability to fit in, as Sara Coleridge's consciousness of paternal disapproval suggests, or she is concerned for less fortunate neighbours and the poor, as Dorothy Wordsworth's *Journals* testify. Amelia Opie, whose autobiographical fragments are included in this anthology, quickly developed a fascination with Bedlam inmates and criminals; while Lady Caroline Lamb's brief memoir tells of being passed from house to house, without any real sense of belonging. Martin Danahay suggests that male-authored nineteenth-century British autobiographies, from Wordsworth's *Prelude* on, largely reject a sense of social obligation: 'The masculine subject in Victorian autobiography emphasizes the autonomy of self at the expense of family and community.'[21] At a time when the masculine vision was apparently privileged above the feminine, women Romantics, by contrast, seem radically unsure of their place in the community unless they are able to create a convincing alternative to heroic self-absorption: a quiet and stable shared domestic life, perhaps, with intellectual stimulus, or a family of their own. Their inner life emerges too as an additional secret resource, not to be displayed in reflective poetry, or cultivated publicly, in the Wordsworth style. This all-absorbing inner world is explored even more fully by their Victorian successors, and here, perhaps, we see the greatest difference between male and female autobiographers in the nineteenth century.

Following in the tradition of the Romantics, Victorian women explored the hidden terrors of the inner life in a way that many Victorian men tended to avoid, as they focused more on their intellectual and spiritual development. What one notices immediately about Victorian women's autobiography is this difference of emphasis. The childhood sections are lengthy and fully alive, surreal in the vividness with which they recall terrifying sights and sounds, often known only to themselves. The best example of this occurs in the opening pages of Harriet Martineau's *Autobiography* (1877), which in its intense evocation of the feel of things looks forward to Virginia Woolf's childhood reminiscences nearly a century later in 'A Sketch of the Past'. Martineau admitted to being afraid of quite ordinary things – such as reflected light from prisms, or the sound of feather mattresses being beaten. The most innocent and harmless objects in Victorian women's autobiography come alive and turn into bogeys to scare the child protagonist, as they do in the Red Room of *Jane Eyre* or more surreally still, in the ever-changing world of Alice's Wonderland.

Many other women, inspired, either as Fanny Kemble was, by Martineau's openness about her fears, or writing coincidentally about similar experiences, confessed with relief to having been victims of all kinds of terrors, and worse, to having suffered alone, without the sympathy and understanding of an adult. For women, the inner life was paramount, frequently displacing any chronological account of external events. Epochs in their childhood are marked less by changes of scene or habitation than by the reading (usually alone or uninstructed) of a memorable book, as they were for their fictional doubles, Jane Eyre and Maggie Tulliver. Mill's childhood was similarly dominated by relations with books, but they were thrust upon him, in a formal course of instruction. Girls' response to literature has always been much more dramatic, because unstructured and derived from genuinely exciting acts of discovery. 'Ever memorable is the day on which I first took a volume of SHAKSPEARE in my hand to read', the American Margaret Fuller recalls;[22] while Harriet Martineau had a similar experience with *Paradise Lost*. As so often with Martineau's early experiences, the look of the volume, its feel and strange language, were what drew her on to explore it further: 'and the common blueish paper, with its old-fashioned type, became as a scroll out of heaven for me'. She was then struck by the word 'Argument', which apparently meant something different here from the usual sense of a dispute; 'but there was something about Satan cleaving Chaos, which made me turn to the poetry'.[23] Mark Pattison, future Rector of Lincoln College, Oxford, was all too conscious that *Paradise Lost* had made a much weaker impression on him: 'Miss Martineau at seven was more advanced than I at seventeen.'[24] Nor did a book have to be poetical to call up an imaginative response. Elizabeth Barrett, who wrote two 'autobiographies' at the ages of twelve and fourteen, recalls the thrill she experienced on reading philosophy: 'Metaphysics were my highest delight and having read a page from Locke my mind not only felt edified but exalted.'[25] Mary Somerville, the mathematician, was thirty-three when she got a similar thrill from discovering 'the mysterious word "Algebra"'.[26] Like Maggie Tulliver sampling her brother Tom's unappreciated Latin lessons, Victorian women autobiographers were genuinely enthralled by their introduction to unwomanly knowledge. Practically all were driven by an urge to educate themselves.

Romantic and Victorian women's autobiography seems closer in tone to the male Romantic prose writers, Leigh Hunt and De Quincey, than to the towering example of Wordsworth, whose sense of his own unique personality seems to have overwhelmed any female would-be imitators. Although he clearly foregrounds the importance of the inner life, 'the models of authorship established by Wordsworth and Carlyle', argues Laura Marcus, provide an uncomfortable fit for women writers'.[27] Though neither *The Prelude* nor *Sartor Resartus* could be regarded as standard autobiography according to the strictest generic definitions, some male writers, at least, were exhilarated by Wordsworth's example, and found it spoke directly to their own experiences. 'When I came in after years to read *The Prelude*', recalls Mark Pattison, 'I recognised, as if it were my own history which was being told, the steps by which the love of the country boy for his hills and moors grew into poetical responsibility for all imaginative presentations of beauty in every direction' (Pattison, p. 35). Women autobiographers found it much harder to reconcile their private experiences with their public persona; to develop their personal rapport with the countryside into a 'poetical responsibility' for the presentation of beauty, or to make an epic poem out of their childhood.

Wordsworth repeatedly sets himself in austerely metaphysical landscapes, chastened by the 'huge and mighty Forms' he recalls moving through his mind after the boat-stealing episode (*The Prelude*, vol. I, p. 425). He believes that nature has prepared an appropriate landscape of 'high objects' for his spiritual purification through a balanced education of pain and fear, and that he is 'led' to certain scenes for his own good. Women autobiographers approach their experiences with far less authority and much greater informality. There is no strong sense that an external force is looking after them, and their revelatory moments often occur when they are with other people. Mary Howitt recalls 'a curious little epoch' in her life (the idea of an epoch being 'little' is typical of the paradoxical nature of experience in much women's writing), when she was returning from a forest ramble with her father and sister Anna, and they passed a pinfold. The spot 'seemed like the line between rational and irrational existence', giving her the first evidence that she could think. 'I remember very well the new light, the gladness, the wealth of which I seemed suddenly possessed' (p. 90). Typically, the experience takes place in a family context, and apparently *a propos* of nothing intellectually significant. A pinfold is a place for securing stray cattle: there is nothing intrinsically uplifting about it, and certainly no suggestion of a guardian power leading her towards increased spiritual enlightenment. The experience seems to have been sudden, spontaneous and inexplicable, an isolated paragraph in Howitt's memoirs, sandwiched between tea-drinking and long summer days in the forest.

Moreover, women like Mary Howitt rejected Wordsworth's and Carlyle's powerful self-mythologizing, while having no female alternative to put in its place. One factor that appears to have influenced the shape of women's childhoods is the lack of any suitable female forerunners in the field before the nineteenth century. Self-writing by women might have been in existence for hundreds of years, but the childhood sections of most seventeenth- and eighteenth-century autobiographies were brief and sketchy. In the eighteenth century, the age of Charlotte Charke, Con Phillips and Laetitia Pilkington, the focus was on amorous escapades and survival in the world of untrustworthy men. By the start of the nineteenth, there was still no canon of female childhoods, or even one single archetypal example to which would-be autobiographers could turn for inspiration (Jane Eyre and Maggie Tulliver were the main nineteenth-century role models). Male autobiographers, by contrast, could look back to St Augustine, Rousseau, Gibbon and Wordsworth. It follows naturally that men appear to have adopted the standard symbolic patterns – the use of biblical typology, especially – even if, as Heather Henderson has recently argued, they used them only to reject and parody them.[28] Women autobiographers had to start from scratch, with a bleak choice between borrowing from inappropriate male models, or rejecting canonical formal patterning altogether. They largely did the latter, favouring the unpredictable sequence of events which mirrored the randomness of their own real lives; a magnification of the seemingly trivial, as we see in Charlotte Yonge's vivid evocation of childhood games. Frances Power Cobbe's first memory was of lying beside her mother on the sofa and admiring her beauty; she also remembered a greyhound snatching a piece of bread and butter from her hand, eating up a box of cakes on a journey, although they were meant as a gift, trying to get to her maid's house on her own, and hearing the *Pilgrim's Progress* read aloud. There is a dreamlike quality about these early reminiscences, connected as they are by mysterious emotional currents and distortions of vision. Though Rousseau also records the quiet movements of a room where he was working, he boasts of 'having once made water in one of our neighbour's cooking-pots while she was at church'.[29] There were obvious reasons why the earlier male models of childhood were inappropriate for Victorian women.

What were the usual features of the nineteenth-century autobiographical account of childhood, and to what extent did women's writings conform to them? Generalization is difficult, as each autobiography is distinctive and different; but it would be fair to say that male autobiographers such as Ruskin and Mill chiefly see themselves as developing minds, the undisputed centre of their parents' lives, their future careers already beckoning them onwards. A period at home is usually followed by arrival at a public school, or a more intense course of private tuition. Male autobiographers generally write with a strong sense of what they were becoming; with women, time is more inclined to stand still, allowing room for digressions and collective family history. While the childhoods of both sexes have some features in common, particularly a sense of loneliness and guilt, an unswerving sense of destiny is less marked in women's writing, which reproduces the meandering private tone of reminiscences. Falls from grace are less dramatic and total than they are in some male autobiographies; small, frequent transgressions are more typical of women's writing, followed by periods of recovery or reaction. In terms of style, nineteenth-century women autobiographers were well rooted in domestic realism. Apart from Southey's wife Caroline Bowles in *The Birth-Day* (1836), Elizabeth Barrett Browning in the fictionalized *Aurora Leigh* (1856) and George Eliot in her 'Brother and Sister' sonnets (1869), they normally wrote their extended childhood memories in prose, rather than in verse, and avoided the popular tropes of Edenic garden scenes, falls from grace, and rivers of growth and development. Their imagery, if it strays from realism, tends to be Gothic or derived from dream and fairy tale, grotesque and inexplicable. Mary Howitt compares herself and her sister Anna, left to rest in the forest, with the Babes in the Wood (p. 90), but her real focus in this episode is the distorted sound of grasshoppers, which a boy tells them are made by bloodhounds dragging chains: 'The horror that fell on us was intense.' Leigh Hunt and De Quincey similarly dwell on bizarre psychological obsessions and incidents, which often involve some exaggeration of vision. Leigh Hunt, for example, recalls seeing some porpoises off the coast of Deal, and considering them 'fearful creatures of some sort ... The very word "porpoise" had an awful, mouthfilling sound'.[30] Mary Howitt, who grew up in a serious and often silent Quaker household, thought the word 'dividends' had something to do with the devil, and was 'grieved and perplexed' to hear her parents using it without any sense of impropriety ( p. 93). Fanny Kemble identifies with a small boy disturbed by the phrase 'ell wide' (suggestive perhaps of gaping hell) which he overheard when his mother and a friend were discussing the purchase of material: 'The words "ell wide", perfectly incomprehensible to the child, seized upon his fancy, and produced some image of terror by which for a long time his poor little mind was haunted' (p. 164).

Kemble saw this as characteristic of German Romanticism, but in fact De Quincey and Hunt were also skilled in infusing familiar things with a sense of the alien or uncanny. De Quincey's *Autobiographic Sketches 1770–1803* and 'Suspiria de Profundis' are more helpful here than his better-known *Confessions of an English Opium-Eater*: for example, when he looked at clouds through the church windows, they seemed 'visions of beds with white lawny curtains; and in the beds lay sick children, dying children, that were tossing in anguish, and weeping clamorously for death.'[31] This revelation of a bizarre psychological landscape, projected onto relatively ordinary, everyday scenes, and existing alongside normal daily routines, heightens the sense of childhood's intense separateness: a state which Victorian women examine far more closely than Victorian men in their autobiographical writing. 'I can truly say that, from ten years old to fourteen or fifteen, I lived a double existence,' recalls Anna Jameson, 'one outward, linking me with the external sensible world, the other inward, creating a world to and for itself, conscious to itself only' (p. 82). Most women autobiographers describe themselves as dreamers, fantasists, storytellers, creating a secret inward world which alternately delighted and tortured them, as it became more real than the real world. Perhaps the most notorious episode occurs in Elizabeth Sewell's *Autobiography* (1907), when Sewell, a highly respectable Tractarian novelist, became obsessed with Jephthah's vow, in the Book of Judges, to kill his daughter as the price of victory in battle. Imagining that every time she thought of making a vow, she was honour bound to keep it, Sewell worried whether she should kill her mother because she thought she had made a vow that she should. At school and at home, Sewell is caught up in a cycle of guilt and confession, 'and I begged that I might be allowed to tell every day the things I had done wrong, because I felt so wicked'. Sewell admits that the situation soon got wildly out of hand: 'My confessions verged on the ludicrous' (p. 159). Nonetheless, she is one of many nineteenth-century women autobiographers who writes with a disproportionate sense of transgression, arising from an amplified inner world; and again, the closest parallel is with De Quincey, who in the *Suspiria* recalls being tricked by a young bookseller's assistant into thinking he had ordered a history of navigation running to about 15,000 volumes. For three years, anxiety about paying for and accommodating the volumes becomes the 'secret affliction' of his life (*Suspiria*, p. 136), a spine-chilling terror of far more poignancy than the usual childish fear of ghosts, and one that Victorian women and Romantic men share a skill in communicating.

Like the children in Mrs Sherwood's *History of the Fairchild Family* (1818), who are taken to see a corpse on a gibbet, as a warning not to squabble with each other, the actress Fanny Kemble, at school in Boulogne, was shown the site of a recent execution. The body had been removed, 'but I saw the guillotine, and certain gutters running red with what I was told (whether truly or not) was blood, and a sad-looking man, busied about the terrible machine, who, it was said, was the executioner's son' (p. 163). Later in her childhood reminiscences, Kemble admits that although she had been appalled at the sight of the blood-stained place of execution, she still had a 'lingering desire for the distinction of a public execution by guillotine (the awful glory of which still survived in my memory)' (p. 166). These visions were certainly empowering for Victorian girls (the least powerful members of society), but usually at a price. As Elizabeth Barrett writes, there was a masochistic streak in their daydreams: 'To suffer! to die! to defend! To save by my death my country or some very very dear friends!' Even at the age of twelve, she had intimations of her relative uselessness in the order of things, and longed to make some grand gesture, however self-destructive.[32]

Victorian women's autobiography is full of such flamboyant gestures in its childhood sections. Refusing to suppress their own presence, they nevertheless find it impossible to articulate their romanticism except in ways that are misunderstood by their families, or else kept secret from them. Childhood, as described by both sexes, is essentially a secret condition – its emotional crises isolating, embarrassing and often impossible to communicate until many years later. Children often feel unable to tell adults about their passionate inner life, for fear of being misunderstood or laughed at. 'Like all children,' recalls the actress Helena Faucit (Lady Martin), 'I kept, as a rule, my greatest delight to myself.' She never revealed, even to her sister, how much her life was wrapped up in fictitious characters: 'I knew I should only be laughed at'.[33] The burden of secrecy was all the heavier for Victorian girls, schooled to the highest standards of propriety: hence the feeling of an emotional cloudburst when their reminiscences were finally written down.

Although nineteenth-century women's autobiography is predominantly secular (indeed, in some cases, such as Harriet Martineau's and Annie Besant's, it recounts a deconversion experience), its fascination with guilt, confession and punishment marks its partial derivation from spiritual autobiography: a genre in which their male predecessors paid some attention to significant childhood experience. Childhood was in any case, at the beginning of the nineteenth century, caught in a conflicting ideology of guilt and innocence: philosophers, teachers and authors being uncertain whether the newborn child was the product of original sin or gifted with vision, innocence and imagination, as Blake and Wordsworth had asserted. In terms of childcare, the century moved towards a more humanitarian approach; indeed, one feature that emerges from women's autobiography is the tremendous care generally taken by both parents over their daughters' physical and intellectual well-being. Queen Victoria was convinced that Prince Albert's influence, as husband and father, had guaranteed her children a far happier upbringing than her own fatherless childhood had been. Nevertheless, autobiography, however secular, reflects a sense of the child's potential for sin, as the protagonist struggles with the temptation to tell falsehoods. Truth-telling and lying are key issues in literature for and about children, as falsehood was the easiest, most tempting sin for children to fall into. William Cowper, in the *Memoir* of his early life, recalls becoming 'an adept in the infernal art of lying', progressing from this to wondering whether the Gospel was true or false, and feeling unable to obey it unless he was certain of its truth. He once 'went so far in a controversy of this kind as to assert that I would gladly submit to have my right hand cut off, so I might but be enabled to live according to the Gospel'.[34] Among the Romantics, Leigh Hunt recalls a similar anxiety, when, one day kneeling in the school chapel during the Litany, 'the thought fell upon me – "suppose eternal punishment should be true." An unusual sense of darkness and anxiety crossed me – but only for a moment. The next instant the extreme absurdity and impiety of the notion restored me to my ordinary feelings.'[35]

Among nineteenth-century women autobiographers, Eliza Lynn Linton (in *The Autobiography of Christopher Kirkland*, 1885), Harriet Martineau, Annie Besant and Elizabeth Sewell inherit this kind of anxiety about Gospel truth, and an introverted, tormented desire to find out for certain their own duties in relation to it. For all the attention given to religion in most Victorian households, children clearly felt unable to ask leading questions about fundamental Christian issues. They were expected to learn religious ideas by rote, and avoid discussion of them: hence their corroding invasion of the child's emotional life, already racked by distorted responses to books, darkness, and sometimes the traumatic deaths of siblings (as recounted by De Quincey and the American Margaret Fuller in particular). As John Burnett has noted, religion occupied a more important place in a child's anxious inner life than sex, which has now succeeded it as the greatest source of pre-pubescent confusion.[36] Most Victorian autobiographers were, in fact, religiously observant as children, even flinging themselves into exaggerated gestures of piety as an outlet for their romantic emotionalism. Their difficulties came later, when they felt unable to accept Christian doctrine in young adulthood or beyond: a further reason, perhaps, for remaining in the safe confines of childhood experience in autobiography.

Another group of Victorian autobiographers to take childhood seriously, and with whom Victorian women have some connections, were the large body of working-class autobiographers, increasingly now anthologized and discussed by critics.[37] The period of childhood for them was necessarily brief: as soon as they were able to do anything useful, most were taken out of school and sent to work, to support their family of younger brothers and sisters. In this respect, they were the opposite of Victorian middle-class girls, kept at home indefinitely, until a 'settlement' was found for them through marriage. Perhaps because of this abrupt termination of childhood, working-class autobiographers value it more intently, and often single out a number of crucial episodes from their earliest days which have acquired landmark characteristics. A sharp visual memory is common to both, as is a strong sense of disadvantage, of not having a secure place in society. This is particularly striking in the extensive childhood memories of Charles Shaw, who worked in the Staffordshire potteries and published his autobiography in 1903. Because education was so important to him, his first chapter recalls his experiences of dame-school and Sunday school, especially the physical appearance of the letters on the page: 'There must have been something intensely vivid about these letters in the alphabet, for to this day when I see the letters Q and S as single capitals I see them rather as when I first saw them in old Betty's alphabet.'[38] Like those of middle-class girls, the needs of working-class children were considered secondary to the welfare of the family group at large, and their role in the family could change abruptly as economic factors dictated. Both debarred from formal membership of the symbolic order, Victorian working-class men and middle-class women concentrated on their private experiences of anxiety or thwarted ambition to cling to any chance of education, knowing how easily it could be snatched away from them. In neither case was the middle-class male programme of public school, university and career an available paradigm, and both were forced to find a different shape for their memories of childhood and youth.

As Victorian women began to publish and read each other's autobiographies, they noticed how similar their childhood experiences had been, especially their imaginative lives. Fanny Kemble was heartened by Martineau's accounts of her irrational fears, and Anna Jameson stressed that her childhood reminiscences were interesting, not because they were original, but because they were representative: 'at least I have met with many children who throve or suffered from the same or similar unseen causes even under external conditions and management every way dissimilar' (p. 78). Some of the childhoods anthologized here were happy: Mary Sherwood's, for example, and Dorothea Herbert's; but even those with some cheerful episodes are predominantly anxious, especially further into the Victorian period itself. While many of these anxieties are commonplace, and experienced by the majority of children whenever they were born, others arise from a fundamental sense of alienation. Autobiographers, whatever their family circumstances, tend to emphasize their solitariness: it would be difficult to tell from John Stuart Mill's *Autobiography*, for instance, that he was the eldest of a large family of brothers and sisters. He seems as alone and self-sufficient as John Ruskin, who was an only child. Victorian male autobiographers say relatively little about their siblings, or even about their mothers (Mill's is notoriously absent); women, on the other hand, pay special attention to the brother and sister relationship, as shown in the autobiographies of Mary Sherwood, Sara Coleridge, Charlotte Yonge, Harriet Martineau, 'Charlotte Elizabeth', and the 'Brother and Sister' sonnet sequence by George Eliot. For most girls, it was a complex relationship: the first experience of sexual difference in the peer group, the first awareness that boys were privileged in their educational opportunities, and often treated as superior to their sisters. The relationship opened up opportunities for rivalry, ambition, jealousy, and at its best, a protective affection, often made more poignant by after-knowledge of their contrasting futures. Relationships with sisters, while important to Martineau and Howitt, generally have a lower profile in women's autobiography, and are less intense. The need to be loved, a central theme of most childhood autobiographies, is directed more intently towards the stronger members of the family – brothers or parents – rather than sisters, who could offer love, but mainly as fellow-sufferers.

Sara Coleridge grew up with a strong sense of inferiority to her brothers, whose strong physical appearance was often remarked on by family friends. Her father was, in any case, surprised that he had fathered a girl: he seems, according to her account of it, to have been prouder of Derwent's stout build than of Sara's fey delicacy. While the birth of younger brothers made an epoch in the lives of Harriet Martineau and Charlotte Yonge, Dorothea Herbert and Mary Sherwood recall efforts to keep up with their elder brothers, and the occasional intellectual triumph over them. Mary Sherwood's brother Marten was so slow at Latin (Tom Tulliver-like), that she was made to learn it alongside him, in order to provide some competition. Their father was unusual in assuming that both his children 'would be what he called *geniuses*' (p. 42), though in fact – surprisingly, perhaps – most Victorian women autobiographers record being encouraged by their fathers to pursue intellectual interests. This may help explain why they subsequently did achieve so much.

School episodes, which figure so largely in male autobiography, are more haphazard in nineteenth-century women's writing. Again, there was no canon of familiar school stories to which they could refer; for the most part, they did not even join well-known prestigious schools, such as Westminster, Harrow or Rugby, which had their published folklore, and famous alumni. The decision to send a girl to school often seems to have arisen in a casual way, rather than as a foregone conclusion, usually after an extended period of education at home, or on the abrupt discovery of academic inadequacy. The journey there was a major event for Mary Howitt and Dorothea Herbert, as for Jane Eyre, while the lessons themselves were often monotonous and pointless. 'Limited and mechanical' was Elizabeth Sewell's view of the lessons at her school, to which she was sent at the age of four (p. 175). Normally, however, stays at school were briefer than for boys, and intellectual attainments considerably more meagre than the advances made by girls reading for themselves at home. 'At the village school,' recalls Mary Somerville, whose turn for reading was disapproved by her Aunt Janet, 'the boys often learnt Latin, but it was thought sufficient for the girls to be able to read the Bible; very few even learnt writing' (p. 52). Although bullying by other pupils was not a key issue, complex relationships with strict, uncomprehending teachers was. Few Victorian women autobiographers have anything good to say about their schooling – Harriet Martineau, who attended a mixed day-school for two years, and then a girls' boarding-school – being a notable exception. The most bizarre images occur in

Elizabeth Sewell's autobiography, in the lengthy episodes at Miss Crooke's school, which she attended from the ages of four to thirteen. 'I had written in a little memorandum book the letters "O. W." meaning "Old Witch", an epithet which some of us had ventured to apply to Miss Crooke', Sewell recalls:

> When the little book was called for (I forget why), I was frightened and threw it away, and then said I had lost it. No mercy was shown me, and the wretchedness of feeling which the punishment caused I shall never forget. It seemed as if I were marked for life, the only one of my family who had ever committed such an offence. (p. 176)

Most of the episodes recounted by these autobiographers of childhood are apparently trivial, but endowed with immense importance by the author. Seeing things vividly is part of childhood for both men and women; certainly, this comes across as powerfully in Dickens's novels as it does in *Jane Eyre*; but it enters Victorian men's autobiographies (Ruskin's is the chief exception to this) less noticeably – not least, perhaps, because of the more structured shape of the male *Bildungsroman*. Girls growing up with little purpose in their lives seem to have had more time to notice things and react strongly to them. Colours, for example, abound in autobiographies by Victorian women: Charlotte Yonge remembers a green spelling book, while Harriet Martineau 'for long could not abide a red book' (p. 121) because her sister Rachel, of whom she was intensely jealous, had been given Gay's *Fables*, bound in red and gold. Martineau also recalls the feel of a flat velvet button on Rachel's bonnet, while Sara Coleridge remembers that her father hated the sight of her scarlet socks. One of Mary Howitt's outstanding memories of school is of the colourful fancy-work made by the girls: 'I shall never forget my admiration of diamonds woven with strips of gold paper on a black ground' (p. 96). Births of siblings are recalled in terms of what rooms or the weather looked like, and the strange appearance of previously familiar places and people. Sensory perception is much more marked in Victorian women's autobiographies than in men's, as if the child is establishing her hold on a world that she already senses as being hostile and uncertain, likely to move from under her feet, as in Harriet Martineau's *Autobiography*: 'I remember standing on the threshold of a cottage, holding fast by the doorpost, and putting my foot down, in repeated attempts to reach the ground' (p. 116). Her world is unstable, shifting, animate: 'sometimes the dim light of the windows in the night seemed to advance till it pressed upon my eyeballs, and then the windows would seem to recede to an infinite distance' (p. 116). The motif of seeing (or not seeing) a comet recurs in autobiographies by Martineau, Howitt, Cobbe and Somerville: perhaps the most extreme sign of a world not fully understood, particularly to Martineau, who was afraid of the starlit sky coming down to crush her. Mary Somerville and Mary Howitt concentrate on their pleasure in simple gardening, on earthbound study of the world around them, while Sara Coleridge carefully reconstructs the interior of her childhood home with all its different rooms assigned to individual people and purposes.

If there is a pattern of childhood in Victorian women's autobiography, it lies in a resistance to pattern, partly through this concept of the unpredictable animate universe, and partly through what Julia Kristeva has described as the 'spasmodic force' of the unconscious disrupting the normal linear progress of autobiography: the subordination of chronology to the pressures of the inner world.[39] In her 'Sketch of the Past', Virginia Woolf recalls having stronger memories of 'sensation' in childhood than an awareness of herself. This is not necessarily to claim that Victorian women prefigure Virginia Woolf and stream-of-consciousness writing, or that they write continuously in heightened language: it is more to suggest that they pinpoint the foreignness of the symbolic order as they enter it, and their language and identities fracture to express their bewilderment. Woolf refers to 'several violent moments of being, always including a circle of the scene which they cut out': these spasmodic scenes, she says, make up the pattern of childhood memory.[40] Indeed, the degree of violence even in nineteenth-century women's autobiography is surprising. These are mostly imaginary acts of violence meditated against members of the family, especially other women, but never performed. Fanny Kemble considered poisoning her sister, and then being executed herself; Elizabeth Sewell thought of killing her mother, and Harriet Martineau of killing herself; even Frances Power Cobbe felt guilty that she had said 'Curse them all!' about her family and governess. Sewell also called her teacher a 'witch'. If, as Carolyn Heilbrun suggests, in *Writing a Woman's Life*, anger has been forbidden to women, this is the way it emerges in Victorian writing: surrounded by guilty apologies, but its impulses targeted at repressive female role models.[41]

There is far more anger about mothers than there is about fathers. There is also a much more openly expressed affection for mothers. Clearly, the mother–daughter relationship provokes the most aggressive responses, as the autobiographers examine the role-models available to them and react against them. The most striking example is Cobbe's: her mother a beautiful invalid, rarely seen outdoors, while Cobbe became an active journalist, reformer and feminist. Strong reactions to mothers, it should be said, are more marked in the later period of this anthology. Among those born in the eighteenth century, such as Mary Sherwood and Mary Howitt, as well as Sara Coleridge, born at the beginning of the nineteenth, closeness to mothers was more characteristic, with less dissent from their values. Sherwood, Howitt and Coleridge became mothers themselves, and combined their writing lives with raising their children. In the later period, conventional domestic life began to look more unattainable. Martineau, Yonge, Cobbe, and Sewell failed to marry at all; Besant and Kemble married unhappily. Few children were born to these later figures, who also led more controversial lives: for example, entering debates over contraception, the Contagious Diseases Acts, Poor Law reform, vivisection and agnosticism. Unsurprisingly, the later figures in this anthology are more critical of their childhood upbringing, and portray themselves as more lonely and unhappy. While it might be true to say that most autobiographers see themselves as lonely and misunderstood children, women writing in the second half of the nineteenth century particularly stress their isolation within the family unit and their alienation from parents who should have understood and supported their needs. At the same time, the autobiographers rarely present themselves as unappreciated angels. Harriet Martineau was unusual in describing herself as particularly difficult and unloveable, but most of the others admitted willingly to behaving badly, looking unappealing, or lacking whatever it was that won the uncritical devotion of adults. Mary Somerville's father returned from sea to find her a 'savage' who needed taming; both she and Mary Sherwood were put in steel braces to improve their posture, while Fanny Kemble, at four, was considered to be 'exceedingly troublesome and unmanageable, my principal crime being a general audacious contempt for all authority ... coupled with a sweet-tempered, cheerful indifference to all punishment' (p. 161). Elizabeth Sewell, who grew up to be an earnest religious novelist, describes herself as a bad-tempered child who often preferred to be alone: 'I am afraid I was by no means a pleasant child. My quick, irritable feelings were constantly bringing me into trouble, and then I shut myself up in my own thoughts and determined to keep aloof from every one' (p. 155). It is unusual for a woman autobiographer of this period not to see herself as in some way at odds with her family and society, as many were to be, more controversially, in their adult lives. Even Charlotte Yonge, who had a happy, if lonely childhood, recalls bouts of screaming and wildness which her uncle found excessive.

Family relationships and the domestic world are their primary concern, with national events largely pushed into the background. In this respect, as Virginia Woolf was to do by relegating the First World War to the sidelines of her novels, or George Eliot in mentioning the 1832 Reform Act as contemporary with *Middlemarch* experiences, they invert the usual patriarchal value-system and put domestic and childhood events at the centre of their writing. Martineau and Howitt both grew up in the shadow of the Napoleonic Wars which they acknowledged largely as a threat to their own freedom and happiness. It was something their parents talked about, and something that added to the Gothic horror of their nightmares. Howitt's first going to school in Croydon coincides with celebrations of the fiftieth anniversary of George III's accession to the throne, and provides a colourful backdrop to her entry into a new life. Military history offers Yonge a chance to glamorize some of her male ancestors, though the real subject of her autobiography is her childhood self, playing with huge families of cousins and dolls.

As for the ending of childhood, this was often more difficult to identify in girls' lives than in boys'. Whereas middle-class boys generally went from public school to university, girls who had been away returned home, in effect to wait for suitors. The pattern of their lives was more circular; some, like Fanny Kemble and Frances Power Cobbe, gaining their release only when a death or financial collapse allowed them into the public sphere. Dorothea Herbert formally abandoned her childhood at the age of fifteen when the marriages of all her old acquaintances made 'the first Epoch' of her life. With no definite programme ahead of her, she spent the next four years 'in a kind of Calm Apathy ... a Non Entity in Existence being quite disengaged from any particular pursuit and divested of any interesting Passion'.[42] What is particularly striking about the adolescence of nineteenth-century women is their passivity. At an age where a century later teenagers would be making decisive choices about their future, Victorian girls were emotionally adrift, bridging the gap between childhood and marriage by helping out in Sunday schools or with younger brothers and sisters, continuing their education at home, or paying calls. Hence, perhaps, the reason why several promising autobiographers end their reminiscences at this stage. Childhood remains crystallized in their memories as a distinctive period with its intensity of vision, its milestone experiences, its bitter pain and extremes of joy. Adult life, for Yonge and Sewell brought few personal changes worth recording – though Sewell kept up her autobiography, assisted by diary entries, into old age; Coleridge, Kemble and Besant faced marital strains; Dorothea Herbert seems to have lost interest in life when she was disappointed in love; Somerville and Kemble resort increasingly to quoted correspondence; Oliphant's early hopes were dashed by the deaths of her husband and sons. The heavy costs paid in personal terms may account for many women autobiographers' reluctance to continue their narrative in approved autobiographical style into old age; as might the controversial nature of their later careers and experiences. With separations, divorces, diseases, deaths and public unpopularity facing many of them in adult life, the appeal of childhood autobiography speaks for itself.

## Notes

1. Queen Victoria to the Princess Royal, 9 June 1858, in *Dearest Child: Private Correspondence of Queen Victoria and the Princess Royal 1858–1861*, ed. Roger Fulford (London: Evans Brothers Ltd, 1964), pp. 111–12.
2. Simone de Beauvoir, *The Second Sex* (1949), ed. H.M. Parshley (Harmondsworth: Penguin, 1983), pp. 644–5.
3. Margaret Oliphant's *Autobiography* (1899) was reissued by Leicester University Press, ed. Q.D. Leavis, in 1974; the University of Chicago Press, ed. Laurie Langbauer, in 1988; and most recently by Oxford University Press, ed. Elisabeth Jay (the complete text) in 1990. *Harriet Martineau's Autobiography* (1877) was reissued by Virago, ed. Gaby Weiner, in 1983. Sara Coleridge's autobiography appears as an appendix to Bradford Keyes Mudge, *Sara Coleridge, A Victorian Daughter: Her Life and Essays* (New Haven and London: Yale University Press, 1989).
4. One of the first books to attempt a chronology of women's autobiography was *Women's Autobiography: Essays in Criticism*, ed. Estelle C. Jelinek (Bloomington and London: Indiana University Press, 1980). Recent books on women's autobiography include Sidonie Smith, *A Poetics of Women's Autobiography* (Bloomington: Indiana University Press, 1987); *The Female Autograph*, ed. Domna C. Stanton (Chicago and

London: University of Chicago Press, 1987); *The Private Self: Theory and Practice of Women's Autobiographical Writing*, ed. Shari Benstock (London: Routledge, 1988); and my own *The Private Lives of Victorian Women: Autobiography in Nineteenth Century England* (London: Harvester Wheatsheaf, 1989).

5.  Henry James, *Essays in London and Elsewhere* (1893), Essay Index Reprint Series (New York: Books for Libraries Press, 1972), p. 107.

6.  *The Autobiography of Margaret Oliphant* (1899), ed. Elisabeth Jay (Oxford: Oxford University Press, 1990), p. 99.

7.  Laura Marcus, *Auto/biographical Discourses: Theory, Criticism, Practice* (Manchester and New York: Manchester University Press, 1994), p. 31.

8.  *Personal Recollections, from Early Life to Old Age, of Mary Somerville*, ed. Martha Somerville (London: John Murray, 1873), p. 1.

9.  Linda Anderson, *Women and Autobiography in the Twentieth Century: Remembered Futures* (London: Harvester Wheatsheaf, 1997), p. 3.

10.  Karl J. Weintraub, 'Autobiography and Historical Consciousness', *Critical Inquiry* I, no. 4 (June 1975), p. 824.

11.  Leslie Stephen, 'Autobiography' (1881), *Hours in a Library*, 3 vols (London: Smith Elder, 1892), vol. I, p. 237.

12.  Georges Gusdorf, 'Conditions and Limits of Autobiography' in *Autobiography: Essays Theoretical and Critical*, ed. James Olney (Princeton: Princeton University Press, 1980), p. 39.

13.  Roy Pascal, *Design and Truth in Autobiography* (London: Routledge and Kegan Paul, 1960), p. 8.

14.  T.H. Huxley, 'Autobiography' (1889), in *Charles Darwin, Thomas Henry Huxley: Autobiographies*, ed. Gavin de Beer (London: Oxford University Press, 1974), p. 101; *The Life of David Hume, Esq. Written by Himself* ( London: W. Strahan and T. Cadell, 1777), p. 1; Mark Pattison, *Memoirs* (London: Macmillan, 1885), p. 1.

15.  Ethel Smyth, *Impressions That Remained*, 2 vols (London: Longmans, Green, 1919), vol. I, p. l.

16.  Anne K. Mellor, *Romanticism and Gender* (London and New York: Routledge, 1993), p. 144.

17.  Wordsworth, letter to Sir George Beaumont, 1 May 1805.

18.  'Author's Introduction to the Standard Novels Edition' (1831), quoted in Mary Shelley, *Frankenstein* (1818; Harmondsworth, Penguin, 1985), p. 52.

19.  Anne K. Mellor, *Romanticism and Gender*, p. 157; Meena Alexander, *Women in Romanticism* (London: Macmillan, 1989), p. 12.

20.  Nancy Chodorow, *Psychoanalysis and the Sociology of Gender* (Berkeley: University of California Press, 1978).

21.  Martin A. Danahay, *A Community of One: Masculine Autobiography and Autonomy in Nineteenth Century Britain* (New York: State University of New York Press, 1993), p. 9.

22.  *Memoirs of Margaret Fuller Ossoli*, 3 vols (London: Richard Bentley and Son, 1852), vol. I, p. 26.

23.  *Harriet Martineau's Autobiography*, ed. Gaby Weiner (London: Virago, 1983), vol. I, p. 42.

24.  Mark Pattison, *Memoirs*, p. 11.

25. 'Glimpses into My Own Life and Literary Character' (1820), in *Two Autobiographical Essays by Elizabeth Barrett*, ed. William S. Peterson, *Browning Institute Studies*, vol. 2 (New York, 1974) p. 126.

26. *Personal Recollections from Early Life to Old Age, of Mary Somerville*, ed. Martha Somerville (London: John Murray, 1873), p. 80.

27. Marcus, p. 29.

28. Heather Henderson, *The Victorian Self: Autobiography and Biblical Narrative* (Ithaca and London: Cornell University Press, 1989), p. 4.

29. *The Confessions of Jean-Jacques Rousseau* (1781; trans. J. M. Cohen, Harmondsworth: Penguin, 1953), p. 21. Phyllis Grosskurth argues that Victorian autobiographers in any case found his extreme egotism 'anathema': 'Where was Rousseau?', in *Approaches to Victorian Autobiography*, ed. George P. Landow (Athens: Ohio University Press, 1979), p. 29.

30. *The Autobiography of Leigh Hunt* (1850; ed. J.E. Morpurgo, London: Cresset Press, 1949), p. 32.

31. Thomas De Quincey, *Suspiria De Profundis* (1845), ed. Grevel Lindop, World's Classics, (Oxford: Oxford University Press, 1985), p. 112.

32. Barrett, 'Glimpses', p. 132.

33. Helena Faucit, Lady Martin, *On Some of Shakespeare's Female Characters* (London and Edinburgh: William Blackwood and Sons, 1885), p. 5.

34. 'Memoir of the Early Life of William Cowper', in *The Letters and Prose Writings of William Cowper*, ed. James King and Charles Ryskamp (Oxford: Clarendon Press, 1979), vol. I, pp. 7, 11.

35. Hunt, *Autobiography*, p. 36.

36. *Destiny Obscure: Autobiographies of Childhood, Education and Family from the 1820s to the 1920s*, ed. John Burnett (London: Allen Lane, 1982), p. 43.

37. David Vincent, *Bread, Knowledge and Freedom: A Study of Nineteenth Century Working-Class Autobiography* (London: Europa Publications, 1981) reviews the themes of working-class autobiography. John Burnett has edited two anthologies, *Destiny Obscure* (1982) and *Useful Toil: Autobiographies of Working People from the 1820s to the 1920s* (London: Allen Lane, 1974).

38. Charles Shaw, *When I was a Child*, ed. John Burnett (London: Caliban Books, 1977), p. 2.

39. Ann Rosalind Jones, referring to Kristeva's 'Le Sujet en Process' in *Polylogue* (1977), suggests women's 'semiotic style is likely to involve repetitive, spasmodic separations from the dominating discourse, which, more often, they are forced to imitate', *The New Feminist Criticism: Essays on Women, Literature and Theory*, ed. Elaine Showalter (London: Virago, 1986), p. 4.

40. Virginia Woolf, 'A Sketch of the Past', in *Moments of Being: Unpublished Autobiographical Writings*, ed. Jeanne Schulkind (London: Hogarth Press, 1976) p. 67. She remembers, like the Victorian women, 'many bright colours; many distinct sounds', p. 79.

41. Carolyn Heilbrun, *Writing a Woman's Life* (London: Women's Press, 1989), p. 13.

42. *Retrospections of Dorothea Herbert 1770–1789*, 2 vols (London: Gerald Howe, 1929), vol. II, p. 141.

# 2

# Amelia Opie

Amelia Opie (1769–1853), novelist and poet, was the daughter of James Alderson, a successful Norwich physician, and his wife, Amelia Briggs (d. 1784). Best remembered for stories of family politics, such as *Father and Daughter* (1801) and *Adeline Mowbray* (1804), she married the painter John Opie in 1798. After his death in 1807, she spent a long widowhood in Norwich and London, mixing with the famous men of her day, including Byron, Scott, Wordsworth and Godwin, and trying to reconcile her sociable, youthful temperament with the teachings of Quakerism, to which she had converted from Unitarianism in 1825. Her two pieces of childhood autobiography, reproduced in the *Memorials of the Life of Amelia Opie* (1854) edited by Cecilia Lucy Brightwell, dwell almost exclusively on her fears, and her fascination with lunatic asylums and law courts. The latter was an interest that remained with her into adulthood, when she attended several treason trials at the Old Bailey, identifying sympathetically with prisoners such as Horne Tooke and Thomas Holcroft. Her alleged reason for writing these passages about her childhood was to acquaint her readers with 'the preparation for [her] future life and occupations, which these days so evidently afforded', an instinct that prompted several other nineteenth-century women to begin writing their autobiographies. What is striking about them now is their bizarre focus and her interest in transgressive experiences: she takes a girl's skeleton on her lap to cure her of fear, and meets a woman disguised as a sailor. Like William and Dorothy Wordsworth, she becomes intrigued by individuals with romantic and lonely histories. Her first remembered experience is of disillusionment at the gap between her imaginings and the reality of things.

One of my earliest recollections is of gazing on the bright blue sky as I lay in my little bed, before my hour of rising came, and listening with delighted attention to the ringing of a peal of bells. I had heard that heaven was beyond those blue skies, and I had been taught that there was the home of the good, and I fancied that those sweet bells were ringing in heaven. What a happy error! Neither illusion nor reality, at any subsequent period of my life, ever gave me such a sensation of pure, heartfelt delight, as I experienced when morning after morning I looked on that blue sky, and listened to those bells, and fancied that I heard the music of the home of the blest, pealing from the dwelling of the most high. Well do I remember the excessive mortification I felt when I was told the truth, and had the nature of bells explained to me; and, though I have since had to awake often from illusions that were dear to my heart, I am sure that I never woke from one with more pain than I experienced when forced to forego this sweet illusion of my imaginative childhood.

I believe I was naturally a fearful child, perhaps more so than other children; but I was not allowed to remain so. Well do I remember the fears, which I used to indulge and prove by tears and screams, whenever I saw the objects that called forth my alarm. The first was terror of black beetles, the second of frogs, the third of skeletons, the fourth of a black man, and the fifth of madmen.

My mother, who was as firm from principle, as she was gentle in disposition, in order to cure me of my first fear, made me take a beetle in my hand, and so convince myself it would not hurt me. As her word was law, I obeyed her, though with a shrinking frame; but the point was carried, and when, as frequently happened, I was told to take up a beetle and put it out of the way of being trodden upon, I learnt to forget even my former fear.

She pursued the same course in order to cure me of screaming at sight of a frog; I was forced to hold one in my hand, and thence I became, perhaps, proud of my courage to handle what my playfellows dared not touch.

The skeleton of which I was afraid was that of a girl, black, probably, from the preparation it had undergone; be that as it may, I was induced to take it on my lap and examine it, and at last, calling it my black doll, I used to exhibit it to my wondering and alarmed companions. Here was vanity again perhaps.

The African of whom I was so terribly afraid was the footman of a rich merchant from Rotterdam, who lived opposite our house; and as he was fond of children, Aboar (as he was called) used to come up to speak to little missey as I stood at the door in my nurse's arms, a civility which I received with screams and tears and kicks. But as soon as my parents heard of this ill behaviour they resolved to put a stop to it, and missey was forced to shake hands with the black the next time he approached her, and thenceforward we were very good friends. Nor did they fail to make me acquainted with negro history; as soon as I was able to understand, I was shewn on the map where their native country was situated; I was told the sad tale of negro wrongs and negro slavery; and I believe that my early and ever-increasing zeal in the cause of emancipation was founded and fostered by the kindly emotions which I was encouraged to feel for my friend Aboar and all his race.

The fifth terror was excited by two poor women who lived near us, and were both deranged though in different degree. The one was called Cousin Betty, a common name for female lunatics; the other, who had been dismissed from bedlam as incurable, called herself 'old happiness', and went by that name. These poor women lived near us and passed by our door every day; consequently I often saw them when I went out with my nurse, and whether it was that I had been told by her, when naught, that the mad woman should get me, I know not, but certain it is, that these poor visited creatures were to me objects of such terror, that when I saw them coming (followed usually by hooting boys) I used to run away to hide myself. But as soon as my mother was aware of this terror she resolved to conquer it, and I was led by her to the door the next time one of these women was in sight; nor was I allowed to stir till I had heard her kindly converse with the poor afflicted one, and then I was commissioned to put a piece of money into her hand. I had to undergo the same process with the other woman; but she tried my nerves more than the preceding one, for she insisted on shaking hands with me, a contact not very pleasing to me: however, the fear was in a measure conquered, and a feeling of deep interest, not unmixed with awe, was excited in my mind, not only towards these women, but towards insane persons in general; a feeling that has never left me, and which, in very early life, I gratified in the following manner:– When able to walk in the street with my beloved parents, they sometimes passed the city asylum for lunatics, called the bedlam, and we used to stop before the iron gates, and see the inmates very often at the windows, who would occasionally ask us to throw halfpence over the wall to buy snuff. Not long after I had discovered the existence of this interesting receptacle, I found my way to it alone, and took care to shew a penny in my fingers, that I might be asked for it, and told where to throw it. A customer soon appeared at one of the windows, in the person of a man named Goodings, and he begged me to throw it over the door of the wall of the ground in which they walked, and he would come to catch it. Eagerly did I run to that door, but never can I forget the terror and the trembling which seized my whole frame, when, as I stood listening for my mad friend at the door, I heard the clanking of his chain! nay, such was my alarm, that, though a strong door was between us, I felt inclined to run away; but better feelings got the mastery, and I threw the money over the door, scarcely staying to hear him say he had found the penny, and that he blessed the giver. I fully believe that I felt myself raised in the scale of existence by this action, and some of my happiest moments were those when I visited the gates of bedlam; and so often did I go, that I became well known to its inmates, and I have heard them say 'Oh! there is the little girl from St. George's' (the parish in which I then lived). At this time my mother used to send me to shops to purchase trifling articles, and chiefly at a shop at some distance from the bedlam, which was as far again from my home. But, when my mother used to ask me where I had been, that I had been gone so long, the reply was, 'I only went round by bedlam, mamma.'

But I did not confine my gifts to pence. Much of my weekly allowance was spent in buying pinks and other flowers for my friend Goodings, who happened to admire a nosegay which he saw me wear; and as my parents were not inclined to rebuke me for spending my money on others, rather than on myself, I was allowed for some time to indulge in this way the interest which early circumstances, those circumstances which always give the bias to the character through life, had led me to feel in beings whom it had pleased the Almighty to deprive of their reason. At this period, and when my attachment to this species of human woe was at its height, a friend of ours hired a house which looked into the ground named before, and my father asked the gentleman to allow me to stand at one of the windows, and see the lunatics walk. Leave was granted and I hastened to my post, and as the window was open I could talk with Goodings and the others; but my feelings were soon more forcibly interested by an unseen lunatic, who had, they told me, been crossed in love, and who, in the cell opposite my window, sang song after song in a voice which I thought very charming.

But I do not remember to have been allowed the indulgence of standing at this window more than twice. I believe my parents thought the excitement was an unsafe one, as I was constantly talking of what I had said to the mad folks, and they to me; and it was so evident that I was proud of their acquaintance, and of my own attachment to them, that I was admonished not to go so often to the gates of the bedlam; and dancing and French school soon gave another turn to my thoughts, and excited in me other views and feelings. Still, the sight of a lunatic gave me a fearful pleasure, which nothing else excited; and when, as youth advanced, I knew that loss of reason accompanied distressed circumstances, I know that I was doubly eager to administer to the pecuniary wants of those who were awaiting their appointed time in madness as well as poverty. Yet, notwithstanding, I could not divest myself entirely of fear of these objects of my pity; and it was with a beating heart that, after some hesitation, I consented to accompany two gentlemen, dear friends of mine, on a visit to the interior of the bedlam. One of my companions was a man of warm feelings and lively fancy, and he had pictured to himself the unfortunate beings, whom we were going to visit, as victims of their sensibility; and as likely to express by their countenances and words the fatal sorrows of their hearts; and I was young enough to share in his anticipations, having, as yet, considered madness not as the result of some physical derangement, but as the result, in most cases, of moral causes. But our romance was sadly disappointed, for we beheld no 'eye in a fine phrensy rolling',[1] no interesting expression of sentimental woe, sufficient to raise its victims above the lowly walk of life in which they had always moved; and I, though I knew that the servant of a friend of mine was in the bedlam who had been 'crazed by hopeless love', yet could not find out, amongst the many figures that glided by me, or bent over the winter fire, a single woman who looked like the victim of the tender passion.

The only woman who had aught interesting about her, was a poor girl, just arrived, whose hair was not yet cut off, and who, seated on the bed in her new cell, had torn off her cap, and had let the dark tresses fall over her shoulders in picturesque confusion! This pleased me; and I was still more convinced I had found what I sought, when, on being told to lie down and sleep, she put her hand to her evidently aching head, as she exclaimed, in a mournful voice, 'Sleep! oh, I cannot sleep!' The wish to question this poor sufferer being repressed by respectful pity, we hastened away to other cells, in which were patients confined in their beds; with one of these women I conversed a little while, and then continued our mournful visits. 'But where (said I to the keeper) is the servant of a friend of mine (naming the patient) who is here because she was deserted by her lover?' 'You have just left her', said the man. 'Indeed', replied I, and hastened eagerly back to the cell I had quitted. I immediately began to talk to her of her mistress and the children, and called her by her name, but she would not reply. I then asked her if she would like money to buy snuff? 'Thank you', she replied. 'Then give me your hand.' 'No, you must lay the money on my pillow.' Accordingly I drew near, when, just as I reached her, she uttered a screaming laugh, so loud, so horrible, so unearthly, that I dropped the pence, and rushing from the cell, never stopped till I found myself with my friends, who had themselves been startled by the noise, and were coming in search of me. I was now eager to leave the place; but I had seen, and lingered behind still, to gaze upon a man whom I had observed from the open door at which I stood, pacing up and down the wintry walk, but who at length saw me earnestly beholding him! He started, fixed his eyes on me with a look full of mournful expression, and never removed them till I, reluctantly I own, had followed my companions. What a world of woe was, as I fancied, in that look! Perhaps I resembled some one dear to him! Perhaps – but it were idle to give all the perhapses of romantic sixteen – resolved to find in bedlam what she thought ought to be there of the sentimental, if it were not. However, that poor man and his expression never left my memory; and I thought of him when, at a later period, I attempted to paint the feelings I imputed to him in the *Father and Daughter*.

On the whole, we came away disappointed, from having formed false ideas of the nature of the infliction which we had gone to contemplate. I have since then seen madness in many different asylums, but I was *never disappointed* again.

Faithful to the views with which I began this little sketch of my childhood and my early youth, I will here relate a circumstance which was romantic enough to add fresh fuel to whatever I had already of romance in my composition; and therefore is another proof that, from the earliest circumstances with which human beings are surrounded, the character takes its colouring through life. Phrenologists watch certain bumps on the head, indicative, they say, of certain propensities, and assert that parents have a power to counteract, by cultivation, the bad propensities, and to increase the good. This may be a surer way of going to work; but, as yet, the truth of their theory is not generally acknowledged. In the meanwhile, I would impress on others what I am fully sensible of myself; namely, that the attention of parents and instructors should be incessantly directed to watching over the very earliest dispositions and tastes of their children or pupils, because, as far as depends on mere human teaching, whatever they are in disposition and pursuit in the earliest dawn of existence, they will probably be in its meridian and in its decline.

When I was scarcely yet in my teens, a highly respected friend of mine, a member of the Society of Friends, informed me that she had a curious story to relate to me and her niece, my favourite friend and companion; she told us that her husband had received a letter from a friend at Lynn, recommending to his kindness a young man, named William Henry Renny, who was a sailor, just come on shore from a distant part, and wanted some assistance on his way (I think) to London. My friend, who was ever ready to lend his aid when needed, and was sure his correspondent would not have required it for one unworthy, received the young man kindly, and ordered him refreshments in the servants' hall; and, as I believe, prepared for him a bed in his own house. But before the evening came, my friend had observed something in the young man's manner which he did not like; he was too familiar towards the servants, and certainly did not seem a proper inmate for the family of a Friend. At length, in consequence of hints given him by some one in the family, he called the stranger into his study, and expressed his vexation at learning that his conduct had not been quite correct. The young man listened respectfully to the deserved rebuke, but with great agitation and considerable excitement, occasioned perhaps, as my candid friend thought, by better meals than he had been used to, and which was therefore a sort of excuse for his behaviour; but little was my friend prepared for the disclosure that awaited him. Falling on his knees, the young man, with clasped hands, conjured his hearer to forgive him the imposition he had practised. 'Oh, sir!' cried he, 'I am an imposter, my name is not William Henry L. but Anna Maria Real, I am not a man, but a woman!' Such a confusion would have astounded any one; judge then how it must have affected the correct man whom she addressed! who certainly did not let the woman remain in her abject position, but desired to hear a true account of who and what she was. She said, that her lover, when very young, had left her to go to sea, and that she resolved to follow him to Russia, whither he was bound; that she did follow him, disguised as a sailor, and had worked out her passage undetected. She found her lover dead, but she liked a sailor's life so well, that she had continued in the service up to that time, when (for some reason which I have forgotten) she left the ship, and came ashore at Lynn, not meaning to return to it, but to resume the garb of her sex. On this latter condition, my friend and his wife were willing to assist her, and endeavour to effect a reformation in her. The first step was to procure her a lodging that evening, and to prevent her being seen, as much as they could, before she had put on woman's clothes. Accordingly, she was sent to lodgings, and inquiries into the truth of her story were instituted at Lynn and elsewhere.

But what an interesting tale was this for me, a Miss just entered into her teens! Of a female soldier's adventures I had some years previously heard, and once had seen Hannah Snelling, a native of Norfolk, who had followed her lover to the wars. Here was a female sailor added to my experience. Every opportunity of hearing any subsequent detail was eagerly seized. What a romantic incident! The romance of real life too! How I wanted to see the heroine; and I was rather mortified that my sober-minded friend would not describe her features to me. Might I (I asked) be at last allowed to see her? and as my parents gave leave, I, accompanied by a young friend, called at the adventurer's lodgings, who was at home! Yes, – she was at home, and to our great consternation we found her in men's clothes still, and working at a trade which she had acquired on board ship, the trade of a tailor! Nor did she leave off though we were her guests, but went on stitching and pulling with most ugly diligence, though ever and anon casting her large, dark, and really beautiful, though fierce eyes, over our disturbed and wondering countenances, silently awaiting to hear why we came. We found it difficult to give a reason, as her appearance and employment so totally extinguished anything like sentiment in our young hearts, upon this occasion. However, we broke the ice at last, and she told us something of her story; which, however touching in the beginning, as that of a disguise and an enterprize prompted by youthful love, became utterly offensive when persisted in after the original motives for it had ceased. Her manner too was not pleasant: I wore a gold watch in my girdle, with a smart chain and seals, and the coveting eye with which she gazed, and at length clapped her hand upon them, begging to see them near, gave me a feeling of distaste; and as I watched her almost terrible eyes, I fancied that they indicated a deranged mind; therefore, hastening to give her the money which I had brought for her, I took my leave, with my friend, resolving not to visit her again. Out of respect to our friends, she went to the Friends' meeting with them, and they were pleased to see her there in her woman's attire; but, when she walked away, with the long strides and bold seeming of a man, it was anything rather than satisfactory, to observe her.

I once saw her walk, and though this romance of real life occupied the minds of my young friend and myself, and was afterwards discussed by us, still the actress in it was becoming, justly, an object with whom we should have loathed any intercourse.

I do not recollect how long she remained under the care of my excellent friends, but I think much of her story was authenticated by the answers to the inquiries made. All that I know with certainty is, that a collection of wild beasts came to town, the shewman of which turned out to be Maria Real's husband, and with him she left Norwich! [*End of first narrative.*]

[*Second narrative.*]

To a girl fond of excitement it will easily be believed that the time of Assizes was one of great interest. As soon as I was old enough to enjoy a procession, I was taken to see the judges come in; and, as youthful pages in pretty dresses ran, at that time of day, by the side of the high sheriff's carriage in which the judges sat, while the coaches drove slowly, and with a solemnity becoming the high and awful office of those whom they contained, it was a sight which I, the older I grew, delighted more and more to witness: with reverence ever did I behold the judges' wigs, the scarlet robes they wore, and even the white wand of the sheriff had an imposing effect on me.

As years advanced, I began to wish to enter the assize court; and as soon as I found that ladies were allowed to attend trials, or causes, I was not satisfied till I had obtained leave to enjoy this indulgence. Accordingly, some one kindly undertook to go with me, and I set off for court: it was to the nisi prius[2] court that I bent my way. I could not bear the thoughts of hearing prisoners tried, as the punishment of death was then in all its force, but I was glad to find myself hearing counsel plead and judges speak where I had no reason to apprehend any fearful consequences to the defendants. By some lucky chance I also soon found myself on the bench, by the side of the judge. Although I could not divest myself of a degree of awful respect when I had reached such a vicinity, it was so advantageous a position for hearing and seeing, that I was soon reconciled to it, especially as the good old man, who sat then as judge, seemed to regard my fixed attention to what was going forward with some complacency.

Sir Henry Gould[3] was the judge then presiding, and he was already on the verge of eighty; but the fire of his fine eye was not quenched by age, nor had his intellect as yet bowed before it; on the contrary, he is said, while in Norwich, to have delivered a charge to the jury, after a trial that had lasted far into the night, in a manner that would have done credit to the youngest judge on the bench.

This handsome and venerable old man, surprised probably at seeing so young a listener by his side, was so kind at last as to enter into conversation with me. Never, I think, had my vanity been so gratified, and when, on my being forced to leave the court, by the arrival of my dinner hour, he said he hoped I was sufficiently pleased to come again, I went home much raised in my own estimation, and fully resolved to go into court again next day. As I was obliged to go alone, I took care to wear the same dress as I wore the preceding day, in hopes that if the judge saw me he would cause way to be made for me. But being obliged to go in at a door where the crowd was very great, I had little hope of being seen, though the door fronted the judge; at last I was pushed forward by the crowd, and gradually got nearer to the table. While thus struggling with obstacles, a man, not quite in the grade of a gentleman, pushed me back rather rudely, and said, 'there miss, go home – you had better go away, what business have you here? this is no place for you; be advised – there go, I tell you!' But miss was obstinate, and stood her ground, turning as she did so towards the judge, who now perceived and recognized her, and instantly ordered one of the servants of the court to make way for that young lady; accordingly way was made, and at his desire I took my place again by the judge's side. It was not in nature, at least not in my weak nature, to resist casting a triumphant glance on my impertinent reprover, and I had the satisfaction of seeing that he looked rather foolish. I do not remember that on either of these days I heard any very interesting causes tried, but I had acquaintances amongst the barristers, and I liked to hear them plead, and I also liked to hear the judge sum up: in short, all was new, exciting and interesting. But

I disliked to hear the witnesses sworn. I was shocked at the very irreverent manner in which the oath was administered and repeated; and evidently the Great Name was spoken with as much levity as if it had been merely that of a brother mortal, not the name of the great King of kings. This was the drawback to my pleasure, but not a sufficient one to keep me from my now accustomed post, and a third time, but early enough to have my choice of places, I repaired to court, and seated myself near the extremity of the bench, hoping to be called to my accustomed seat when my venerable friend arrived. It was expected that the court would be that day crowded to excess, for the cause coming on was one of the deepest interest. One of our richest and oldest aldermen was going to be proceeded against for usury, and the principal witness against him was a gentleman who owed him considerable obligation. The prosecutor was unknown to me; the witness named above I knew sufficiently to bow to him as he passed our house, which he did every day; and he was reckoned a worthy and honourable man. These circumstances gave me an eager desire to be a witness of the proceedings, and I was gratified at being able to answer some questions which the judge asked me when, as before, he had beckoned me to sit by him.

The cause at length began, and it was so interesting that I listened with almost breathless attention, feeling, for the first time, what deep and agitating interest a court of justice can sometimes excite, and what a fearful picture it can hold up to the young of human depravity; for, as this cause went on, the witness for the accused, and the witness for the accuser, both swore in direct opposition to each other! One of them therefore was undoubtedly perjured! and I had witnessed the commission of this awful crime!

Never shall I forget that moment! as it seemed very soon to be the general conclusion, that my acquaintance was the person perjured. I felt a pain wholly unknown before, and though I rejoiced that my friend, the accused, was declared wholly innocent of the charge brought against him, I was indeed sorry that I should never be able to salute my old acquaintance with such cordiality in future, when he passed my window, as this stain rested on his reputation; but that window he was never to pass again!

The next morning before I was up, (for beginning influenza confined me to my bed,) the servant ran into the room to inform me that poor – had been found dead in his bed, with strong suspicions of suicide by poison!

Instantly I dressed myself, forgetting my illness, and went in search of more information. Well do I remember the ghastly expression of the wretched man's countenance as he left the court. I saw his bright grey eye lifted up in a sort of agony to heaven, with, as I supposed, the conviction that he was retiring in disgrace, and I had been told what his lips uttered, while his eyes so spoke. 'What! are you going', said a friend to him. 'Yes; why not? What should I stay for now?' and his tone and manner bore such strong evidence of a desponding mind, that these words were repeated as confirming the belief that he had destroyed himself.

I never can forget with what painful feelings I went back to my chamber, the sensation of illness forgotten, by the sufferings of my mind!

What would I not have given to hear that the poor man who had thus rushed unbidden into the presence of his heavenly judge, urged by the convictions of having been condemned in the presence of an earthly one, was innocent of this second crime! It had been terrible to believe him guilty of the first!

My mind was so painfully full of this subject, that it was always uppermost with me; and, to increase my suffering, the unhappy man's grave was dug immediately opposite our windows, and although I drew down the blinds all day long, I heard the murmuring voices of the people talking over the event, some saying he was an injured man, and venting curses on the heads of those who had brought him to that pass. The verdict having been that 'he was found dead in his bed', the interment took place in the usual manner; and it did so early in the morning. I took care to avoid the front of the house till all was over; and when the hour in the following morning arrived, at which I used to go to the window, and receive the bow and smile of our neighbour, I remembered with bitter regret that I should see him no more, as he lay beneath the wall before me.

Even while I am writing, the whole scene in the court, and the frightful results, live before me with all the vividness of early impressions; and I can scarcely assert, that, at any future stage of life, I ever experienced emotions more keen or more enduring.

Judge Gould came to Norwich again the next year, and as I heard he had inquired for me, I was not long in going to court. One of his first questions was concerning the result of the Usury cause, which he had found so interesting, and he heard with much feeling what I had to impart. I thought my kind friend seemed full a year older; and when I took leave of him I did not expect to see him again. Perhaps the invitation which he gave me, was a proof of a decay of faculties; for he said that if ever I came to London, he lived in such a square, (I forget the place,) and should be pleased to introduce me to his daughter Lady Cavan. I did go to London before he died, but I had not courage enough to call on Sir Henry Gould; I felt it was likely that he had forgotten me, and that he was unlikely to exclaim, like my friends at the bedlam, 'Oh! here's the young girl from St. George's!'

*Source*: Cecilia Lucy Brightwell (ed.), *Memorials of the Life of Amelia Opie* (Norwich: Fletcher and Alexander; London: Longman, Brown and Co., 1854)

### Notes

1. *A Midsummer Night's Dream*, v.i.12.
2. *Nisi prius* – 'unless previously': a name given to the jury sittings in civil cases.
3. Sir Henry Gould (1710–94). According to the *Dictionary of National Biography* he 'had the reputation of being a sound but not an eloquent lawyer' (vol. VIII, p. 286). His daughter, Honora Margaretta (d. 1813), married Richard Lambart, 7th Earl of Cavan.

# 3

# Dorothea Herbert

Dorothea Herbert (1770–1829) was the eldest daughter of a clergyman, the Revd Nicholas Herbert (d. 1803), and the Hon. Martha Cuffe (d. 1811). Raised in Ireland, at Carrick-on-Suir, and subsequently educated in Dublin, she fell in love with a man called John Roe, who after apparently encouraging her to become emotionally involved with him, married someone else. 'I shall always regard him as My Husband,' she wrote in the second volume of her *Retrospections*, 'though his renegade Amour has placed a Barrier of Vicious Obstacles to my Claims' (p. 411). Her *Retrospections of Dorothea Herbert 1770–1789* remained an unpublished manuscript in the Mandeville family until 1929, when they were edited by Gerald Howe. Little else is known about her, though the title page suggests she wrote plays, poems and novels. The following extracts describe an ebullient, boisterous childhood, with a particularly vivid account of the games played in her large family of brothers and sisters. Drunkenness seems to have been a common experience, and the whole tone of these childhood recollections is distinctly indecorous. The first section begins with a list of the servants employed in her parents' home:

Besides them we had first a bad Nurse 2dly a Mad Nurse, and 3rdly a sickly Nurse for my little Ladyship (Its a Wonder Poor Miss Dolly ever got over such an Ordeal) and Nurses apiece for all the rest – Not forgetting old Mary Neal who drynursed us all and lived with us upwards of forty Years without ever stirring from the Nursery Window, where she sat crying about us or damning us unmercifully for our boldness whilst she sat mending our Stockings and Rocking the Cradles, Yet at Eighty Years of Age she was upright as a palm tree in Carriage and was indeed a rare Instance of fidelity and honest Attachment ...

There were six or seven of us almost always in Mischief – Tom invented Pop Guns that often blinded us – Fanny the Art of Dyeing by which we compleatly spoiled a set of new scarlet Stuff Gowns we had just Got – We then washed them, and when that was of no avail we threw them out to Bleach ... When the Boys first returnd from School it gave a new turn to Affairs – They spouted to us and we stood gaping round till we were all Book Mad – Dido and Aeneas – Hector and Paris fired our Brains, a Sixpenny Voyage of Lord Anson,[1] and Old Robinson Crusoes Tale compleated our Mania – One time we fancied ourselves thrown on a Desart Island till a fight who should be Crusoe and who Fryday ended our play – Another time we were a set of sailors thrown on the Delightful Island of Juan Fernandez – We spent whole weeks in an old blue Bed under cure for the Sea Scurvy and eat such quantities of Cabbage Stumps, Celery, and other Antiscorbutic Thrash that we really got scorbutic Disorder with worms and a Variety of Complaint that obliged us to submit to Continual Doses of Physick which old Mary administered with tear swoln Eyes to half a Dozen of us at Once.

Thus passed our Hours of Relaxation from School Studies which were emulatively pursued in the forenoon – Mr Wimpe [the Parish Clerk] made us spell for Slaps – but Tom having one Day egregiously cut up Fanny She very deliberately went and hang'd herself in the Garret – She was however cut down by her more fortunate Competitor and with Proper Care recover'd – It were endless to recount all our prowess –.

... At this time [1778] we were at home as happy as Uncultivated Nature could be – dressing out as Shepherds and Shepherdesses with flower wrought vestments, and Parasoles of Sycamore Leaves studded with Daisies and Buttercups – Here was a groupe of lovely Shepherdesses basking on a Sunny Hillock with two or three pet Kids browzing beside them – There a groupe of Shepherds with their Dogs and Crooks – regaling of a frugal Meal of stolen Cold Meat with a Wretched Sallad – 'Their Drink the Chrystal Well' – Except at the Season the Whiskey Currants were thrown out when we were all as fuddled as Couple Beggars – Nay one time the Pigs, Servants, and Children were reeling about the Yard where the heaps were thrown. Having once got a relish for the delightful Haut gout we often found a pretence to stay at home from Church, when the Jephsons [a neighbouring family] and we used to say family prayers – dress'd out in our Mothers fine flowerd Damasks with sticks across for large Hoops – We first tossd up a Marmalade of orange peels and Stolen Honey – then we got to the Cellar and made a delightful warm jug of Punch in the fine hot Summers

Mornings – After that we made Pews with the Chairs and then most devoutly fell to Prayers never missing one Amen – At length our revelry was ended by my Mothers catching us one Sunday Morning in such a State of Intoxication that not one of us could stir from our Chairs or utter a Monosyllable – This stopd all our future Piety and feasting – Our tastes were indeed rather Eccentric – We would eat nothing but pig potatoes, Pap or Stirabout for our breakfast and we ended the Day with a Desert of raw Turneps, Cabbage Stumps, or Celery Tops – In this wild state my Aunt Cuffe and her accomplish'd Grace found us – they were much shocked at first but we soon brought Grace over and conferr'd on her the honour of being head Cook and Confectioner having just Politeness enough to shew our Guest this Mark of Distinction.

Nothing now was heard of but hot Mutton Pies and so forth with all the Varieties of Creams and Candies that the Dairy and Garden could allow – some were contriving small Ovens that we might do without the cross Cook – others Stills, baking Dishes and Pudding Cloths, till my Aunt Cuffe one Day found our Confectioner regaling under a Tree of green Gooseberries – on which she was confined, and put in Coventry by her Mother and never after allowed to come down till Dinner time – This was a terrible Blow to poor Grace, who almost forgot her Town Education amongst her Country Cousins.

*Source*: *Retrospections of Dorothea Herbert 1770–1789*, 2 vols (London: Gerald Howe, 1929).

**Notes**

1. George Anson (1697–1762), British Admiral known for his voyages round the world in the 'Centurion' from 1740–44.

# 4

# Mary Martha Sherwood

Mary Martha Sherwood (1775–1851) is best known for her *History of the Fairchild Family* (1818), a popular children's book, which inculcated religious principles – sometimes by rather shocking means (notoriously, after they have been squabbling, Mr Fairchild takes the children to see a corpse hanging on a gibbet: 'one who first hated and afterwards killed his brother': 'Story on the Sixth Commandment'). The second child of George Butt (1741–95), divine and poet, and his wife Martha Sherwood, Mary Butt was born at Stanford in Worcestershire, attended the Abbey School, Reading, and on 30 June 1803 married her cousin, Captain Henry Sherwood (d. 1849). In the course of an eventful married life, Mrs Sherwood travelled widely, lived in India with her husband, whose regiment was posted there, and had eight children, of whom only three survived to adulthood. She wrote approximately three hundred stories and tracts, and her *History of the Fairchild Family* ran to three parts, from 1818 to the final part in 1847. The following extract is taken from the *Life of Mrs Sherwood* (1854) edited by her daughter, Sophia Kelly. 'There has been a singular Providence attending me through life,' Mrs Sherwood states, 'and preparing me in a remarkable manner for that which it was the Divine will I should do' (*Life*, p. 2). She is one of few women in this collection to describe a relatively happy childhood.

The very first recollection of existence which I have, is being carried down a hanging stone staircase at the parsonage at Stanford, in my mother's arms, and seeing the half-circular window over the hall door. It seems that I then began first to make observations on my own thoughts, but I must have reflected before that time, otherwise I should not have known where I was, or by whose arms I was supported. It is wonderful to observe the expandings of the human intellect, from the first dawn of infant light, till that far-distant period which prophecy unfolds, beyond all calculation hitherto used by man, even to the end of ages, when the human intellect being no longer darkened by sin, shall have been submitted to the teachings of the Lord the Spirit, through periods of time of which we now can form only very imperfect conceptions. But in writing the history of another, however intimate we may have been with that other, it is impossible to trace the openings of the mind as we can do in taking the review of our own life, that is, if memory is accurate, and power is given for clear discernment. In speaking of myself, I wish to remark that one of the peculiar blessings of my education I consider to have been this, that whilst sufficient nourishment was administered to my mind, and that all I saw was elegant and beautiful, and all I heard was highly intellectual and pure, speaking after the manner of men, no attempt at display or personal vanity was excited in me, at least during the first ten or eleven years of my life. To this special circumstance I attribute the regular development of my intellect.

It is not while I live that the world, if I can help it, shall ever see these memoranda. I therefore would wish to consider myself, when writing this, as one with whom all present things are past, – as one, as it were, speaking from the dead, – as one who never more can hear the voice of fame, with whom the praise or blame of man are just as the breezes which passed over the earth in the days before the 'hearing ear of man was planted'. Ps. xciv.9.

As I said before, I assuredly entered life under the most happy circumstances, being blessed with a remarkably fine constitution, and a frame decidedly healthy. I was a large child, and grew so rapidly that I was at my full height, which is above the standard of women in general, at thirteen years of age. My appearance was so healthy and glowing, that my father, in fond fancy, used to call me Hygeia.[1] I had very long hair of a bright auburn, which my mother had great pleasure in arranging; and, as I was a very placid child, my appearance indicated nothing of that peculiarity of mind, which, whether good or bad, was soon afterwards made manifest. I have often heard my mother tell a singular story about my brother and myself, when he was three years old, and I scarcely two. Our parents took us to Lichfield, to visit at the palace; Miss Seward was there, and Mr. Lovel Edgeworth, and the elder Dr. Darwin.[2] We were brought into the room to be looked at, and Dr. Darwin took up my brother, as I have seen a Frenchman do a frog, by one leg, exclaiming at the same time, 'What a fine animal! what a noble animal!' My brother was then a beautiful child, and no doubt he made no small resistance, on being treated thus philosophically; but he was hardly rescued when Mr. Edgeworth's eye fell on me, and having looked at me some time, he patted his own forehead, and having paid some compliments to my father on my well-nurtured animal nature, he added, with no great tenderness to his feelings, 'But you may depend upon it, Mr Butt, you may depend upon it she wants it here', and the little taps on his own brow were reiterated. This hint made my poor mother for a while very uneasy, – of all this I however remember nothing.

My parents, probably owing to the remark of Mr. Edgeworth, had very little opinion of my intellectual abilities till I was six years of age; hence my mind was allowed to develop itself in health, and strength, and consistency; nor was any attempt made to induce efforts beyond the state of my infant faculties, which kind of excitement or mismanagement has often blighted a fine mind before it has hardly blossomed, and by which superiority is either precluded, or if obtained and possessed for a short time, is terminated often and suddenly, either by death or the loss of reason. Much and long experience has taught me to dread, above many things, the system which now prevails so largely, of hurrying the young mind, by which smatterers in knowledge may be made, but never solid, useful characters.

I was, from very early infancy, a creature who had a peculiar world of images about me; and the first exercise of my imagination operated upon one set of fancies. My mother used to sit much in her beautiful dressing-room, and there she often played sweetly on her guitar, and sung to it. Her voice sounded through the hall, which was lofty; and I loved to sit on the steps of the stairs and listen to her singing. She had possessed a canary bird when she first married, and it had died, and she had preserved it and put it into a little coffin in an Indian cabinet in her dressing-room. My first idea of death was from this canary bird and this coffin; and as I had no decided idea of time, as regarded its length, I felt that this canary bird had lived, and what appeared to me, ages before, when my mother had sung and played on the guitar before my birth; and I had numerous fancies about those remote ages, fancies I could not define nor explain; but they possessed a spell over my mind that had power to keep me quiet many a half-hour as I sat by myself, dreamily pondering on their strange enchantment. I had also some very curious thoughts about an echo, which answered our invocations in various parts of the lovely grounds of Stanford. Echo I fancied to be a beautiful winged boy, and I longed to see him, though I knew it was in vain to attempt to pursue him to his haunts; neither was Echo the only unseen being who filled my imagination.

There are circumstances which happened just before I entered my fifth year, which enable me to fix the time when I had such and such thoughts, and when I made such and such observations. I was not four, when one day after dinner, a gentleman, who shall be nameless, took me on his knee and said something to me which I did not understand, but which was of a nature which should not have been said to any one, especially a female, and more especially if that female is of tender years. He looked me full in the face when he spoke, and I answered, 'I don't like you, you are naughty.' My parents were astonished; and the gentleman set me down in some alarm. I perfectly remember the whole circumstance. My mother asked me why I called him naughty? 'Because', I answered, 'his eyes are wicked.' Thus early I began to notice the expression of the eye; and to this hour does the human eye speak so intelligibly to me, that I am often obliged to restrain myself from pronouncing too severe a judgment on the expression it reveals. And I hope also, that I am kept humble from a sense of what perhaps might be read in my own countenance by those disposed and enabled to read aright, for the Almighty himself has declared that 'the imaginations of man's heart are evil continually'. I have many sweet recollections of parental kindnesses, even before my fourth year. I remember my mother teaching me to read with my brother, in a book where was a picture of a white horse feeding by starlight. My first idea of the quiet beauty of a star-light scene was taken from that print. I remember our mother telling us stories in the dusk of a winter's evening, one of which I have recorded in my history of *The Fairchild Family*. It is the tale of the old lady who invites many children to spend a day with her. I also recollect some walks with my father in the woods, and how he carried me in his arms over difficult places. Where are these beloved parents now? Their mortal remains sleep, indeed, in Stanford Church. They were laid there, and there our natural senses tell us that they still are, though mouldered and fallen into dust; but where are their immortal spirits? None of our natural senses can tell us this; but faith, which is the evidence of things not seen, has assured me that they are with Christ, our Lord having obtained their salvation, not because they loved him, but because he loved them and made his love manifest to them, whilst yet they were in the flesh. I had my little notions of religion before I was four years old. My brother had a dream and he told it to me. He had seen heaven over the highest trees of Stanford Park; and he had seen hell, such as little children fancy it. We had sundry discussions on the subject; and we determined to seek the one and avoid the other. The cartoon of St. Stephen in the hall no doubt helped forward our ideas; and because our Saviour was painted there in the clouds, we were taught by it to understand that we were to look to him as a friend; and what more was necessary, and what more would be necessary, than such a childlike sincerity and confidence as we then had? Had it pleased God at that time to have taken me and my dear brother, we should, I dare avow, have been in a much better state, if we only depended on ourselves, than we were years afterwards. Our blessed Saviour's words are, 'Unless ye be converted and become as little children, ye cannot enter the kingdom of God.'[3]

But I must now proceed to the first grand event of my life, the journey to see my grandfather Butt, at Pipe Grange, near Lichfield. I must here remark, I had been attacked with a severe illness, called, formerly, Saint Anthony's fire, which had much affected my eyes. When we were in the carriage going to Lichfield, my mother pointed out to my brother the Abberley and Woodbury hills, which formed some of the grandest features of the view from our home; and she told him that we were going over those hills and far away. Had she spoken prophetically of what was to be the future destiny of her little girl, she would have spoken truth; but a little way was far in the imagination of my beloved mother, who lived and died without ever seeing the sea. I was so blind that I could not see the hills; but even then I had my thoughts of hills; and these ideas thus early acquired and strongly impressed, have accompanied me through life.

I had entered my fifth year, when with my grandfather at Pipe Grange; I remember little of the following summer; but one event in the winter I can recall, connected with a Mr. B—y, the last representative of an old Worcestershire family, who possessed Abberley Lodge. This Mr. B—y had a town house in the College Yard, Worcester, and he was an old bachelor, remarkable for that sort of ugliness which children hate, being strongly marked with the smallpox, and having a circle like rows of heavy red beads round his eyes; he was also what the world falsely calls a man of pleasure, and his manner of life in private had, no doubt, imparted a sort of coarseness to his expression, which added not a little to his ugliness; but withal, he was a man of the most polished manners of the old school; and he sometimes came in form to dine with my parents. Being brought in one day after dinner, as I was making my way round the table, he caught me, to my inexpressible horror, and placed me on his knee, asking me if I would be his wife. I looked at my mother, to take a hint from her respecting what I ought to say, and thinking that I must not dare say no, I replied that I would have him in six years, wondering at the laughter which this my answer produced. Six years I thought would never end; but they did end too soon for my peace; for, on the occasion of my reaching my eleventh birthday, Mr. B—y came in form to demand me, and it was with some difficulty that I got a respite for a few more years, though I then firmly believed that I must necessarily some time or other fulfil my engagement. This, when I thought of it, or met the old gentleman, was such a subject of dread to me, that I always ran away and hid myself when I saw his carriage coming to the house.

And now I must record the first trouble of my infancy. When my brother Marten was five years old, we went out one autumn evening to take a walk with our father and mother, and Caesar our dog was with us. As we children ran along, tempted by the dog to go forwards and forwards, we came to a five-barred gate, of a good height, which impeded our progress; though Caesar jumped over it, and tried by many wiles to persuade us to follow him. My brother first attempted to open the gate; but being unable to do so, he began to climb upon it from one bar to another. With some difficulty he got upon the top of the gate, whilst I was talking and patting Caesar, and there he stood, shouting and spreading out his little arms as if they were wings. Our parents called to him; but the noise he made prevented his hearing their voices, and swinging his arms still more, he lost his balance, and down he fell: his head struck upon a stone with such force that he could neither move nor cry. My poor father was soon on the spot, and he carried my brother home; but it was a long time before he recovered his senses, for his head was severely injured, and I have no doubt my mother had much trouble in nursing him while this illness continued. It was on account of this that he got his way much more than he would otherwise have done, and a system of indulgence was commenced which would to most boys have proved exceedingly injurious; but my brother was gifted naturally with such a very sweet temper, and was so affectionate, that I never suffered from any partiality shown to him by my mother in preference to myself. Still, it was owing to this indulgence that some of our plays were allowed, which I believe would not have been permitted under other circumstances, judging, as I now do, from the quiet character of my mother. Some of his exploits I still remember with amazement.

My brother, no doubt, had heard of the unique, but certainly undignified, amusement that was in fashion in my mother's early days. This fashion consisted of spreading a large strong table-cloth on the upper steps of any wide, old-fashioned staircase, and this being done, all the ladies present, who were disposed for merriment, seated themselves on this table-cloth, in rows upon the steps. Then the gentlemen seized hold of the cloth and pulled it down the stairs, and a struggle would ensue, which usually ended with the tumbling down of the ladies, table-cloth and all, to the bottom of the stairs, to the utter confusion of all order and decorum.

As my brother had no table-cloth at his command, he used to put me into a drawer and kick me down the nursery stairs. He also used to heap chairs and tables one on the other, and set me at the top of them, and then throw them all down. He used to put a bridle round my neck, and drive me about with a whip: but being a very hardy child, and not easily hurt, I suppose I had myself to blame for some of his excesses; for, with all this, he was the kindest of brothers to me, and I loved him very, very much. Many of his thoughts and expressions were singularly sweet; and I remember once, when we had climbed up a high bank among the woods at Stanford, which overlooked the pleasure-grounds, he showed me my mother walking along a path shaded by filbert trees, and he made me look till I almost cried to think how much I loved her. It was wonderful how many of my tenderest feelings were elicited by him in our infancy.

But I have forgotten to mention the anecdote of the berries of the mountain-ash. When my brother was lying ill of the wound in his head, from the fall off the five-barred gate, he did not like the doctor to dress his head, and our father promised him, if he would be a good boy and let it be done, he would get him a bagful of blue beans. Marten had seen some berries on the mountain-ash tree on the day of the accident, and he asked for the berries instead. Our beloved father promised he would get them for him; but it so happened that, being called from home, time passed on, and the birds and winter caused the red berries to pass away also. On our father's return, my brother reminded him of his promise, and this tender parent at once set off in his search for the berries. Many, many miles did he ride, many many trees were examined – but they were all stripped of their berries; still he persevered in his search, and at last. after much labour, he found one tree, from which he gathered all the berries, and brought them home to Marten. My brother never forgot the beautiful lesson taught him by our mother, upon the trouble our beloved father had taken to get the berries for his child. 'Marten,' she said, 'you see that when your dear papa makes a promise, he will take the greatest pains in the world to keep that promise, and this is the reason wherefore he desires it. He is a follower of that perfect Saviour whose ways he dearly loves; and that Saviour never departs from his holy word, but performs everything which he has promised to his redeemed ones.' By my brother's especial desire, I made a little tale of this fact, called *The Mountain Ash*, and it was published by Thomas Melrose, of Berwick-upon-Tweed, and first came out in 1834.

I was in my sixth year when I first began to make stories, but what they were I have not the least idea. I was too young to write them down; but when I had thought of anything belonging to my story, I used to follow my mother with a slate and pencil, and get her to put my ideas down for me. She afterwards, I found, copied these stories with pen and ink, and kept them by her for the love she bore her child.

Through the great care of this tender and good mother, I was preserved, during all my childhood, in an ignorance of vice, to a degree I could hardly have believed to have been possible. This ignorance of things as they are, might perhaps have been promoted by the tendency of my mind always to run upon an imaginary world, and, in consequence, to take less note of the ordinary occurrences about me than most persons do in common life.

The society in which I mixed as a child was such as to give a decided turn to the thoughts and the tastes. Indeed, as long as I have lived, I have never heard any persons converse as my father and mother were accustomed to converse. My mother never suffered her children to interrupt conversation. We were compelled to listen, whether willing or not. My father not only conversed in a superior way himself, but he gave the tone to all his visitors and to all his pupils. I can hardly say how young I was when I got ideas of other countries, and other times, and other modes of life, such as, by the modern style of education, could never possibly be obtained; and this through the simple means of listening to my father's conversation. Whilst this system of improvement was always going forward whenever the family were assembled, there was a private discipline of such undeviating strictness carried on with me by my excellent mother, that it might have appeared that no other person in the world could have been better fitted to bring a mere child of many imaginations under control than was my ever honoured parent. Lady Jane Grey speaks of the severities to which she was subjected by her noble parents. I had neither nips, nor bobs, nor pinches; but I experienced what I thought much worse. It was the fashion then for children to wear iron collars round the neck, with a backboard strapped over the shoulders: to one of these I was subjected from my sixth to my thirteenth year. It was put on in the morning, and seldom taken off till late in the evening; and I generally did all my lessons standing in stocks, with this stiff collar round my neck. At the same time I had the plainest possible food, such as dry bread and cold milk. I never sat on a chair in my mother's presence. Yet I was a very happy child; and when relieved from my collar, I not unseldom manifested my delight by starting from our hall door, and taking a run for at least half a mile through the woods which adjoined our pleasure-grounds.

It would not be easy to judge the character of a child so favourably circumstanced as I was; neither can I myself decide whether I had then any ideas of religion beyond what parents may teach – in fact, beyond what may be acquired by the unregenerate mind: the time of trial was then remote, and the evil nature restrained by the gentle, yet firm, hand of a tender and wise mother ...

My brother and I were great readers, though our books were few. *Robinson Crusoe*, two sets of *Fairy Tales*, *The Little Female Academy*,[4] and *Aesop's Fables* formed the whole of our infant library. *Robinson Crusoe* was always in my brother's hands when he was disposed to read; and his wont was to place himself with me at the foot of the stairs, and to ascend one step every time he turned over a page. Of course, I did as he did. Another curious custom we had was, that on the first day of every month we used to take two sticks with certain notches cut upon them, and hide them in a hollow tree in the wood, as far from the house as we were permitted to go: no person was to see us do this, and no one was to know we did it. How easily in a heathen country might a caprice of this kind grow into a superstition, and how soon might these notched sticks have become objects of veneration! Where we got the idea I do not recollect; but anything at that time which took hold of the imagination was delightful to me, and equally congenial to the mind of my brother. Though educated under the same roof with my brother till he was nine or ten years old, yet we were by no means under the same management. I have described the discipline to which I was subjected, and for which I have many times thanked my God and my beloved mother. A very different process, however, was going on with Marten. All this time, whilst I was with my mother in her dressing-room, he was with my father in his study; and, no authority being used, he made such small progress in his Latin, that it was at last suggested that I should be made to learn Latin with him. My dear mother, in order that, by her regularity, she might make up for the intermitting habits of my father, set herself to learn Latin, and thus she became our tutor. Still, however, as she constantly obliged me to get my lessons, whilst no such authority was exercised over my brother, it proved that I soon got before him. Besides, it is generally observed that, all things being equal, girls learn more rapidly than boys during the years of childhood. With me and my brother, however, all things were not equal.

About this time, my father shut me and my brother up, one morning, in his study, that each of us might write a story, with a view to prove our natural talents; for he had begun to suspect that both Marten and Mary would be what he called *genuises*. I forget what I produced; but my brother began a story which he called 'The Travels of the Lady Viatoria', and wrote the adventures of one day. During this first trial, we had each made a beginning, and my father shut us up again the next day. I added a little more to whatever I had begun, and my brother carried his lady on another day, carefully providing her with meals at the wonted hours, and a good bed at night.

Another and another day we were shut up, and my story came to a conclusion. But the Lady Viatoria's adventures might have gone to the length of the tale of 'The Suitor of the Princess of Shiraz',[5] so well known in oriental history, if the experiment had not terminated. I never knew to which of his children my father gave the first palm of genius ... In the year 1784, my brother was sent to Dr. Valpy's[6] school at Reading, for my father was wisely persuaded that his education could not go on well at home ... Thus was I separated from my brother; and as my sister's nurse, a very nice person, who used to be very kind to me, also went just at the same time, I remember being very unhappy, seriously unhappy, probably for the first time of my life. Then it was I first had an idea of that feeling of bereavement which every one who lives to my age must often, often have experienced. But I ought to say, that before these losses occurred I had gone with my father and mother to visit Madame de Pelivé at Ludlow. I have never seen that place since then; but it left so strong an impression on my mind, that I was able full twelve years after to describe it with so much accuracy, in my history of *Susan Grey*, that the inhabitants of Ludlow often show the old house where Mrs. Neale is said to have lived. It was early in the autumn that we went to Ludlow, and it was at my return that I felt the sadness I speak of, for, from the time in which my brother went to school, he never could be to me what he was before. The hours of infancy were gone, and with them its thousand delights, known only when the mind is fresh and young. It often happens that something of this freshness is renewed in after life, in parents, when the sympathies with their children lead them to delight again, for their sakes, in the same description of trifles which amused themselves in their infancy ... I do not remember that at that period of my life I attempted to write any stories; indeed, probably I had not time, but I was the most indefatigable narrator of stories. With Margaret [a cousin] and my sister Lucy, for my auditors, I repeated stories, – one story often going on at every possible interval for months together. In company I was remarkably silent and very much at a loss for words; but I do not remember feeling this want when telling my stories to my young companions. I knew nothing then of life as it is, but my mind was familiar with fairies, enchanters, wizards, and all the imagery of heathen gods and goddesses which I could get out of any book in my father's study. But what I could have made of these heroes of Olympus, without finding out the hateful points in their characters, I cannot now explain. The eighteen months during which Margaret was with us appear to me to have been very long and happy. At length, in the autumn, her father and step-mother came and took her away. My grief at the loss of Margaret was deep and long, and all that winter I continued to mourn for her. Soon after this I remember that I began to write fairy tales and fables; but I do not think that I made much of them.

I grew so rapidly in my childhood, that at thirteen I had attained my full height, which is considered above the usual standard of women. I stooped very much when thus growing. As my mother always dressed me like a child in a pinafore, I must certainly have been a very extraordinary sort of personage, and every one cried out on seeing me as one that was to be a giantess. As my only companion of nearly my own age, Miss Winnington, was small and delicate, I was very often thoroughly abashed at my appearance; and therefore never was I so happy as when I was out of sight of visitors, in my own beloved woods of

Stanford. In those sweet woods I had many little embowered corners, which no one knew but myself, and there, when my daily tasks were done, I used to fly with a book and enjoy myself in places where I could hear the cooing of doves, the note of the blackbird, and the rush of two waterfalls coming from two sides of the valley and meeting within the range where I might stroll undisturbed by any one. It must be noticed, that I never made these excursions without carrying a huge wooden doll with me, which I generally slung with a string round my waist under my pinafore, as I was thought by the neighbours too big to like a doll. My sister, as a child, had not good health, and therefore she could bear neither the exposure nor fatigue I did. Hence the reason wherefore I was so much alone. From this cause, too, she was never submitted to the same discipline that I was; she was never made so familiar with the stocks and iron collar, nor the heavy tasks; for after my brother was gone to school, I still was carried on in my Latin studies, and even before I was twelve I was obliged to translate fifty lines of Virgil every morning, standing in these same stocks with the iron collar pressing on my throat. It only wanted one to tell me that I was hardly used to turn this healthful discipline into poison; but there was no such person to give this hint, and hence the suspicion never, as I remember, arose in my mind that other children were not subjected to the same usage as myself. If my sister was not so, I put it down to her being much younger, and thus I was reconciled to the difference made between us ... My father had a large and fine edition of the *Tatler*, which had been my delight ever since I was eight years of age, and I have reason to think that the account there given me of Miss Bickerstaff[7] had a very strong effect upon my mind, for it was about this time that, as I stood alone in the wood at Stanford, I suddenly asked myself: Whether it was necessary that geniuses should be slovenly and odd? My father had always told me that I was to grow up a genius, and of course I believed him, for what child ever doubts the assurance given by an elder, that he or she is, or is to be, something very extraordinary? But even then I felt if it were necessary to be very singular, I would rather not be a genius, nor do I ever remember, either at that time, or at any other time of my life, that the desire of literary fame was remarkably strong in my mind; I mean as remarkably strong as I have generally seen it in others.

I would at any time of my youth rather have been a heroine of romance than a celebrated authoress.

*Source*: *The Life of Mrs Sherwood*, ed. Sophia Kelly (London: Darton and Co., 1854).

## Notes

1. The Greek goddess of health.
2. Anna Seward (1747–1809), known as 'the Swan of Lichfield', and author of the

*Memoirs of the Life of Dr Darwin* (1804); Erasmus Darwin (1731–1802), poet and physician, author of *The Botanic Garden* (1792) and *Zoonomia* (1794–96). He was the grandfather of Charles Darwin, author of *The Origin of Species* (1859). The Edgeworth mentioned must be the educationist Richard Lovell (1744–1817), rather than his son Lovell, who was not born until 1776.

3.      Matthew 18:3.

4.      *The Governess, or The Little Female Academy*, by Sarah Fielding (1749), one of the first educational books specifically for girls.

5.      Scheherazade, heroine of the *Thousand and One Nights*, who ended each of her stories on a cliffhanger, so that her husband, who had intended to put her to death, was obliged to spare her for another day.

6.      Richard Valpy (1754–1836) became Headmaster of the Reading school in 1781, where he considerably raised standards, but had a reputation for being a hard flogger.

7.      Isaac Bickerstaff, pseudonym of Richard Steele as Editor of the *Tatler*, describes his half-sister Jenny as vain of her intelligence, 'which inclines her to be a little, but a very little, sluttish' (1 October 1709). Jenny's surname is Distaff, however, not Bickerstaff.

# 5

# Mary Somerville

Mary Somerville (1780–1872), the best-known female mathematician of the nineteenth century, after whom Somerville College, Oxford, was named, grew up in Burntisland, near Edinburgh, and was the daughter of a vice-admiral, Sir William Fairfax, and his second wife, Margaret Charters. Like most Victorian women autobiographers, she was deeply dissatisfied with her formal education, and learnt  more by private reading and cadging lessons from male tutors. She married twice – on each occasion a cousin, the first of whom, Samuel Greig, was unsympathetic to her scientific interests. Greig died in 1807, leaving her with two sons; five years later, she married another cousin, William Somerville, who was an army doctor. This was a much more successful marriage intellectually. Moving to London in 1816, she entered the scientific community, and attracted excited attention with her 1831 English version of Laplace's *Mécanique Celeste*. As a public persona, Mrs Somerville was admired even more for her ladylike behaviour as a wife and mother whose scientific accomplishments apparently took second place to the smooth running of her home, and she was often cited as an example of the ideal woman in contrast to the 'shrieking sisterhood' of the mid-Victorian period. Yet the child, Mary Fairfax, frustrated by not being allowed to read freely or acquire a sound education (something she remedied with her own two daughters), presents herself as an angry rebel, alternately afraid of the dark and determined to educate herself by whatever means came to hand.

My father was very good looking, of a brave and noble nature, and a perfect gentleman both in appearance and character. He was sent to sea as midshipman at ten years of age, so he had very little education; but he read a great deal, chiefly history and voyages. He was very cool, and of instant resource in moments of danger.

One night, when his little vessel had taken refuge with many others from an intensely violent gale and drifting snow in Yarmouth Road, they saw lights disappear, as vessel after vessel foundered. My father, after having done all that was possible for the safety of the ship, went to bed. His cabin door did not shut closely, from the rolling of the ship, and the man who was sentry that night told my mother years afterwards, that when he saw my father on his knees praying, he thought it would soon be all over with them; then seeing him go to bed and fall asleep, he felt no more fear. In the morning the coast was strewed with wrecks. There were no life-boats in those days; now the lives of hundreds are annually saved by the noble self-devotion of British sailors.

My mother was the daughter of Samuel Charters, Solicitor of the Customs for Scotland, and his wife Christian Murray, of Kynynmont, whose eldest sister married the great grandfather of the present Earl Minto. My grandmother was exceedingly proud and stately. She made her children stand in her presence. My mother, on the contrary, was indulgent and kind, so that her children were perfectly at ease with her. She seldom read anything but the Bible, sermons, and the newspaper. She was very sincere and devout in her religion, and was remarkable for good sense and great strength of expression in writing and conversation. Though by no means pretty, she was exceedingly distinguished and ladylike both in appearance and manners.

My father was constantly employed, and twice distinguished himself by attacking vessels of superior force. He captured the first, but was overpowered by the second, and being taken to France, remained two years a prisoner on parole, when he met with much kindness from the Choiseul family. At last he was exchanged, and afterwards was appointed lieutenant on board a frigate destined for foreign service. I think it was the North American station, for the war of Independence was not over till the beginning of 1783. As my mother knew that my father would be absent for some years, she accompanied him to London, though so near her confinement that in returning home she had just time to arrive at the manse of Jedburgh, her sister Martha Somerville's house, when I was born, on the 26th December, 1780. My mother was dangerously ill, and my aunt, who was about to wean her second daughter Janet, who married General Henry Elliot, nursed me till a wetnurse could be found. So I was born in the house of my future husband, and nursed by his mother – a rather singular coincidence.

During my father's absence, my mother lived with great economy in a house not far from Burntisland which belonged to my grandfather, solely occupied with the care of her family, which consisted of her eldest son Samuel, four or five years old, and myself. One evening while my brother was lying at play on the floor, he called out, 'O, mamma, there's the moon rinnin' awa.' It was the celebrated meteor of 1783.

Some time afterwards, for what reason I do not know, my father and mother went to live for a short time at Inveresk, and thence returned to Burntisland, our permanent home ...

My mother taught me to read the Bible, and to say my prayers morning and evening; otherwise she allowed me to grow up a wild creature. When I was seven or eight years old I began to be useful, for I pulled the fruit for preserving; shelled the peas and beans, fed the poultry, and looked after the dairy, for we kept a cow.

On one occasion I had put green gooseberries into bottles and sent them to the kitchen with orders to the cook to boil the bottles uncorked, and, when the fruit was sufficiently cooked, to cork and tie up the bottles. After a time all the house was alarmed by loud explosions and violent screaming in the kitchen; the cook had corked the bottles before she boiled them, and of course they exploded. For greater preservation, the bottles were always buried in the ground; a number were once found in our garden with the fruit in high preservation which had been buried no one knew when. Thus experience is sometimes the antecedent of science, for it was little suspected at that time that by shutting out the air the invisible organic world was excluded – the cause of all fermentation and decay.

I never cared for dolls, and had no one to play with me. I amused myself in the garden, which was much frequented by birds. I knew most of them, their flight and their habits. The swallows were never prevented from building above our windows, and, when about to migrate, they used to assemble in hundreds on the roof of our house, and prepared for their journey by short flights. We fed the birds when the ground was covered with snow, and opened our windows at breakfast-time to let in the robins, who would hop on the table to pick up crumbs. The quantity of singing birds was very great, for the farmers and gardeners were less cruel and avaricious than they are now – though poorer. They allowed our pretty songsters to share in the bounties of providence. The shortsighted cruelty, which is too prevalent now, brings its own punishment, for, owing to the reckless destruction of birds, the equilibrium of nature is disturbed, insects increase to such an extent as materially to affect every description of crop. This summer (1872), when I was at Sorrento, even the olives, grapes, and oranges were seriously injured by the caterpillars – a disaster which I entirely attribute to the ruthless havoc made among every kind of bird.

My mother set me in due time to learn the catechism of the Kirk of Scotland, and to attend the public examinations in the kirk. This was a severe trial for me; for, besides being timid and shy, I had a bad memory, and did not understand one word of the catechism. These meetings, which began with prayer, were attended by all the children of the town and neighbourhood, with their mothers, and a great many old women, who came to be edified. They were an acute race, and could quote chapter and verse of Scripture as accurately as the minister himself. I remember he said to one of them – 'Peggie, what lightened the world before the sun was made?' After thinking for a minute, she said – 'Deed, sir, the question is mair curious than edifying.'

Besides these public examinations, the minister made an annual visit to each household in his parish. When he came to us, the servants were called in, and we all knelt while he said a prayer; and then he examined each individual as to the state of his soul and conduct. He asked me if I could say my 'Questions' – that is, the catechism of the Kirk of Scotland – and asked a question at random to ascertain the fact. He did the same to the servants.

When I was between eight and nine years old, my father came home from sea, and was shocked to find me such a savage. I had not yet been taught to write, and although I amused myself reading the *Arabian Nights*, *Robinson Crusoe*, and the *Pilgrim's Progress*, I read very badly, and with a strong Scotch accent; so, besides a chapter of the Bible, he made me read a paper of the *Spectator* aloud every morning, after breakfast; the consequence of which discipline is that I have never since opened that book. Hume's *History of England*, was also a real penance to me.[1] I gladly accompanied my father when he cultivated his flowers, which even now I can say were of the best quality. The tulips and other bulbous plants, ranunculi, anemones, carnations, as well as the annuals then known, were all beautiful. He used to root up and throw away many plants I thought very beautiful; he said he did so because the colours of their petals were not sharply defined, and that they would spoil the seed of the others. Thus I learnt to know the good and the bad – how to lay carnations, and how to distinguish between the leaf and fruit buds in pruning fruit trees; this kind of knowledge was of no practical use, for as my after-life was spent in towns, I never had a garden, to my great regret.

George the Third was so popular, that even in Burntisland nosegays were placed in every window on the 4th of June, his birthday; and it occasionally happened that our garden was robbed the preceding night of its gayest flowers.

My father at last said to my mother, – 'This kind of life will never do, Mary must at least know how to write and keep accounts.' So at ten years old I was sent to a boarding-school, kept by a Miss Primrose, at Musselburgh, where I was utterly wretched. The change from perfect liberty to perpetual restraint was in itself a great trial; besides, being naturally shy and timid, I was afraid of strangers, and although Miss Primrose was not unkind she had an habitual frown, which even the elder girls dreaded. My future companions, who were all older than I, came round me like a swarm of bees, and asked if my father had a title, what was the name of our estate, if we kept a carriage, and other such questions, which made me first feel the difference of station. However, the girls were very kind, and often bathed my eyes to prevent our stern mistress from seeing that I was perpetually in tears. A few days after my arrival, although perfectly straight and well-made, I was enclosed in stiff stays with a steel busk in front, while, above my frock, bands drew my shoulders back till the shoulder-blades met. Then a steel rod, with a semi-circle which went under the chin, was clasped to the steel busk in my stays. In this constrained state I, and most of the younger girls, had to prepare our lessons. The chief thing I had to do was to learn by heart a page of Johnson's dictionary, not only to spell the words, give their parts of speech and meaning, but as an exercise of memory to remember their order of succession. Besides I had to learn the first principles of writing, and the rudiments of French and English grammar. The method of teaching was extremely tedious and inefficient. Our religious duties were attended to in a remarkable way. Some of the girls were Presbyterians, others belonged to the Church of England, so Miss Primrose cut the matter short by taking us all to the kirk in the morning and to church in the afternoon.

In our play-hours we amused ourselves with playing at ball, marbles, and especially at 'Scotch and English', a game which represented a raid on the debatable land, or Border between Scotland and England, in which each party tried to rob the other of their playthings. The little ones were always compelled to be English, for the bigger girls thought it too degrading.

Lady Hope, a relative of my mother, frequently invited me to spend Saturday at Pinkie. She was a very ladylike person, in delicate health, and with cold manners. Sir Archibald was stout, loud, passionate, and devoted to hunting. I amused myself in the grounds, a good deal afraid of a turkey-cock, who was pugnacious and defiant ...

Soon after my return home I received a note from a lady in the neighbourhood, inquiring for my mother, who had been ill. This note greatly distressed me, for my half-text writing was as bad as possible, and I could neither compose an answer nor spell the words. My eldest cousin, Miss Somerville, a grown-up young lady, then with us, got me out of this scrape, but I soon got myself into another, by writing to my brother in Edinburgh that I had sent him a bank-*knot* (note) to buy something for me. The school at Musselburgh was expensive, and I was reproached with having cost so much money in vain. My mother said she would have been contented if I had only learnt to write well and keep accounts, which was all that a woman was expected to know.

This passed over, and I was like a wild animal escaped out of a cage. I was no longer amused in the gardens, but wandered about the country. When the tide was out I spent hours on the sands, looking at the star-fish and sea-urchins, or watching the children digging for sand-eels, cockles, and the spouting razor-fish. I made a collection of shells, such as were cast ashore, some so small that they appeared like white specks in patches of black sand. There was a small pier on the sands for shipping limestone brought from the coal mines inland. I was astonished to see the surface of these blocks of stone covered with beautiful impressions of what seemed to be leaves; how they got there I could not imagine, but I picked up the broken bits, and even large pieces, and brought them to my repository. I knew the eggs of many birds, and made a collection of them. I never robbed a nest, but bought strings of eggs, which were sold by boys, besides getting sea-fowl eggs, from sailors who had been in whalers or on other northern voyages. It was believed by these sailors that there was a gigantic flat fish in the North Sea, called a kraken. It was so enormous that when it came to the surface, covered with tangles and sand, it was supposed to be an island, till, on one occasion, part of a ship's crew landed on it and found out their mistake. However, much as they believed in it, none of the sailors at Burntisland had ever seen it. The sea-serpent was also an article of our faith.

In the rocks at the end of our garden there was a shingly opening, in which we used to bathe, and where at low tide I frequently waded among masses of rock covered with sea-weeds. With the exception of dulse and tangle I knew the names of none, though I was well acquainted with and admired many of these beautiful plants. I also watched the crabs, live shells, jelly-fish, and various marine animals, all of which were objects of curiosity and amusement to me in my lonely life.

The flora on the links and hills around was very beautiful, and I soon learnt the trivial names of all the plants. There was not a tree nor bush higher than furze in this part of the country, but the coast to the north-west of Burntisland was bordered by a tree and brushwood-covered bank belonging to the Earl of Morton, which extended to Aberdour. I could not go so far alone, but had frequent opportunities of walking there and gathering ferns, fox-gloves, and primroses, which grew on the mossy banks of a little stream that ran into the sea. The bed of this stream or burn was thickly covered with the freshwater mussel, which I knew often contained pearls, but I did not like to kill the creatures to get the pearls ...

When the bad weather began I did not know what to do with myself. Fortunately we had a small collection of books, among which I found Shakespeare, and read it at every moment I could spare from my domestic duties. These occupied a great part of my time; besides, I had to *shew* (sew) my sampler, working the alphabet from A to Z, as well as the ten numbers, on canvas.

My mother did not prevent me from reading, but my aunt Janet, who came to live in Burntisland after her father's death, greatly disapproved of my conduct. She was an old maid who could be very agreeable and witty, but she had all the prejudices of the time with regard to women's duties, and said to my mother, 'I wonder you let Mary waste her time in reading, she never *shews* (sews) more than if she were a man.' Whereupon I was sent to the village school to learn plain needlework. I do not remember how long it was after this that an old lady sent some very fine linen to be made into shirts for her brother, and desired that one should be made entirely by me. The shirt was so well worked that I was relieved from attending the school, but the house linen was given into my charge to make and to mend. We had a large stock, much of it very beautiful, for the Scotch ladies at that time were very proud of their napery, but they no longer sent it to Holland to be bleached, as had once been the custom. We grew flax, and our maids spun it. The coarser yarn was woven in Burntisland, and bleached upon the links; the finer was sent to Dunfermline, where there was a manufactory of table-linen.

I was annoyed that my turn for reading was so much disapproved of, and thought it unjust that women should have been given a desire for knowledge if it were wrong to acquire it. Among our books I found Chapone's *Letters to Young Women*, and resolved to follow the course of history there recommended, the more so as we had most of the works she mentions.[2] One, however, which my cousin lent me was French, and here the little I had learnt at school was useful, for with the help of a dictionary I made out the sense. What annoyed me was my memory not being good – I could remember neither names nor dates. Years afterwards I studied a Memoria Technica, then in fashion, without success; yet in my youth I could play long pieces of music on the piano without the book, and I never forget mathematical formulae. In looking over one of my MSS., which I had not seen for forty years, I at once recognised the formulae for computing the secular inequalities of the moon.

We had two small globes, and my mother allowed me to learn the use of them from Mr. Reed, the village schoolmaster, who came to teach me for a few weeks in the winter evenings. Besides the ordinary branches, Mr. Reed taught Latin and navigation, but these were out of the question for me. At the village school the boys often learnt Latin, but it was thought sufficient for the girls to be able to read the Bible; very few even learnt writing. I recollect, however, that some men were ignorant of book-keeping; our baker, for instance, had a wooden tally, in which he made a notch for every loaf of bread, and of course we had the corresponding tally. They were called nick-sticks.

My bedroom had a window to the south, and a small closet near had one to the north. At these I spent many hours, studying the stars by the aid of the celestial globe. Although I watched and admired the magnificent displays of the Aurora, which frequently occurred, they seemed to be so nearly allied to lightning that I was somewhat afraid of them. At an earlier period of my life there was a comet, which I dreaded exceedingly ...

Our house on one occasion being full, I was sent to sleep in a room quite detached from the rest and with a different staircase. There was a closet in this room in which my father kept his fowling pieces, fishing tackle, and golf clubs, and a long garret overhead was filled with presses and stores of all kinds, among other things a number of large cheeses were on a board slung by ropes to the rafters. One night I had put out my candle and was fast asleep, when I was awakened by a violent crash, and then a rolling noise over my head. Now the room was said to be haunted, so that the servants would not sleep in it. I was desperate, for there was no bell. I groped my way to the closet – lucifer matches were unknown in those days – I seized one of the golf clubs, which are shod with iron, and thundered on the bedroom door till I brought my father, followed by the whole household, to my aid. It was found that the rats had gnawed through the ropes by which the cheeses were suspended, so that the crash and rolling were accounted for, and I was scolded for making such an uproar.

Children suffer much misery from being left alone in the dark. When I was very young I was sent to bed at eight or nine o'clock, and the maid who slept in the room went away as soon as I was in bed, leaving me alone in the dark till she came to bed herself. All that time I was in an agony of fear of something indefinite, I could not tell what. The joy, the relief, when the maid came back, were such that I instantly fell asleep. Now that I am a widow and old, although I always have a night-lamp, such is the power of early impressions that I rejoice when daylight comes ...

When I was about thirteen my mother took a small apartment in Edinburgh for the winter, and I was sent to a writing school, where I soon learnt to write a good hand, and studied the common rules of arithmetic. My uncle William Henry Charters, lately returned from India, gave me a pianoforte, and I had music lessons from an old lady who lived in the top story [sic] of one of the highest houses in the old town ... On returning to Burntisland I spent four or five hours daily at the piano; and for the sake of having something to do, I taught myself Latin enough, from such books as we had, to read Caesar's *Commentaries*. I went that summer on a visit to my aunt at Jedburgh, and for the first time in my life, I met in my uncle, Dr. Somerville, with a friend who approved of my thirst for knowledge. During long walks with him in the early mornings, he was so kind, that I had the courage to tell him that I had been trying to learn Latin, but I feared it was in vain; for my brother and other boys, superior to me in talent, and with every assistance, spent years in learning it. He assured me, on the contrary, that in ancient times many women – some of them of the highest rank in England – had been very elegant scholars, and that he would read Virgil with me if I would come to his study for an hour or two every morning before breakfast, which I gladly did.

I never was happier in my life than during the months I spent at Jedburgh. My aunt was a charming companion – witty, full of anecdote, and had read more than most women of her day, especially Shakespeare, who was her favourite author. My cousins had little turn for reading, but they were better educated than most girls. They were taught to write by David Brewster, son of the village schoolmaster, afterwards Sir David, who became one of the most distinguished philosophers and discoverers of the age, member of all the scientific societies at home and abroad, and at last President of the University of Edinburgh.[3] He was studying in Edinburgh when I was at Jedburgh; so I did not make his acquaintance then; but later in life he became my valued friend. I did not know till after his death, that, while teaching my cousins, he fell in love with my cousin Margaret. I do not believe she was aware of it. She was afterwards attached to an officer in the army; but my aunt would not allow her to go to that *out-landish* place, Malta, where he was quartered; so she lived and died unmarried. Steam has changed our ideas of distance since that time.

My uncle's house – the manse – in which I was born, stands in a pretty garden, bounded by the fine ancient abbey, which, though partially ruined, still serves as the parish kirk. The garden produced abundance of common flowers, vegetables, and fruit. Some of the plum and pear trees were very old, and were said to have been planted by the monks. Both were excellent in quality, and very productive. The view from both garden and manse was over the beautiful narrow valley through which the Jed flows. The precipitous banks of red sandstone are richly clothed with vegetation, some of the trees ancient and very fine, especially the magnificent one called the capon tree, and the lofty king of the wood, remnants of the fine forests which at one time had covered the country. An inland scene was new to me, and I was never tired of admiring the tree-crowned scaurs or precipices, where the rich glow of the red sandstone harmonized so well with the autumnal tints of the foliage.

We often bathed in the pure stream of the Jed. My aunt always went with us, and was the merriest of the party; we bathed in a pool which was deep under the high scaur, but sloped gradually from the grassy bank on the other side. Quiet and transparent as the Jed was, it one day came down with irresistible fury, red with the debris of the sandstone scaurs. There had been a thunderstorm in the hills up-stream, and as soon as the river began to rise, the people came out with pitchforks and hooks to catch the hayricks, sheaves of corn, drowned pigs, and other animals that came sweeping past. My cousins and I were standing on the bridge, but my aunt called us off when the water rose above the arches, for fear of the bridge giving way. We made expeditions every day; sometimes we went nutting in the forest; at other times we gathered mushrooms on the grass parks of Stewart-field, where there was a wood of picturesque old Scotch firs, inhabited by a colony of rooks. I still kept the habit of looking out for birds, and had the good fortune to see a heron, now a rare bird in the valley of the Jed. Some of us went every day to a spring called the Allerly well, about a quarter of a mile from the manse, and brought a large jug of sparkling water for dinner. The evenings were cheerful; my aunt sang Scotch songs prettily, and told us stories and legends about Jedburgh, which had been a royal residence in the olden time. She had a tame white and tawny-coloured owl, which we fed every night, and sometimes brought into the drawing-room. The Sunday evening never was gloomy, though properly observed. We occasionally drank tea with acquaintances, and made visits of a few days to the Rutherfords of Edgerton and others; but I was always glad to return to the manse ...

They sent me to Strange's dancing school. Strange himself was exactly like a figure on the stage; tall and thin, he wore a powdered wig, with cannons at the ears, and a pigtail. Ruffles at the breast and wrists, white waistcoat, black silk or velvet shorts, white silk stockings, large silver buckles, and a pale blue coat completed his costume. He had a little fiddle on which he played, called a kit. My first lesson was how to walk and make a curtsey. 'Young lady, if you visit the queen you must make three curtsies, lower and lower and lower as you approach her. So-0-0', leading me on and making me curtsey. 'Now, if the queen were to ask you to eat a bit of mutton with her, what would you say?' Every Saturday afternoon all the scholars, both boys and girls, met to practise in the public assembly rooms in George's Street. It was a handsome large hall with benches rising like an amphitheatre. Some of the elder girls were very pretty, and danced well, so these practisings became a lounge for officers from the Castle, and other young men. We used always to go in full evening dress. We learnt the *minuet de la cour*, reels and country dances. Our partners used to give us gingerbread and oranges. Dancing before so many people was quite an exhibition, and I was greatly mortified one day when ready to begin a minuet, by the dancing-master shaking me roughly and making me hold out my frock properly.

Though kind in the main, my uncle and his wife were rather sarcastic and severe, and kept me down a good deal, which I felt keenly, but said nothing. I was not a favourite with my family at that period of my life, because I was reserved and unexpansive, in consequence of the silence I was obliged to observe on the subjects which interested me. Three Miss Melvilles, friends, or perhaps relatives, of Mrs. Charters, were always held up to me as models of perfection, to be imitated in everything, and I wearied of hearing them constantly praised at my expense ...

I was often invited with my mother to the tea-parties given either by widows or maiden ladies who resided at Burntisland. A pool of commerce used to be keenly contested till a late hour at these parties, which bored me exceedingly, but I there became acquainted with a Miss Ogilvie, much younger than the rest, who asked me to go and see fancy works she was doing, and at which she was very clever. I went next day, and after admiring her work, and being told how it was done, she showed me a monthly magazine with coloured plates of ladies' dresses, charades, and puzzles. At the end of a page I read what appeared to me to be simply an arithmetical question; but on turning the page I was surprised to see strange-looking lines mixed with letters, chiefly X'es and Y's, and asked; 'What is that?' 'Oh,' said Miss Ogilvie, 'it is a kind of arithmetic: they call it Algebra; but I can tell you nothing about it.' And we talked about other things; but on going home I thought I would look if any of our books could tell me what was meant by Algebra.

In Robertson's *Navigation* [4] I flattered myself that I had got precisely what I wanted; but I soon found that I was mistaken. I perceived, however, that astronomy did not consist in star-gazing, and as I persevered in studying the book for a time, I certainly got a dim view of several subjects which were useful to me afterwards. Unfortunately not one of our acquaintances or relations knew anything of science or natural history; nor, had they done so, should I have had courage to ask any of them a question, for I should have been laughed at. I was often very sad and forlorn; not a hand held out to help me.

My uncle and aunt Charters took a house at Burntisland for the summer, and the Miss Melville I have already mentioned came to pay them a visit. She painted miniatures, and from seeing her at work, I took a fancy to learn to draw, and actually wasted time in copying prints; but this circumstance enabled me to get elementary books on Algebra and Geometry without asking questions of any one, as will be explained afterwards. The rest of the summer I spent in playing on the piano and learning Greek enough to read Xenophon and part of Herodotus; then we prepared to go to Edinburgh ...

Nasmyth, [5] an exceedingly good landscape painter, had opened an academy for ladies in Edinburgh, a proof of the gradual improvement which was taking place in the education of the higher classes; my mother very willingly allowed me to attend it. The class was very full. I was not taught to draw, but looked on while Nasmyth painted; then a picture was given me to copy, the master correcting the faults. Though I spoilt canvas, I had made some progress by the end of the season.

Mr. Nasmyth, besides being a good artist, was clever, well-informed, and had a great deal of conversation. One day I happened to be near him while he was talking to the Ladies Douglas about perspective. He said, 'You should study Euclid's Elements of geometry, the foundation not only of perspective, but of astronomy and all mechanical science.' Here, in the most unexpected manner, I got the information I wanted, for I at once saw that it would help me to understand some parts of Robertson's *Navigation*; but as to going to a bookseller and asking for Euclid the thing was impossible! Besides I did not yet know anything definite about Algebra, so no more could be done at that time; but I never lost sight of an object which had interested me from the first.

I rose very early. and played four or five hours, as usual, on the piano, and had lessons from Corri, an Italian, who taught carelessly, and did not correct a habit I had of thumping so as to break the strings; but I learned to tune a piano and mend the strings, as there was no tuner at Burntisland. Afterwards I got over my bad habit and played the music then in vogue: pieces by Pleyel, Clementi, Steibelt, Mozart, and Beethoven, the last being my favourite to this day. I was sometimes accompanied on the violin by Mr. Thomson, the friend of Burns; more frequently by Stabilini; but I was always too shy to play before people, and invariably played badly when obliged to do so, which vexed me ...

On returning to Burntisland, I played on the piano as diligently as ever, and painted several hours a day. At this time, however, a Mr. Craw came to live with us as tutor to my youngest brother, Henry. He had been educated for the kirk, was a fair Greek and Latin scholar, but unfortunately for me, was no mathematician. He was a simple, good-natured kind of man, and I ventured to ask him about algebra and geometry, and begged him, the first time he went to Edinburgh, to buy me something elementary on these subjects, so he soon brought me *Euclid* and Bonnycastle's *Algebra*,[6] which were the books used in the schools at that time. Now I had got what I so long and earnestly desired. I asked Mr. Craw to hear me demonstrate a few problems in the first book of *Euclid*, and then I continued the study alone with courage and assiduity, knowing I was on the right road. Before I began to read algebra I found it necessary to study arithmetic again, having forgotten much of it. I never was expert at addition, for, in summing up a long column of pounds, shillings, and pence, in the family account book, it seldom came out twice the same way. In after life I, of course, used logarithms for the higher branches of science.

I had to take part in the household affairs; and to make and mend my own clothes. I rose early, played on the piano, and painted during the time I could spare in the daylight hours, but I sat up very late reading *Euclid*. The servants, however, told my mother 'It was no wonder the stock of candles was soon exhausted, for Miss Mary sat up reading till a very late hour'; whereupon an order was given to take away my candle as soon as I was in bed. I had, however, already gone through the first six books of *Euclid*, and now I was thrown on my memory, which I exercised by beginning at the first book, and demonstrating in my mind a certain number of problems every night, till I could nearly go through the whole. My father came home for a short time, and somehow or other, finding out what I was about, said to my mother, 'Peg, we must put a stop to this, or we shall have Mary in a strait jacket one of these days. There was X., who went raving mad about the longitude!'

*Source*: Mary Somerville's *Personal Recollections, from Early Life to Old Age* was published with selections from her correspondence by her daughter Martha in 1873.

**Notes**

1. David Hume's (1711–76) *History of England*, which began with Caesar's invasion and continued to 1688, came out in six volumes from 1754 to 1762.

2. Hester Chapone (1727–1801), literary bluestocking, author of *Letters on the Improvement of the mind. Addressed to a Young Lady* (1773).

3. Sir David Brewster (1781–1868), physicist, noted for his studies in optics and light absorption. He invented the kaleidoscope in 1816, and became President of Edinburgh University in 1859.

4. *The Elements of Navigation* (1754) by the mathematician John Robertson (1712–76).

5. Alexander Nasmyth (1758–1840) painted portraits as well as landscapes. Among his sitters was the poet Robert Burns. He was also an architect who specialized in bridge design.

6. *Introduction to Algebra* by John Bonnycastle (1750?–1821).

# 6

# Lady Caroline Lamb

Lady Caroline Lamb (1785–1828), only daughter of Frederick Ponsonby, 3rd Earl of Bessborough, and Lady Henrietta Frances Spencer, had a troubled and unsettled childhood, neglected by her parents. At the age of three she was sent to Italy for six years with a servant, returning at nine to be cared for by her aunt at Devonshire House. She was married to the Hon. William Lamb, Lord Melbourne, in 1805, but quickly became infatuated with Byron. It was she who famously described Byron as 'mad, bad, and dangerous to know', breaking up with him in 1813, and portraying him in her novel *Glenarvon* (1816). Her entry in the *Dictionary of National Biography* describes her as 'excitable to the verge of insanity' (vol. XI, p. 422). Her childhood reminiscences are in Lady Morgan's *Memoirs* (1862), first as recorded by Lady Morgan herself in her journal, and then in an undated letter from Lady Caroline to Lady Morgan.

## I: From Lady Morgan's Journal:

Lady Caroline Lamb sent for me. Her story: Her mother had a paralytic stroke: went to Italy: she remained there till nine years old, brought up by a maid called Fanny. She was then taken to Devonshire House, and brought up with her cousins. She gave curious anecdotes of high life, – children neglected by their mothers – children served on silver in the morning, carrying down their plate to the kitchen –no one to attend to them – servants all at variance – ignorance of children on all subjects – thought all people were drunks or beggars – or had never to part with their money – did not know bread, or butter, was made – wondered if horses fed on beef – so neglected in her education, she could not write at ten years old.

(Vol. II, p. 198–9)

## II: Letter from Lady Caroline Lamb to Lady Morgan:

My history, if you ever care and like to read it, is this – My mother, having boys, wished ardently for a girl; and I, who evidently ought to have been a soldier, was found a naughty girl – forward, talking like Richard the Third.

I was a trouble, not a pleasure, all my childhood, for which reason, after my return from Italy, where I was from the age of four until nine, I was ordered by the late Dr. Warre neither to learn anything nor see any one, for fear the violent passions and strange whims they found in me should lead to madness; of which, however, he assured every one there were no symptoms. I differ, but the end was, that until fifteen I learned nothing. My instinct – for we all have instincts – was for music – in it I delighted; I cried when it was pathetic, and did all that Dryden's ode[1] made Alexander do – of course I was not allowed to follow it up. My angel mother's ill-health prevented my living at home; my kind aunt Devonshire[2] took me; the present Duke loved me better than himself, and every one paid me those compliments shown to children who are precious to their parents, or delicate and likely to die. I wrote not, spelt not; but I made verses, which they all thought beautiful – for myself, I preferred washing a dog, or polishing a piece of Derbyshire spar, or breaking in a horse, to any accomplishment in the world. Drawing-room (shall I say withdrawing-room, as they now say?) looking-glasses, finery, or dress-company for ever were my abhorrence. I was, I am, religious; I was loving (?) but I was and am unkind. I fell in love when only twelve years old, with a friend of Charles Fox – a friend of liberty whose poems I had read, whose self I had never seen, and when I did see him, at thirteen, could I change? No, I was more attached than ever. William Lamb was beautiful, and far the cleverest person then about, and the most daring in his opinions, in his love of liberty and independence. He thought of me but as a child, yet he liked me much; afterwards he offered to marry me, and I refused him because of my temper, which was too violent; he, however, asked twice, and was not refused the second time, and the reason was that I adored him. I had three children; two died; my only child is afflicted; it is the will of God.[3] I have wandered from right, and been punished.

## Notes

1. In Dryden's 'Alexander's Feast, or, The Power of Musique: An Ode in Honour of St Cecilia's Day', Alexander the Great experiences a full range of emotions in response to different kinds of music in praise of wine, love and revenge.

2. Her mother's elder sister, Georgiana (née Spencer) (1757–1806) married to William Cavendish, 5th Duke of Devonshire, and mother of the 6th Duke.

3. Her surviving son, George Augustus, died in 1836.

# 7

# 'Charlotte Elizabeth'

'Charlotte Elizabeth' was the pseudonym of Charlotte Elizabeth Tonna, Evangelical social-problem novelist. Born in Norwich in 1790, the daughter of a clergyman, Michael Browne, who was a minor canon of Norwich Cathedral, she married Captain George Phelan (d. 1837) in 1813, but separated from him around 1824. Lewis Tonna, whom she married in 1841, was also a writer of religious works. Best known for her novels *Helen Fleetwood* (1841), written in support of the Ten Hours Movement in factories, and *The Wrongs of Women* (1843–44), Charlotte Elizabeth Tonna also edited a succession of religious journals, and published her *Personal Recollections* (1841) in the form of letters to an imaginary friend, illustrating the mental and spiritual discipline she had undergone. Mrs Tonna died in 1846. She regarded her mission as 'the cause of Protestantism', as she declares at the start of her autobiography, and felt it was significant that she was born 'just opposite the dark old gateway of that strong building [in Norwich] where the glorious martyrs of Mary's day were imprisoned'.

The stern-looking gateway, opening on St Martin's Plain, was probably one of the very first objects traced on the retina of my infant eye, when it ranged beyond the inner walls of the nursery: and often, with tottering step, I passed beneath that arch into the splendid garden of our noble episcopal palace; and certainly, if my Protestantism may not be traced to that locality, my taste may; for from all the elaborate display of modern architecture, all the profuse luxuriance and endless variety of modern horticulture, I now turn away, to feast in thought on the recollection of that venerable scene. The palace itself is a fine specimen of the chaste old English style; but the most conspicuous, the most unforgettable feature was the cathedral itself, which formed the boundary of one-half of the garden: a mass of sober magnificence, rising in calm repose against the sky, which, to my awe-struck gaze and childish imagination, seemed to rest upon its exquisitely-formed spire. Seated on the grass, busying my fingers with the daisies that were permitted to spring around, I have been lost in such imaginings as I suppose not many little children indulge in, while permitting my eyes to rove over the seemingly interminable mass of old grey stone, and then to fall upon the pleasant flowers around me. I loved silence, for nothing that fell on the ear seemed in accordance with what so charmed the eye: and thus a positive evil found entrance in the midst of much enjoyment. I acquired that habit of dreamy excursiveness into imaginary scenes, and among unreal personages, which is alike inimical to rational pursuits, and opposed to spiritual-mindedness. To a period so early as the middle of my fourth year I can revert with a most perfect, most vivid recollection of my habitual thoughts and feelings; and at that age, I can unhesitatingly declare, my mind was deeply tinctured with a romance not derived from books, nor from conversation, but arising, as I verily believe, out of the singular adaptation to each other of my natural taste and the scenery amidst which it began to develope [sic] itself. Our abode was changed to another part of the city before this period arrived; but the bishop's garden was still our haunt, and my supreme delight.

An immense orchard, shrubbery, and flower-garden, were attached to my father's new residence, to which he had removed on account of its proximity to the church of which he was rector. This, too, was an old-fashioned house, mantled with a vine, and straggling out, in irregular buildings, along the slope of the garden. The centre of an immense grass-plat, studded with apple, pear, and plum-trees, was occupied by the most gigantic mulberry I ever beheld, the thick trunk of which resembled that of a knotted oak, while in its forest of dark branches nestled a number of owls and bats. Oh, how I loved to lurk beneath its shadow on a summer evening, and await the twilight gloom, that the large owl might come forth and wheel around the tree, and call out his companions with a melancholy hoot; while the smaller bat, dipping lower in his fight, brushed by me, accustomed to my presence. I had entered betimes upon the pernicious study of nursery tales, as they then were, and without having the smallest actual belief in the existence of fairies, goblins, or any such things, I took unutterable delight in surrounding myself with hosts of them, decked out in colours of my own supplying, gorgeous or terrible beyond the conception of my classic authorities. The faculty of realizing whatever I pictured to myself was astonishingly great; and you must admit that the localities in which I was placed were but too favourable to the formation of a character, which I have no doubt the enemy was secretly constructing within me, to mislead, by wild, unholy fiction, such as should come within the range of its influence. To God be all the glory that I am not now pandering with this pen to the most grovelling of the most impious of man's perverted feelings!

But above all other tastes, all other cravings, one passion reigned supreme, and that acme of enjoyment to me was music. This also was met by indulgence as unlimited as its cravings; for not only did my father possess one of the finest voices in the world, and the very highest degree of scientific knowledge, taste, and skill in the management of it, but our house was seldom without an inmate in the person of his most intimate friend and brother clergyman, a son of the celebrated composer, Mr. Linley, who was as highly gifted in instrumental as my father was in vocal music. The rich tones of his old harpsichord seem at this moment to fill my ear and swell my heart; while my father's deep, clear, mellow voice breaks in, with some noble recitative or elaborate air of Handel, Haydn, and the rest of a school that may be superseded, but never, never can be equalled by modern composers. Or the harpsichord was relinquished to another hand, and the breath of our friend came forth through the reed of his hautboy in strains of such overpowering melody, that I have hid my face on my mother's lap to weep the feelings that absolutely wrung my little heart with excess of enjoyment. This was not a snare; or, if it might have been made one, the Lord broke it in time, by taking away my hearing. I would not that it had been otherwise, for while a vain imagination was fostered by the habit I have before adverted to, this taste for music, and its high gratification, most certainly elevated the mind. I do firmly believe that it is a gift from God to man, to be prized, cherished, cultivated. I believe that the man whose bosom yields no response to the concord of sweet sounds, falls short of the standard to which man should aspire as an intellectual being; and though Satan does fearfully pervert this solace of the mind to most vile purposes, still I heartily agree with Martin Luther, that, in the abstract, 'the devil hates music'.

Before I had completed my sixth year, I came under the rod of discipline which was to fall so long and so perseveringly upon me ere I should 'hear the rod and who had appointed it'.[1] Enthusiastic in every thing, and already passionately fond of reading, I had eagerly accepted the offer of a dear uncle, a young physician, to teach me French. I loved him; for he was gentle and kind, and very fond of me; and it was a great happiness to trip through the long winding street that separated us, to turn down by the old Bridewell, so celebrated as an architectural curiosity, being built of dark flint stones, exquisitely chisselled [sic] into the form of bricks, and which even then I could greatly admire, and to take my seat on my young uncle's knee, in the large hall of his house, where stood a very large and deep-toned organ, some sublime strain from which was to reward my diligence, if I repeated accurately the lesson he had appointed. Thus between love for my uncle, delight in his organ, and a natural inclination to acquire learning, I was stimulated to extraordinary efforts, and met the demand on my energies in a very unsafe way. I placed my French book under my pillow every night, and starting from repose at the earliest break of dawn, strained my sleepy eyes over the page, until, very suddenly, I became totally blind.

This was a grievous blow to my tender parents: the eclipse was so complete that I could not tell whether it was midnight or midnoon, so far as perception of light was concerned, and the case seemed hopeless. It was, however, among the 'all things' that God causes to work together for good, while Satan eagerly seeks to use them for evil. It checked my inordinate desire for mere acquirements, which I believe to be a bad tendency, particularly in a female, while it threw me more upon my own resources, such as they were, and gave me a keen relish for the highly intellectual conversation that always prevailed in our home. My father delighted in the society of literary men: and he was himself of a turn so argumentative, so overflowing with rich conversation, so decided in his political views, so alive to passing events, so devotedly and so proudly the Englishman, that with such associates as he gathered about him at his own fireside, I don't see how the little blind girl, whose face was ever turned up towards the unseen speaker, and whose mind opened to every passing remark, could avoid becoming a thinker, a reasoner, a tory and a patriot. Sometimes a tough disputant crossed our threshold; one of these was Dr. Parr, and brilliant were the flashes resulting from such occasional collision with antagonists of that calibre.[2] I am often charged with the offence of being too political in my writings: the fact is, I write as I think and feel; and what else can you expect from a child reared in such a nursery?

But another consequence of this temporary visitation was an increased passion for music. The severe remedies used for my blindness frequently laid me on the sofa for days together, and then my fond father would bring home with him, after the afternoon service of the cathedral, of which he was also a canon, a party of the young choristers. My godfather would seat himself at the harpsichord; the boys, led by my father, perform the vocal parts; and such feasts of sacred music were served up to me, that I have breathed to my brother in an ecstatic whisper the confession, 'I don't want to see; I like music better than seeing.'

That brother I have not before named: but that only brother was a second self. Not that he resembled me in any respect, for he was beautiful to a prodigy, and I an ordinary child; he was wholly free from any predilection for learning, being mirthful and volatile in the highest degree; and though he listened when I read to him the mysterious marvels of my favourite nursery books, I doubt whether he ever bestowed an after-thought on any thing therein contained. The brightest, the sweetest, the most sparkling creature that ever lived, he was all joy, all love. I do not remember to have seen him for one moment out of temper or out of spirits for the first sixteen years of his life; and he was to me what the natural sun is to the system. We were never separated; our studies, our plays, our walks, our plans, our hearts were always one. That holy band which the Lord has woven, that inestimable blessing of fraternal love and confidence, was never broken, never loosened between us, from the cradle to his grave; and God forbid I should say or think that the grave has broken it! If I have not from the outset included that precious brother in my sketch, it was because I should almost as soon have deemed it necessary to include by name my own head or my own heart. He too was musical, and sang sweetly, and I cannot look back on my childhood without confessing that its cup ran over with the profusion of delights that my God poured into it.

About this time, when my sight, after a few months' privation, was fully restored, I first imbibed the strength of Protestantism as deeply as it can be imbibed apart from spiritual understanding. Norwich was infamously conspicuous in persecuting unto death the saints of the Most High, under the sanguinary despotism of Popish Mary; and the spot where they suffered, called the Lollard's Pit, lies just outside the town, over Bishop's bridge, having a circular excavation against the side of Mousehold-hill. This, at least to within a year or two ago, was kept distinct, an opening by the road-side. My father often took us to walk in that direction, and pointed out the pit, and told us that there Mary burnt good people alive for refusing to worship wooden images. I was horror-stricken, and asked many questions, to which he did not always reply so fully as I wished; and one day, having to go out while I was enquiring, he said, 'I don't think you can read a word of this book, but you may look at the pictures: it is all about the martyrs.' So saying, he placed on a chair the old folio of Foxe's Acts and Monuments, in venerable black letter, and left me to examine it.[3]

Hours passed, and still found me bending over, or rather leaning against that magic book. I could not, it is true, decypher the black letter; but I found some examinations in Roman type, and devoured them; while every wood-cut was examined with aching eyes and a palpitating heart. Assuredly I took in more of the spirit of John Foxe, even by that imperfect mode of acquaintance, than many do by reading his book through; and when my father next found me at what became my darling study, I looked up at him with burning cheeks and asked, 'Papa, may I be a martyr?'

'What do you mean, child?'

'I mean, papa, may I be burned to death for my religion, as these were? I want to be a martyr.'

He smiled, and made me this answer, which I have never forgotten, 'Why, Charlotte, if the government ever gives power to the Papists again, as they talk of doing, you may very probably live to be a martyr.'

I remember the stern pleasure that this reply afforded me: of spiritual knowledge not the least glimmer had ever reached me in any form, yet I knew the Bible most intimately, and loved it with all my heart, as the most sacred, the most beautiful of earthly things. Already had its sublimity caught my admiration; and when listening to the lofty language of Isaiah, as read from his stall in the cathedral by my father in Advent, and the early Sundays of the year, while his magnificent voice sent the prophetic denunciations pealing through those vaulted aisles, I had received into my mind, and I think into my heart, that scorn of idolatry which breathes so thrillingly in his inspired page. This I know, that at six years old the foundation of a truly scriptural protest was laid in my character; and to this hour it is my prayer that whenever the Lord calls me hence, or whenever the Lord himself comes to earth, he may find his servant not only watching but working against the diabolical iniquity that filled the Lollard's Pit with the ashes of his saints.

And now upon that all-important topic, the Bible, I would remark, that among the most invaluable blessings of my life I remember the judicious conduct of my parents in regard to it. We generally find that precious volume made a book of tasks; sometimes even a book of penalties: the consequence of so doing cannot but be evil. With us, it was emphatically a reward-book. That identical book is now before me, in its rich red cover, elegantly emblazoned with the royal arms; for it is the very Bible that was placed before Queen Charlotte at her coronation in 1761; and which, becoming the perquisite of a Prebendary of Westminster, was by his wife presented to my mother to whom she stood sponsor. This royal Bible was highly prized; and it was by special favour that it was opened for us when we had been good, and were deemed worthy of some mark of approval. My father, then, whose voice made music of every thing, would read to us the history of Abel, of Noah, Moses, Gideon, or some other of the exquisite narratives of the Old Testament. I do not say that they were made the medium of conveying spiritual instruction; they were unaccompanied by note or comment, written or oral, and merely read as histories, the fact being carefully impressed on our minds that God was the author, and that it would be highly criminal to doubt the truth of any word in that book; but I do assert that such a mode of bringing a child acquainted with the Scriptures is infinitely preferable to setting him tasks to learn out of it, or even of encumbering with human explanations what God has made so very plain, so very attractive ...

Never did children more abhor a lie; we spurned at its meanness, while trembling at its guilt; and nothing bound us more closely and exclusively together than the discoveries we were always making of a laxity among other children in this respect. On such occasions we would shrink into a corner by ourselves, and whisper, 'Do they think God does not hear that?' Self-righteousness, no doubt, existed in a high degree: we were baby Pharisees, rejoicing in the external cleanliness of cup and platter; but I look back with great thankfulness on the mercy that so far instructed us; an habitual regard to truth has carried me safely through many a trial, and, as a means, guarded me from many a snare. It cannot be too early or too strongly inculcated; nor should any effort be considered too great, any difficulty as too discouraging, any reprobation as too strong, or, I will add, any punishment too severe, when the object in view is to overcome this infamous vice in a child. Once I remember having been led into a lie, at the instigation, and through the contrivance of a servant girl, for whose benefit it was told. Suspicion instantly arose, from my dreadful embarrassment of manner; a strict investigation commenced; the girl told me to face it out, for that nobody else knew of it, and she would not flinch. But my terrors of conscience were insupportable; I could ill bear my father's steady eye fixed on mine, still less the anxious, wondering, incredulous expression of my brother's innocent face, who could not for a moment fancy me guilty. I confessed at once; and with a heavy sigh my father sent to borrow from a neighbour an instrument of chastisement never before needed in his own house. He took me to another room, and said, 'Child, it will pain me more to punish you thus, than any blows I can inflict will pain you; but I must do it; you have told a lie; a dreadful sin, and a base, mean, cowardly action. If I let you grow up a liar you will reproach me for it one day; if I now spared the rod I should hate the child.' I took the punishment in a most extraordinary spirit; I wished every stroke had been a stab; I wept because the pain was not great enough; and I loved my father at that moment better than even I, who almost idolized him, had ever loved him before. I thanked him, and thank him still; for I never transgressed in that way again. The servant was called, received her wages, and a most awful lecture, and was discharged the same hour. Yet, of all these things what sank deepest into my very soul were the sobs and cries of my fond little brother, and the lamentable tones of his soft voice, pleading through the closed door, 'Oh, Papa, don't whip Charlotte! Oh, forgive poor Charlotte!'

It is sweet to know we have a Brother indeed who always pleads, and never pleads in vain for the offending child; a Father whose chastisements are not withheld, but administered in tender love; judgement being his strange work, and mercy that wherein he delights, and the peaceable fruits of righteousness the end of his corrections. The event to which I have referred may appear too trivial a thing to record; but it is by neglecting trivial things that we ruin ourselves and our children ...

A boarding school had never been thought of for me; my parents loved their children too well to meditate their expulsion from the paternal roof; and the children so well loved their parents and each other that such a separation would have been insupportable to them. Masters we had in the necessary branches of education, and we studied together so far as I was permitted to study; but before it was deemed safe to exercise my eyes with writing apparatus, I had stealthily possessed myself of a patent copy-book, by means of which, tracing the characters as they shone through the paper, I was able to write with tolerable freedom before any one knew that I could join two letters; and I well remember my father's surprise, not unmixed with annoyance, when he accidentally took up a letter which I had been writing to a distant relation, giving a circumstantial account of some domestic calamity which had no existence but in my brain; related with so much pathos too, that my tears had fallen over the slate whereon this my first literary attempt was very neatly traced. He could not forbear laughing; but ended with a grave shake of the head, and a remark to the effect, that I was making more haste than good speed.

At this time, seven years of age, I became entangled in a net of dangerous fascination. One evening my brother was taken to the theatre, while I, on account of a cold, had to stay at home. To compensate for this, I was permitted to read the play to him; and that play was *The Merchant of Venice*. I will not dwell upon the effect: I had already become fond of such theatrical spectacles as were considered suitable for children – pantomime and broad farce – and like a child I gazed upon the glitter, and enjoyed the bustle: but now, seated in a corner, all quiet abut me, and nothing to interfere with the mental wold, I drank a cup of intoxication under which my brain reeled for many a year. The character of Shylock burst upon me, even as Shakespeare had conceived it. I revelled in the terrible excitement that it gave rise to; page after page was stereotyped upon a most retentive memory, without an effort, and during a sleepless night I feasted on the pernicious sweets thus hoarded in my brain.

Pernicious indeed they were, for from that hour my diligence in study, my docility of conduct, every thing that is usually regarded as praiseworthy in a child sprung from a new motive. I wanted to earn a reward, and that was no longer a sweet story from the Bible, but permission to carry into my retreat a volume of Shakspeare [sic]. A taste so unusual at my age was hailed with applause; visitors questioned me on the different plays, to ascertain my intimate acquaintance with the characters; but no one, not even my father, could persuade me to recite a line, or to listen when another attempted it, or to witness the representation of any play of Shakspeare. This I mention to prove what a powerful hold the enemy of all godliness must have expected to take on a spirit so attuned to romance. Reality became insipid, almost hateful to me; conversation, except that of the literary men, to whom I have alluded, a burden: I imbibed a thorough contempt for women, children, and household affairs, entrenching myself behind invisible barriers that few, very few, could pass. Oh, how many wasted hours, how much of unprofitable labour, what wrong to my fellow-creatures, what robbery of God must I refer to this ensnaring book. My mind became unnerved, my judgment perverted, my estimate of people and things wholly falsified, and my soul wrapped in the vain solace of unsubstantial enjoyments during years of sorrow, when but for this I might have early-sought the consolations of the gospel. Parents know not what they do, when from vanity, thoughtlessness, or overindulgence, they foster in a young girl what is called a poetical taste. Those things highly esteemed among men, are held in abomination with God; they thrust Him from his creature's thoughts, and enshrine a host of polluting idols in his place.

My father, I am sure, wished to check the evil which, as a sensible man, he could not but foresee; my state of health, however, won a larger portion of indulgence than was good for me. The doctors, into whose hands I had fallen, were of the school now happily very much exploded; they had one panacea for almost every ill, and that was the perilous drug, mercury. With it they rather fed than physicked me; and its deleterious effects on the nervous system were doubly injurious to me, as increasing tenfold the excitability that required every curb. Among all the marvels of my life the greatest is that of my having grown up to be one of the healthiest of human beings, and with an inexhaustible flow of even mirthful spirits, for certainly I was long kept hovering on the verge of the grave by the barbarous excess to which medical experiments were carried; and I never entertained a doubt that the total loss of my hearing, before I was ten years old, was owing to a paralysis induced by such severe treatment. God, however, had his own purposes to work out, which neither Satan nor man could hinder. He overruled all for the furtherance of his own gracious designs.

Shut out by this last dispensation from my two delightful resources, music and conversation, I took refuge in books with tenfold activity. By this time I had added the British poets generally to my original stock, together with such reading as is usually prescribed for young ladies; and I underwent the infliction of reading aloud to my mother the seven mortal volumes of Sir Charles Grandison. It was in the fulfilment of this awful task that I acquired a habit particularly mischievous and ensnaring, that of reading mechanically with a total abstraction of mind from what I was about. This became the easier to me from the absence of all external sound; and its consequences are exceedingly distressing to this day, as experienced in a long indulged, and afterwards most bitterly lamented wandering of the mind in prayer and in reading the scriptures. In fact, through the prevalence of this habit, my devotions, always very punctually performed, became such an utter lip-service as frequently to startle and terrify my conscience when I found myself saying prayers and thinking idle songs or scraps of plays; but I regarded such transient pangs of remorse as a satisfaction for the sin, and never dreamed of resisting the general habit.

Thus far, I had led a town life, residing in the heart of a populous city, enjoying indeed that noble garden, and but daily more and more absorbed in books of fancy. Happily my health became so affected that a removal into the country was judged necessary, and I forgave the doctors all their past persecution of me in consideration of their parting injunctions; which were, that I was to have unbounded liberty; to live entirely in the open air, save when the weather forbade; to be amused with all rural occupations; and especially to frequent farm-yards, for the purpose of inhaling the breath of cows. My father exchanged parochial duty with a friend, taking his village congregation, and engaging a house very near the church.

That tall white house, – what a place it holds in my fond recollection! It was perfectly an old parsonage, and behind it lay a garden larger than our city orchard, sloping gently down, with a profusion of fruit and flowers, bounded by high walls, and the central walk terminating in a door, beyond which lay the scene of our greatest enjoyment. A narrow slip of grass, fringed with osiers, and alders, and willows, alone separated the wall from a very clear, lovely stream, which, winding half round an extensive common, turned a mill. This small river abounded with fish, and we soon became expert anglers; besides which, on creeping to some distance by a path of our own discovery, we could cross the stream on a moveable plank, and take a wide range through the country. This removal was a double resource; it invigorated my bodily frame, until I outgrew and out-bloomed every girl of my age in the neighbourhood, while really laying a foundation for many years of uninterrupted health, and a constitution to defy the change of climate for which I was destined; while it won me from the sickening, enervating habit of sedentary enjoyment over the pages of a book, which, added to the necessary studies and occupations, was relaxing alike the tone of the bodily and mental frame. From the polluted works of man I was drawn to the glorious works of God; and never did bird of the air or beast of the field more luxuriate in the pure bright elements of nature than I did. All the poetical visions of liberty that had floated in my brain seemed now realized; all pastoral descriptions faded before the actual enjoyment of rural life. Sometimes wreathing garlands of wild flowers, reclined on a sunny bank, while a flock of sheep strolled around, and the bold little lambs came to peep in our faces, and then gallop away in pretended alarm; sometimes tearing our clothes to tatters in an ardent hunt for the sweet filberts that hung high above our heads on trees well fortified behind breastworks of bramble and thorn; sometimes cultivating the friendship while we quaffed the milk of the good-natured cows under the dairymaid's operation, whose breath I was instructed to inhale; all was freedom, mirth, and peace. Often would my father take his noble pointers, preparatory to the shooting season, at once to try their powers and to ascertain what promise of future sport the fields presented. These were destructive expeditions in one sense. I remember the following dialogue, repeated to me by my brother, when we made our appearance at home after a day's demolition of wearing apparel.

'Mr. B. this will never do; that girl cannot wear a frock twice without soiling it; nor keep it whole for a week: the expense will ruin us.'

'Well, my dear, if I am to be ruined by expence, let it come in the shape of the washerwoman's and linen-draper's bills; not in those of the apothecary and undertaker.'

My dear father was right; and it would be a happy thing for girls in general if somewhat of appearance, and of acquirement too, was sacrificed to what God has so liberally provided, and to the enjoyment of which a blessing is undoubtedly annexed. Where, among females, do we find the stamina of constitution and the elasticity of spirit which exist in those of our rural population who follow out-door employment? It positively pains me to see a party of girls, a bonneted and tippeted double-file of humanity,

> That like a wounded snake drags its slow length along[4]

under the keen surveillance of a governess, whose nerves would never be able to endure the shock of seeing them bound over a stream or scramble through a fence, or even toss their heads and throw out their limbs as all young animals, except that oppressed class called young ladies, are privileged to do. Having ventured, in a fit of my country daring, to break the ice of this very rigid and frigid subject, I will recount another instance of the paternal good sense to which I owe, under God, the physical powers without which my little talent might have lain by in a napkin all my days.

One morning, when his daughter was about eight years old, my father came in, and found sundry preparations going on, the chief materials for which were buckram, whalebone, and other stiff articles; while the young lady was under measurement by the hands of a female friend.

'Pray, what are you going to do to the child?'

'Going to fit her with a pair of stays.'

'For what purpose?'

'To improve her figure; no young lady can grow up properly without them.'

'I beg your pardon; young gentlemen grow up very well without them, and so may young ladies.'

'Oh, you are mistaken. See what a stoop she has already, depend on it this girl will be both a dwarf and a cripple if we don't put her into stays.'

'My child may be a cripple, Ma'am, if such is God's will; but she shall be one of His making, not our's [sic].'

All remonstrance was vain; stays and every species of tight dress were strictly prohibited by the authority of one whose will was, as every man's ought to be, absolute in his own household. He also carefully watched against any evasion of the rule; a ribband drawn tightly round my waist would have been cut without hesitation, by his determined hand; while the little girl of the anxious friend whose operations he had interrupted, enjoyed all the advantages of that system from which I was preserved. She grew up a wand-like figure, graceful and interesting, and died of decline at nineteen, while I, though not able to compare shapes with a wasp or an hour-glass, yet passed muster very fairly among mere human forms, of God's moulding; and I have enjoyed to this hour a rare exemption from headaches, and other lady-like maladies, that appear the almost exclusive privilege of women in the higher classes ...

Compressure of the feet was with equal strictness forbidden by my judicious father. This vain custom is perhaps not so fatal as the other, but it produces many evils ... All cramping is decidedly bad: wholesome restraints there are, which parents are bound to lay upon their children, and the latter to submit to; and among other things I am sure a defined method, and regular habits, in education, work, and play, together with a most strict attention to scrupulous punctuality, are not only valuable, but indispensable to a right government of the mind and conduct in after life. I have daily cause to lament the unavoidable neglect of such a system in my own case, during three important years; but unavoidable it was, unless my life had been sacrificed to the maintenance of such order. Accordingly, mine was the life of a butterfly; and whatever of the busy bee has since appeared in my proceedings must be ascribed to divine grace alone. I often recal [sic] those days of summer sunshine to which I have alluded; and the scarcely less joyous winter season, when, ploughing the light snow, we raced with our inseparable companion, the favourite pointer, or built up a brittle giant for the glory of demolishing him with balls of his own substance, or directed the soft missiles against each other. Accompanied by our father, but never alone, we made excursions upon our frozen stream; and very sweet it was to the fond hearts of my tender parents to watch the mantling glow of health, the elastic vigour of increasing stature, and the unbounded play of most exuberant spirits in the poor child whom they had expected to enclose in an early grave. How often, seated on the low wide brick-work corner of the immense fireplace in a neighbouring farm-house, have I been smoked among hams and tongues, while watching the progress of baking a homely cake upon those glowing wood embers, or keeping guard over a treasury of apples, nuts, and elderberry wine, all steaming together in the lusciousness of a promised feast! Patriotism is with me no inert principle: it verily lives, and acts, and pervades my whole spirit; and I believe its energetic character, except as God deigns to work by his especial influence, is traceable to that early acquaintance with what is most purely English among us – the homes and the habits of our own bold yeomanry.

I grew up a healthy, active, light-hearted girl, wholly devoted to reading and to rural occupations. The latter, particularly gardening, seemed as a counterpoise to the sedentary temptation that would have proved physically injurious: but laying in, as I daily did, a plentiful store of romantic adventure or fascinating poetry for rumination when abroad, my mind was unprofitably occupied at all times, to the exclusion of better things ... And now, the chambers of imagery being well furnished, I became in thought the heroine of all the foolish, improbable adventures I met with. Shakspeare [sic] and others having furnished me with dresses and decorations, every day of my life had its drama. Adventures the most improbable, situations the most trying, and conversations the most nonsensical among a visionary acquaintance of my own creating, became the constant amusement of my mind; or if I took a fancy to any new companion, that individual was metamorphosed into something equally unreal, and was soon looked upon in the light, not of sober reality, but of fanciful extravagance. Of course, my estimate alike of persons and of things was egregiously false; and with a fair portion of common sense naturally belonging to me, I became most emphatically a fool. Even when employed at the pencil, which I dearly loved, I could not trace a figure on the paper, or a landscape on the canvas, that did not presently become the subject of a separate romance; and it never occurred to me that there was danger, much less sin, in this. I loved dancing to excess, and took much delight in all that was brilliant and beautiful; but upon the whole I preferred the uninterrupted course of my own vain thoughts, and then admired myself for being of a less dissipated turn than my young friends. Of course, I am now speaking of the time when, according to the world's usage, and rather earlier than usual, that is to say, at sixteen, I was introduced into public, by making my appearance at a grand election ball; and moreover, publicly receiving the compliments of the most polished and distinguished of our successful candidates, for sundry political squibs, said to be full of drollery and point, which had been traced home to me. Alas for the girl who makes such a debut! We were now again resident in the town, or rather within the precincts, as they are called, surrounding that venerable cathedral which had been the object of my babyish contemplation, and which is endeared to me beyond any other spot in my native place.

My beloved companion, my brother, had always manifested the most decided predeliction for a military life. Often had he, in earliest childhood, toddled away from the gate after the fife and drum of a recruiting party; and often did he march and countermarch me, till I could not stand for fatigue, with a grenadier's cap, alias a muff, on my head, and my father's large cane shouldered by way of a firelock. The menaced invasion had added fuel to his martial fire, and when any other line of life was pointed out to him, his high spirits would droop, and the desire of his heart shew itself with increasing decision. Our parents were very anxious to settle him at home, for my sake, who seemed unable to live without him; and I am sure that my influence would have prevailed, even over his long-cherished inclination, so dearly did he love me; but here the effect of that pernicious reading shewed itself, and forged the first link in a long chain of sorrows. I viewed the matter through the lying medium of romance; glory, fame, a conqueror's wreath or a hero's grave, with all the vain merit of such a sacrifice as I must myself make in sending him to the field – these wrought on me to stifle in my aching bosom the cry of natural affection, and I encouraged the boy in his choice, and helped him to urge on our parents this offering up of their only son, the darling of all our hearts, to the Moloch of war.

Finding that he could not be dissuaded, my father gave a reluctant consent; and let me here record an instance of generous kindness on the part of the Bishop. He went to London, and by dint of personal, persevering importunity, obtained in a few days a commission in the army, at a time when seven hundred applicants, many of them backed by strong interest, were waiting for the same boon. The suddenness of the thing was quite stunning: we calculated on a delay of this sore trial; but it was done, and he was ordered to repair immediately, not to the depot, but to his regiment, then hotly engaged in the Peninsula. The Bishop's kindness did not end here: he carried his generosity farther in other ways, and likewise gave him introductions of great value. I love to record it of one whose public conduct as a Protestant prelate I am compelled to lament, but whose private character was most lovely.

Upheld by the intoxicating power of senseless romance, not by confidence in God, nor even by the reality of the patriotism that I persuaded myself was at the root of it all, I bore to see that beloved companion of my life depart for the scene of most bloody conflict. He was not nearly full grown; a blooming beautiful boy, reared, and up to that time tenderly, guarded under the parental roof, in almost exclusive companionship with me. There was, indeed, but one heart between us, and neither could fancy what it would be to rejoice or to suffer alone. Of this I had given a proof in the preceding year. He took the measles, and was exceedingly ill, and great precautions were used to preserve me from the infection; but, unable to brook a separation from him, I baffled their vigilance, burst into his apartment, and laying my cheek to his, resisted for a while all efforts to remove me. To my infinite delight, I sickened immediately, and considered it an ample compensation for all attendant suffering, that I was allowed to sit constantly in the same room with him.

How strong, how sweet, how sacred is the tie that binds an only sister to an only brother, when they have been permitted to grow up together, untrammelled by the heartless forms of fashion; unrivalled by alien claimants in their confiding affection; undivided in study, in sport, and in interests! Some object, that such union renders the boy too effeminate and the girl too masculine. In our case it did neither. He was the manliest, the hardiest, most decided, most intrepid character imaginable; but in manners sweet, gentle, and courteous, as they will be who are accustomed to look with protecting tenderness on an associate weaker than themselves. And as for me, though I must plead guilty to the charge of being more healthy, more active, and perhaps more energetic than young ladies are usually expected to be, still I never was considered unfeminine; and the only peculiarity resulting from this constant companionship with one of the superior sex, was to give me a high sense of that superiority, with a habit of deference to man's judgment, and submission to man's authority, which I am quite sure God intended the woman to yield. Every way has this fraternal tie been a rich blessing to me. The love that grew with us from our cradles never knew diminution from time or distance. Other ties were formed, but they did not supersede or weaken this. Death tore away all that was mortal and perishable, but this tie he could not sunder. As I loved him while he was on earth, so do I love him now that he is in heaven; and while I cherish in his boys the living likeness of what he was, my heart evermore yearns towards him where he is, anticipating the day when the Lord shall come, and bring that beloved one with him.

Parents are wrong to check as they do the outgoings of fraternal affection, by separating those whom God has especially joined as the offspring of one father and one mother. God has beautifully mingled them, by sending now a babe of one sex, now of the other, and suiting, as any careful observer may discern, their various characters to form a domestic whole. The parents interpose, packing off the boys to some school where no softer influence exists to round off, as it were, the rugged points of the masculine disposition, and where they soon lose all the delicacy of feeling peculiar to a brother's regard, and learn to look on the female character in a light wholly subversive of the frankness, the purity, the generous care for which earth can yield no substitute, and the loss of which only transforms him who ought to be the tender preserver of woman into her heartless destroyer. The girls are either grouped at home, with the blessed privilege of a father's eye still upon them, or sent away in a different direction from their brothers, exposed, through unnatural and unpalateable restraints, to evils not perhaps so great, but every whit as wantonly incurred as the others. The shyness, miscalled retiring modesty, with which one young lady shrinks from the notice of a gentleman as though there were danger in his approach, and the conscious, coquettish air, miscalled ease, with which another invites his notice, are alike removed from the reality of either modesty or ease. Both result from a fictitious mode of education: both are the consequences of nipping in the bud those sisterly feelings that lay a fair foundation for the right use of those privileges to which she looks forward as a member of society; and if the subject be viewed through the clear medium of Christian principle its lights will become more brilliant, its shadows more dark, the longer and the closer we contemplate it.

*Source*: 'Charlotte Elizabeth', *Personal Recollections* (London: R.B. Seeley and W. Burnside, 1841).

**Notes**

1. Micah 6:9.
2. Samuel Parr (1747–1825), headmaster and theologian who had been a curate in Norwich, but lived in Hatton, Warwickshire.
3. Commonly known as *Foxe's Book of Martyrs* (1563) by John Foxe (1517–87), a supporter of the Reformation, who left the country when Mary I became Queen. 'Charlotte Elizabeth' admired the book so much that she wrote an abridged version of it.
4. Alexander Pope, *An Essay on Criticism* (1711), vol. l, p. 357.

# 8

# Anna Jameson

Although Anna Jameson (1794–1860) did not attempt a formal autobiography, she has been included in this collection because she wrote an extended essay on the imaginative and emotional life of children, using an autobiographical framework. Born in Dublin, Anna Murphy was the eldest of five daughters of the Irish miniaturist painter Dennis Brownell Murphy, and subsequently developed a keen interest in the fine arts, publishing gallery guides and *Memoirs of the Early Italian Painters* (1845). She worked as a governess for two different families, until in 1825 she married a barrister, Robert Jameson. Temperamentally unsuited, they had already broken off their engagement once, and soon discovered that they could not live with each other. Attempts were made to patch things up (she followed him to Canada, where he had gone to take up a legal appointment in 1833), but their marriage finally failed, and she concentrated on earning her own living by writing. Anna Jameson wrote widely on a range of cultural subjects: her *Characteristics of Women* (1832) was about Shakespeare's heroines, and *Winter Studies and Summer Rambles in Canada* (1838) at least made good use of the time she had spent trying to salvage her relationship with her husband. She became involved with the women's movement of the 1850s, and knew many of the prominent women of the day. The following essay, 'A Revelation of Childhood', published in *A Commonplace Book of Thoughts, Memories, and Fancies, Original and Selected* (1854), is a plea for a fuller and more humane understanding of childhood, in the guidance of which she felt women should be given a larger formal role.

We are all interested in this great question of popular education; but I see others much more sanguine than I am. They hope for some immediate good result from all that is thought, written, spoken on the subject day after day. I see such results as possible, probable, but far, far off. All this talk is of systems and methods, institutions, school houses, schoolmasters, schoolmistresses, school books; the ways and the means by which we are to instruct, inform, manage, mould, regulate, that which lies in most cases beyond our reach – the spirit sent from God. What do we know of the mystery of child-nature, child-life? What, indeed, do we know of any life? All life we acknowledge to be an awful mystery, but child-life we treat as if it were no mystery whatever – just so much material placed in our hands to be fashioned to a certain form according to our will or our prejudices, – fitted to certain purposes according to our notions of expediency. Till we know how to *reverence* childhood we shall do no good. Educators commit the same mistake with regard to childhood that theologians commit with regard to our present earthly existence; thinking of it, treating of it, as of little value or significance in itself, only transient, and preparatory to some condition of being which is to follow – as if it were something separate from us and to be left behind us as the creature casts its skin. But as in the sight of God this life is also something for its own sake, so in the estimation of Christ, childhood was something for its own sake, – something holy and beautiful in itself, and dear to him. He saw it not merely as the germ of something to grow out of it, but as perfect and lovely in itself as the flower which precedes the fruit. We misunderstand childhood, and we misuse it; we delight in it, and we pamper it; we spoil it ingeniously, we neglect it sinfully; at the best we trifle with it as a plaything which we can pull to pieces and put together at pleasure – ignorant, reckless, presumptuous that we are!

And if we are perpetually making the grossest mistakes in the physical and practical management of childhood, how much do we know of that which lies in the minds of children? we know only what we put there. The world of instincts, perceptions, experiences, pleasures, and pains, lying there without self-consciousness, – sometimes helplessly mute, sometimes so imperfectly expressed, that we quite mistake the manifestation – what do we know of all this? How shall we come at the understanding of it? The child lives, and does not contemplate its own life. It can give no account of that inward, busy, perpetual activity of the growing faculties and feelings which it is of so much importance that we should know. To lead children by questionings to think about their own identity, or observe their own feelings, is to teach them to be artificial. To waken self-consciousness before you awaken conscience is the beginning of incalculable mischief. Introspection is always, as a habit, unhealthy; introspection in childhood, fatally so. How shall we come at a knowledge of life such as it is when it first gushes from its mysterious fountain head? We cannot re-ascend the stream. We all, however we may remember the external scenes lived through in our infancy, either do not, or cannot, consult that part of our nature which remains indissolubly connected with the inward life of that time. We so forget it, that we know not how to deal with the child-nature when it comes under our power. We seldom reason about children from natural laws, or psychological data. Unconsciously we confound our matured experience with our memory: we attribute to children what is not possible, exact from them what is impossible; – ignore many things which the child has neither words to express, nor the will nor the power to manifest. The quickness with which children perceive, the keenness with which they suffer, the tenacity with which they remember, I have never seen fully appreciated. What misery we cause to children, what mischief we do them by bringing our own minds, habits, artificial prejudices and senile experiences, to bear on their young life, and cramp and overshadow it – it is fearful!

Of all the wrongs and anomalies that afflict our earth, a sinful childhood, a suffering childhood, are among the worst ...

I say nothing here of teaching, though very few in truth understand that lowest part of our duty to children. Men, it is generally allowed, *teach* better than women because they have been better taught the things they teach. Women *train* better than men because of their quick instinctive perceptions and sympathies, and greater tenderness and patience. In schools and in families I would have some things taught by men and some by women: but we will here put aside the art, the act of teaching: we will turn aside from the droves of children in national schools and reformatory asylums, and turn to the individual child, brought up within the guarded circle of a home or a select school, watched by an intelligent, a conscientious influence. How shall we deal with that spirit which has come out of nature's hands unless we remember what we were ourselves in the past? What sympathy can we have with that state of being which we regard as immature, so long as we commit the double mistake of sometimes attributing to children motives which could only spring from our adult experience, and sometimes denying to them the same intuitive tempers and feelings which actuate and agitate our maturer life? We do not sufficiently consider that our life is not made up of separate parts, but is *one* – is a progressive whole. When we talk of leaving our childhood behind us, we might as well say that the river flowing onward to the sea had left the fountain behind.

I will here put together some recollections of my own child-life; not because it was in any respect an exceptional or remarkable existence, but for a reason exactly the reverse, because it was like that of many children; at least I have met with many children who throve or suffered from the same or similar unseen causes even under external conditions and management every way dissimilar. Facts, therefore, which can be relied on, may be generally useful as hints towards a theory of conduct. What I shall say here shall be simply the truth so far as it goes; not something between the false and the true, garnished for effect, – not something half-remembered, half-imagined, – but plain, absolute, matter of fact.

No; certainly I was not an extraordinary child. I have had something to do with children, and have met with several more remarkable for quickness of talent, and precocity of feeling. If any thing in particular, I believe I was particularly naughty, –at least so it was said twenty times a day. But looking back now, I do not think I was particular even in this respect; I perpetrated not more than the usual amount of mischief – so called – which every lively active child perpetrates between five and ten years old. I had the usual desire to know, and the usual dislike to learn; the usual love of fairy tales, and hatred of French exercises. But not of what I learned, but of what I did not learn; not of what they taught me, but of what they could not teach me; not of what was open, apparent, manageable, but of the under current, the hidden, the unmanaged or unmanageable, I have to speak, and you, my friend, to hear and turn to account, if you will, and how you will. As we grow old the experiences of infancy come back upon us with a strange vividness. There is a period when the overflowing, tumultuous life of our youth rises up between us and those first years; but as the torrent subsides in its bed we can look across the impassable gulf to that haunted fairy land which we shall never more approach, and never more forget!

In memory I can go back to a very early age. I perfectly remember being sung to sleep, and can remember even the tune which was sung to me – blessings on the voice that sang it! I was an affectionate, but not, as I now think, a loveable nor an attractive child. I did not, like the little Mozart, ask of everyone around me, 'Do you love me?' The instinctive question was, rather, 'Can I love you?' Yet certainly I was not more than six years old when I suffered from the fear of not being loved where I had attached myself, and from the idea that another was preferred before me, such anguish as had nearly killed me. Whether those around me regarded it as a fit of ill-temper, or a fit of illness, I do not know. I could not then have given a name to the pang that fevered me. I knew not the cause, but never forgot the suffering. It left a deeper impression than childish passions usually do; and the recollection was so far salutary, that in after life I guarded myself against the approaches of that hateful, deformed, agonising thing which men call jealousy, as I would from an attack of cramp or cholera. If such self-knowledge has not saved me from the pain, at least it has saved me from the demoralising effects of the passion, by a wholesome terror, and even a sort of disgust.

With a good temper, there was the capacity of strong, deep, silent resentment, and a vindictive spirit of rather a peculiar kind. I recollect that when one of those set over me inflicted what then appeared a most horrible injury and injustice, the thoughts of vengeance haunted my fancy for months: but it was an inverted sort of vengeance. I imagined the house of my enemy on fire, and rushed through the flames to rescue her. She was drowning, and I leaped into the deep water to draw her forth. She was pining in prison, and I forced bars and bolts to deliver her. If this were magnanimity, it was not the less vengeance; for, observe, I always fancied evil, and shame, and humiliation to my adversary; to myself the role of superiority and gratified pride. For several years this sort of burning resentment against wrong done to myself and others, though it took no mean or cruel form, was a source of intense, untold suffering. No one was aware of it. I was left to settle it; and my mind righted itself I hardly know how: not certainly by religious influences – they passed over my mind, and did not at the time sink into it, – and as for earthly counsel or comfort, I never had either when most needed. And as it fared with me then, so it has been in after life; so it has been, must be, with all those who, in fighting out alone, the pitched battle between principle and passion, will accept no intervention between the infinite within them and the infinite above them; so it has been, *must* be, with all strong natures. Will it be said that victory in the struggle brings increase of strength? It may be so with some who survive the contest; but then, how many sink! how many are crippled morally for life! how many, strengthened in some particular faculties, suffering in losing the harmony of the character as a whole! This is one of the points in which the matured mind may help the childish nature at strife with itself. It is impossible to say how far this sort of vindictiveness might have penetrated and hardened into the character, if I had been of a timid or retiring nature. It was expelled at last by no outer influences, but by a growing sense of power and self-reliance.

In regard to truth – always such a difficulty in education, – I certainly had, as a child, and like most children, confused ideas about it. I had a more distinct and absolute idea of honour than of truth, – a mistake into which our conventional morality leads those who educate and those who are educated. I knew very well, in a general way, that to tell a lie was *wicked*; to lie for my own profit or pleasure, or to the hurt of others, was, according to my infant code of morals, worse than wicked – it was *dishonourable*. But I had no compunction about telling fictions; – inventing scenes and circumstances, which I related as real, and with a keen sense of triumphant enjoyment in seeing the listener taken in by a most artful and ingenious concatenation of impossibilities. In this respect 'Ferdinand Mendez Pinto, that liar of the first magnitude',[1] was nothing in comparison to me. I must have been twelve years old before my conscience was first awakened up to a sense of the necessity of truth as a principle, as well as its holiness as a virtue. Afterwards, having to set right the minds of others cleared my own mind on this and some other important points.

I do not think I was naturally obstinate, but remember going without food all day, and being sent hungry and exhausted to bed, because I would not do some trifling thing required of me. I think it was to recite some lines I knew by heart. I was punished as wilfully obstinate: but what no one knew then, and what I know now as the fact, was, that after refusing to do what was required, and bearing anger and threats in consequence, I lost the power to do it. I became stone: the will was petrified, and I absolutely could not comply. They might have hacked me in pieces before my lips could have unclosed to utterance. The obstinacy was not in the mind, but on the nerves; and I am persuaded that what we call obstinacy in children, and grown-up people, too, is often something of this kind, and that it may be increased, by mismanagement, by persistence, or what is called firmness, in the controlling power, into disease, or something near to it.

There was in my childish mind another cause of suffering besides those I have mentioned, less acute, but more permanent and always acknowledged. It was fear – fear of darkness and supernatural influences. As long as I can remember anything, I remember those horrors of my infancy. How they had been awakened I do not know; they were never revealed. I had heard other children ridiculed for such fears, and held my peace. At first these haunting, thrilling, stifling terrors were vague; afterwards the form varied; but one of the most permanent was the ghost in Hamlet. There was a volume of Shakspeare lying about, in which was an engraving I have not seen since, but it remains distinct in my mind as a picture. On one side stood Hamlet with his hair on end, literally 'like quills upon the fretful porcupine', and one hand with all the fingers outspread. On the other strided the ghost, encased in armour with nodding plumes; one finger pointing forwards, and all surrounded with a supernatural light. O that spectre! for three years it followed me up and down the dark staircase, or stood by my bed: only the blessed light had power to exorcise it. How it was that I knew, while I trembled and quaked, that it was unreal, never cried out, never expostulated, never confessed, I do not know. The figure of Apollyon looming over Christian, which I had found in an old edition of the *Pilgrim's Progress*, was also a great torment. But worse, perhaps, were certain phantasms without shape, – things like the vision in Job – '*A spirit passed before my face; it stood still, but I could not discern the form thereof*'[2] :– and if not intelligible voices, there were strange unaccountable sounds filling the air around with a sort of mysterious life. In daylight I was not only fearless, but audacious, inclined to defy all power and brave all danger, – that is, all danger I could see. I remember volunteering to lead the way through a herd of cattle (among which was a dangerous bull, the terror of the neighbourhood) armed only with a little stick; but first I said the Lord's Prayer fervently. In the ghastly night I never prayed; terror stifled prayer. These visionary sufferings, in some form or other, pursued me till I was nearly twelve years old. If I had not possessed a strong constitution and strong understanding, which rejected and contemned my own fears, even while they shook me, I had been destroyed. How much weaker children suffer in this way, I have since known; and have known how to bring them help and strength, through sympathy and knowledge, the sympathy that soothes and does not encourage – the knowledge that dispels, and does not suggest, the evil.

People, in general, even those who have been much interested in education, are not aware of the sacred duty of *truth*, exact truth in their intercourse with children. Limit what you tell them according to the measure of their faculties; but let what you say be the truth. Accuracy not merely as to fact, but well-considered accuracy in the use of words, is essential with children. I have read some wise book on the treatment of the insane, in which absolute veracity and accuracy in speaking is prescribed as a *curative* principle; and deception for any purpose is deprecated as almost fatal to the health of the patient. Now, it is a good sanitary principle, that what is curative is preventive; and that an unhealthy state of mind, leading to madness, may, in some organisations, be induced by that sort of uncertainty and perplexity which grows up where the mind has not been accustomed to truth in its external relations. It is like breathing for a continuance an impure or confined air.

Of the mischief that may be done to a childish mind by a falsehood uttered in thoughtless gaiety, I remember an absurd and yet a painful instance. A visitor was turning over, for a little girl, some prints, one of which represented an Indian widow springing into the fire kindled for the funeral pile of her husband. It was thus explained to the child, who asked innocently, whether, if her father died, her mother would be burned? The person to whom the question was addressed, a lively, amiable woman, was probably much amused by the question, and answered, giddily, 'Oh, of course, – certainly!' and was believed implicitly. But thenceforth, for many weary months, the mind of that child was haunted and tortured by the image of her mother springing into the devouring flames, and consumed by fire, with all the accessories of the picture, particularly the drums beating to drown her cries. In a weaker organisation, the results might have been permanent and serious. But to proceed.

These terrors I have described had an existence external to myself: I had no power over them to shape them by my will, and their power over me vanished gradually before a more dangerous infatuation, – the propensity to reverie. The shaping spirit of imagination began when I was about eight or nine years old to haunt my inner life. I can truly say that, from ten years old to fourteen or fifteen, I lived a double existence; one outward, linking me with the external sensible world, the other inward, creating a world to and for itself, conscious to itself only. I carried on for whole years a series of actions, scenes, and adventures; one springing out of another, and coloured and modified by increasing knowledge. This habit grew so upon me, that there were moments – as when I came to some crisis in my imaginary adventures, – when I was not more awake to outward things than in sleep, – scarcely took cognisance of the beings around me. When punished for idleness by being placed in solitary confinement (the worst of all punishments for children), the intended penance was nothing less than a delight and an emancipation, giving me up to my dreams. I had a very strict and very accomplished governess, one of the cleverest women I have ever met with in my life; but nothing of this was known or even suspected by her, and I exulted in possessing something which her power could not reach. My reveries were my real life: it was an unhealthy state of things.

Those who are engaged in the training of children will perhaps pause here. It may be said, in the first place, How are we to reach those recesses of the inner life which the God who made us keeps from every eye but his own? As when we walk over the field in spring we are aware of a thousand influences and processes at work of which we have no exact knowledge or clear perception, yet must watch and use accordingly, – so it is with education. And secondly, it may be asked, if such secret processes be working unconscious mischief, where the remedy? The remedy is employment. Then the mother or the teacher echoes with astonishment, 'Employment! the child is employed from morning till night; she is learning a dozen sciences and languages; she has masters and lessons for every hour of the day: with her pencil, her piano, her books, her companions, her birds, her flowers, – what can she want more?' An energetic child even at a very early age, and yet farther as the physical organisation is developed, wants something more and something better; employment which shall bring with it the bond of a higher duty than that which centres in self and self-improvement; employment which shall not merely cultivate the understanding, but strengthen and elevate the conscience; employment for the higher and more generous faculties; employment addressed to the sympathies; employment which has the aim of utility, not pretended, but real, obvious, direct utility. A girl who as a mere child is not always being taught or being amused, whose mind is early restrained by the bond of definite duty, and thrown out of the limit of self, will not in after years be subject to fancies that disturb or to reveries that absorb, and the present and the actual will have that power they ought to have as combined in due degree with desire and anticipation.

The Roman Catholic priesthood understand this well: employment, which enlists with the spiritual the sympathetic part of our being, is a means through which they guide both young and adult minds. Physicians who have to manage various states of mental and moral disease understand this well; they speak of the necessity of employment (not mere amusement) as a curative means, but of employment with the direct aim of usefulness, apprehended and appreciated by the patient, else it is nothing. It is the same with children. Such employment, chosen with reference to utility, and in harmony with the faculties, would prove in many cases, either preventive or curative. In my own case, as I now think, it would have been both.

There was a time when it was thought essential that women should know something of cookery, something of medicine, something of surgery. If all these things are far better understood now than heretofore, is that a reason why a well-educated woman should be left wholly ignorant of them? A knowledge of what people call 'common things' – of the elements of physiology, of the conditions of health, of the qualities, nutritive or remedial, of substances commonly used as food or medicine, and the most economical and most beneficial way of applying both, – these should form part of the system of every girls' school – whether for the higher or the lower classes. At present you shall see a girl studying chemistry, and attending Faraday's lectures, who would be puzzled to compound a rice-pudding or a cup of barley-water: and a girl who could work quickly a complicated sum in the Rule of Three, afterwards wasting a fourth of her husband's wages through want of management.

In my own case, how much of the practical and the sympathetic in my nature was exhausted in airy visions!

As to the stuff out of which my waking dreams were composed, I cannot tell you much. I have a remembrance that I was always a princess-heroine in the disguise of a knight, a sort of Clorinda or Britomart,[3] going about to redress the wrongs of the poor, fight giants, and kill dragons; or founding a society in some far-off solitude or desolate island, which would have rivalled that of Gonsalez [sic],[4] where there were to be no tears, no tasks, and no laws – except those which I made myself, – no caged birds nor tormented kittens.

Enough of the pains, and mistakes, and vagaries of childhood; let me tell of some of its pleasures equally unguessed and unexpressed. A great, an exquisite source of enjoyment arose out of an early, instinctive, boundless delight in external beauty. How this went hand in hand with my terrors and reveries, how it could coexist with them, I cannot tell now – it was so; and if this sympathy with the external, living, beautiful world, had been properly, scientifically cultivated, and directed to useful definite purposes, it would have been the best remedy for much that was morbid: this was not the case, and we were, unhappily for me, too early removed from the country to a town residence. I can remember, however, that in very early years the appearances of nature did truly 'haunt me like a passion';[5] the stars were to me as the gates of heaven; the rolling of the wave to the shore, the graceful weeds and grasses bending before the breeze as they grew by the wayside; the minute and delicate forms of insects; the trembling shadows of boughs and leaves dancing on the ground in the highest noon; these were to me perfect pleasures of which the imagery now in my mind is distinct. Wordsworth's poem of 'The Daffodils', the one beginning –

> I wandered lonely as a cloud,

may appear to some unintelligible or overcharged, but to me it was a vivid truth, a simple fact; and if Wordsworth had been then in my hands I think I must have loved him. It was this intense sense of beauty which gave the first zest to poetry: I loved it, not because it told me what I did not know, but because it helped me to words in which to clothe my own knowledge and perceptions, and reflected back the pictures unconsciously hoarded up in my mind. This was what made Thomson's *Seasons* a favourite book when I first began to read for my own amusement, and before I could understand one half of it; St. Pierre's *Indian Cottage (La Chaumiere Indienne)*[6] was also charming, either because it reflected my dreams, or gave me new stuff for them in pictures of an external world quite different from that I inhabited, – palm-trees, elephants, tigers, dark-turbaned men with flowing draperies; and the *Arabian Nights* completed my Oriental intoxication, which lasted for a long time.

I have said little of the impressions left by books, and of my first religious notions. A friend of mine had once the wise idea of collecting together a variety of evidence as to the impressions left by certain books on childish or immature minds: If carried out, it would have been one of the most valuable additions to educational experience ever made. For myself I did not much care about the books put into my hands, nor imbibe much information from them. I had a great taste, I am sorry to say, for forbidden books; yet it was not the forbidden books that did the mischief, except in their being read furtively. I remember impressions of vice and cruelty from some parts of the Old Testament and Goldsmith's *History of England*, which I shudder to recall. Shakspeare was on the forbidden shelf. I had read him all through between seven and ten years old. He never did me any moral mischief. He never soiled my mind with any disordered image. What was exceptionable and coarse in language I passed by without attaching any meaning whatever to it. How it might have been if I had read Shakspeare first when I was fifteen or sixteen, I do not know; perhaps the occasional coarsenesses and obscurities might have shocked the delicacy or puzzled the intelligence of that sensitive and inquiring age. But at nine or ten I had no comprehension of what was unseemly; what might be obscure in words to wordy commentators, was to me lighted up by the idea I found or interpreted for myself – right or wrong.

No; I repeat, Shakspeare – bless him! – never did me any moral mischief. Though the Witches in *Macbeth* troubled me, – though the Ghost in *Hamlet* terrified me (the picture that is, – for the spirit in Shakspeare was solemn and pathetic, not hideous), – though poor little Arthur cost me an ocean of tears, – yet much that was obscure, and all that was painful and revolting was merged on the whole in the vivid presence of a new, beautiful, vigorous, living world. The plays which I now think the most wonderful produced comparatively little effect on my fancy: *Romeo and Juliet*, *Othello*, *Macbeth*, struck me then less than the historical plays, and far less than the *Midsummer Night's Dream* and *Cymbeline*. It may be thought, perhaps, that Falstaff is not a character to strike a child, or to be understood by a child: – no; surely not. To me Falstaff was not witty and wicked – only irresistibly fat and funny; and I remember lying on the ground rolling with laughter over some of the scenes in *Henry the Fourth*, – the mock play, and the seven men in buckram. But *The Tempest* and *Cymbeline* were the plays I liked best and knew best.

Altogether I should say that in my early years books were known to me, not as such, not for their general contents, but for some especial image or picture I had picked out of them and assimilated to my own mind and mixed up with my own life. For example, out of Homer's *Odyssey* (lent to me by the parish clerk) I had the picture of Nasicaa and her maidens going down in their chariots to wash their linen: so that when the first time I went to the Pitti Palace, and could hardly see the pictures through blinding tears, I saw that picture of Rubens, which all remember who have been at Florence, and it flashed delight and refreshment through those remembered childish associations.[7] The Syrens [sic] and Polypheme left also vivid pictures on my fancy. The *Iliad*, on the contrary, wearied me, except the parting of Hector and Andromache, in which the child, scared by its father's dazzling helm and nodding crest, remains a vivid image in my mind from that time.

The same parish clerk – a curious fellow in his way, – lent me also some religious tracts and stories, by Hannah More. It is most certain that more moral mischief was done to me by some of these than by all Shakspeare's plays together. These so-called pious tracts first introduced me to a knowledge of the vices of vulgar life, and the excitements of a vulgar religion, – the fear of being hanged and the fear of hell became coexistent in my mind; and the teaching resolved itself into this, – that it was not by being naughty, but by being found out, that I was to incur the risk of both. My fairy world was better!

About Religion: – I was taught religion as children used to be taught in my younger days, and are taught it still in some cases, I believe – through the medium of creeds and catechisms. I read the Bible too early, and too indiscriminately, and too irreverently. Even the New Testament was too early placed in my hands; too early made a lesson book, as the custom then was. The letter of the Scriptures – the words – were familiarised to me by sermonising and dogmatising, long before I could enter into the spirit. Meantime, happily, another religion was growing up in my heart, which, strangely enough, seemed to me quite apart from that which was taught, – which, indeed, I never in any way regarded as the same which I was taught when I stood up wearily on a Sunday to repeat the collect and say the catechism. It was quite another thing. Not only the taught religion and the sentiment of faith and adoration were never combined, but it never for years entered into my head to combine them; the first remained extraneous, the latter had gradually taken root in my life, even from the moment my mother joined my little hands in prayer. The histories out of the Bible (the Parables especially) were, however, enchanting to me, though my interpretation of them was in some instances the very reverse of correct or orthodox. To my infant conception our Lord was a being who had come down from heaven to make people good, and to tell them beautiful stories. And though no pains were spared to indoctrinate me, and all my pastors and masters took it for granted that my ideas were quite satisfactory, nothing could be more confused and heterodox.

It is a common observation that girls of lively talents are apt to grow pert and satirical. I fell into this danger when about ten years old. Sallies at the expense of certain people, ill-looking, or ill-dressed, or ridiculous, or foolish, had been laughed at and applauded in company, until, without being naturally malignant, I ran some risk of becoming so from sheer vanity.

The fables which appeal to our higher moral sympathies may sometimes do as much for us as the truths of science. So thought our Saviour when he taught the multitude in parables.

A good clergyman who lived near us, a famous Persian scholar, took it into his head to teach me Persian (I was then about seven years old), and I set to work with infinite delight and earnestness. All I learned was soon forgotten; but a few years afterwards, happening to stumble on a volume of Sir William Jones's works – his Persian grammar – it revived my Orientalism, and I began to study it eagerly.[8] Among the exercises given was a Persian fable or poem – one of those traditions of our Lord which are preserved in the East. The beautiful apologue of 'St. Peter and the Cherries', which Goethe has versified or imitated, is a well known example. This fable I allude to was something similar, but I have not met with the original these forty years, and must give it here from memory.

[*She tells the story of Jesus finding something complimentary to say about the body of a dead dog that everyone else was abusing.*]

I can recall, at this hour, the vivid, yet softening and pathetic impression left on my fancy by this old Eastern story. It struck me as exquisitely humorous, as well as exquisitely beautiful. It gave me a pain in my conscience, for it seemed thenceforward so easy and so vulgar to say satirical things, and so much nobler to be benign and merciful, and I took the lesson so home, that I was in great danger of falling into the opposite extreme, – of seeking the beautiful even in the midst of the corrupt and the repulsive. Pity, a large element in my composition, might have easily degenerated into weakness, threatening to subvert hatred of evil in trying to find excuses for it; and whether my mind has ever completely righted itself, I am not sure.

Educators are not always aware, I think, how acute are the perceptions, and how permanent the memories of children. I remember experiments tried upon my temper and feelings, and how I was made aware of this, by their being repeated, and, in some instances, spoken of, before me. Music, to which I was early and peculiarly sensitive, was sometimes made the medium of these experiments. Discordant sounds were not only hateful, but made me turn white and cold, and sent the blood backward to my heart; and certain tunes had a curious effect, I cannot now account for: for though, when heard for the first time, they had little effect, they became intolerable by repetition; they turned up some hidden emotion within me too strong to be borne. It could not have been from association, which I believe to be a principal element in the emotion excited by music. I was too young for that. What associations could such a baby have had with pleasure or with pain? Or could it be possible that associations with some former state of existence awake up to sound? That our life 'hath elsewhere its beginning, and cometh from afar',[9] is a belief, or at least an instinct, in some minds, which music, and only music, seems to thrill into consciousness. At this time, when I was about five or six years old, Mrs. Arkwright – she was then Fanny Kemble,[10] – used to come to our house, and used to entrance me with her singing. I had a sort of adoration for her, such as an ecstatic votary might have had for a Saint Cecilia. I trembled with pleasure when I only heard her step. But her voice! – it has charmed hundreds since; whom has it ever moved to a more genuine passion of delight than the little child that crept silent and tremulous to her side? And she was fond of me, – fond of singing to me, and it must be confessed, fond also of playing these experiments on me. The music of 'Paul and Virginia'[11] was then in vogue, and there was one air – a very simple air – in that opera, which, after the first few bars, always made me stop my ears and rush out of the room. I became at last aware that this was sometimes done by particular desire to please my parents, or amuse and interest others by the display of such vehement emotion. My infant conscience became perplexed between the reality of the feeling and the exhibition of it. People are not always aware of the injury done to children by repeating before them things they say, or describing things they do: words and actions, spontaneous and unconscious, become thenceforth artificial and conscious. I can speak of the injury done to myself between five and eight years old. There was some danger of my becoming a precocious actress, –danger of permanent mischief such as I have seen done to other children, – but I was saved by the recoil of resistance and resentment excited in my mind.

This is enough. All that has been told here refers to a period between five and ten years old.

*Source*: Anna Jameson, 'A Revelation of Childhood', in *A Commonplace Book of Thoughts, Memories, and Fancies, Original and Selected* (London: Longman, Brown, Green and Longmans, 1854).

## Notes

1. A quotation from William Congreve's *Love for Love* (1695) referring to Ferdinand Mendez Pinto (1509–83), Portuguese traveller in the East and author of *Peregrinacao* (1614). He was thought to have exaggerated what he saw.

2. Job 4:15–16: 'Then a spirit passed before my face; the hair of my flesh stood up:/ It stood still, but I could not discern the form thereof.'

3. Britomart is a female knight of chastity from book III of Spenser's *Faerie Queene* (1590–96), a type of Elizabeth I. Clorinda is leader of the pagan forces in Tasso's *Gerusalemme Liberata* (1580–81). She dies after being wounded by Tancred, the man she loves.

4. Gonzalo is the idealistic elderly courtier shipwrecked in Shakespeare's *Tempest*, who describes the perfect commonwealth he would create: 'And yet he would be king on't', Sebastian, another shipwrecked prince, comments (Act 2, scene 1).

5. From Wordsworth's 'Tintern Abbey', lines 77–8.

6. *La Chaumiere Indienne* (1791) by Bernardin de Saint-Pierre (1737–1814) tells how a traveller finds truth and wisdom in an Indian's cottage.

7. 'Ulysses and Nausicaa' (1625–35) by Peter Paul Rubens (1577–1640), a landscape painting illustrating the scene from Homer's *Odyssey* book 6 when the Phaeacian princess Nausicaa washing linen in the river meets the shipwrecked Ulysses and takes him home to her father's palace.

8. Sir William Jones (1746–94), orientalist and pioneer in Sanskrit learning, author of a *Grammar of the Persian Language* (1771).

9. Wordsworth's 'Ode – Intimations of Immortality' contains the lines: 'The Soul that rises with us, our life's Star, / Hath had elsewhere its setting, / And cometh from afar' (stanza v).

10. Not the Fanny Kemble included in this anthology, but her cousin Frances, daughter of her father's brother, Stephen Kemble. She married Captain Robert Arkwright, grandson of the inventor Richard Arkwright.

11. The comic opera *Paul et Virginia, ou Le temple de la vertue* (1794) was composed by Jean-Francois Le Sueur (1760–1837) after the novella (1788) by Bernardin de Saint-Pierre.

# 9

# Mary Howitt

Mary Howitt (1799–1888) grew up as a Quaker in Uttoxeter. The second daughter of Samuel Botham (d. 1823), a businessman and surveyor, and his wife Anne (née Wood), she was particularly close to her older sister, Anna. After being educated at schools in Croydon and Sheffield, she married William Howitt in 1821: together they led an active literary life, besides raising their five children. Her wide-ranging work included translations of Frederika Bremer's novels and Hans Christian Andersen's fairy tales in the 1840s, besides writing children's books, tales and poems of her own, such as *Hymns and Fireside Verses* (1839). Her *Autobiography*, which was published in 1889, edited by her daughter Margaret, begins with a long account of her ancestors on both sides of the family. The following extract begins in chapter 2 of the *Autobiography*, when Howitt was about seven, and her father was surveyor of Needwood Chase during its period of disafforestation and enclosure:

As he laid out the ground he sometimes permitted his children to accompany him, thus enabling us from infancy to become acquainted with the spirit of Nature. Indeed a great amount of enjoyment came to Anna and me out of the Forest enclosure. Our knowledge of the world around us became less circumscribed. Our mother, a good walker in those days, would sometimes take us to meet our father at certain points arranged beforehand, perhaps at the house of some Forest farmer, where we could have tea, and return home pleasantly in the evening. Our father, always on foot over his land measurements, seemed never tired, and always glad to see us ...

Then I recollect a curious little epoch in my life, as we were returning one evening from a Forest ramble with my father. It was the first evidence to my mind that I could think. I remember very well the new light, the gladness, the wealth of which I seemed suddenly possessed. It has curiously connected itself in my mind with passing a pinfold. That particular spot seemed like the line between rational and irrational existence; and so childish was I in intellectual life, that it seemed to me as if before I passed the pinfold I could only say and think 'Bungam' – such was the expression in my mind – but that after passing it I had the full use of all intelligible speech.

Many a long happy summer day had we spent already in the Forest, when, I being then five or six years old, our father took Anna and me with him to be out from morning till evening. Towards noon we were wearied by our long ramble, and were left to recover from our fatigue under the spreading shade of an enormous oak. Around us lay a small opening in a forest glade, covered with short herbage. This was enclosed by thickets of black holly, which in contrast with the light foreground seemed intensely sombre; under these grew the greenwood laurel, with its clusters of poisonous-looking berries, and whole beds of fair white stellaria. In other spots flourished enchanter's night-shade and the rare four-leaved Herb Paris, bearing its berry-like flower at the central angles of its four leaves.

There was an undefined feeling half of pleasure, half of pain, in being left alone in so wild a spot. We heard the crow of the distant pheasant, the coo of the wood-pigeon, and the laugh-like cry of the woodpecker. We watched the hare run past from thicket to thicket. At the same time we remarked the strange unceasing low sound, a perpetual chirr-chirr-chirring somewhere near us.

We asked a stout Forest lad carrying a bundle of fagots to explain it. He seemed amazed to find two children, like Babes in the Wood, seated hand in hand at the foot of an old oak. Speaking in a low but distinctly articulated whisper, he said, 'It's my Lord Vernum's blood-hounds. They are out hunting, and yon sounds are the chains they drag after them.' So saying, he dashed off like a wild stag. The horror that fell on us was intense. Indeed, had we been left to ourselves and our terror I know not what would have become of us; but our cry of, 'Father! father!' speedily brought him to us. 'It is the grasshopper, and nothing more,' he said, 'which has caused this foolish alarm.' Listening for a moment, he traced it by its sound among the short dry sunny grass, then held it in his hand before us.

My parents, on returning from the Forest of Dean, had temporarily resided in a small semi-detached house belonging to them, having let the old home on a short lease. By March 1802, however, they must have removed to their usual habitation in Balance Street, with my grandfather for an inmate, as my very earliest recollection is a dim remembrance of the old man delivering, in the kitchen, some piece of intelligence which was received by the assembled household with expressions of joy. I was told later that it must have been his announcing the Peace of Amiens.[1]

My grandfather did not long remain under the same roof, for having, in a moment of great excitement, wounded the little Anna with the large scissors he used to cut out the strong veins of the leaves, which he dried, and feeling it a sad mischance, he was made willing to remove himself and his medicaments. He took up his abode with some good, simple people in a comfortable cottage on the enclosed land, that had formerly been the Heath. At this distance he acquired for us children a certain interest and charm. The walk to his dwelling was pleasant. His sunny sitting-room, with the small stove from which pungent odours issued, the chafing-dishes, metallic tractors, the curious glasses and retorts and ancient tomes excited our imagination; in after years we perceived that it must have resembled the study of an alchemist. Here, amongst his drying herbs and occult possessions, he taught the poorest, most neglected boys to read, from a sense of Christian duty, which was generally regarded as a queer crotchet; for it was before the days of Bell and Lancaster,[2] and when ragged schools were unimagined.

How well do I remember him! His features were good, but his countenance severe; over his very grey hair he wore a grey worsted wig, with three stiff rows of curls behind, and was attired in a dark-brown collar-less suit of a very old-fashioned cut, wearing out of doors a cocked hat, also of an old Quaker type, a short great-coat or spencer, and in winter grey-ribbed worsted leggings, drawn to the middle of the thigh. Although a stickler for old customs, he was one of the very first in the Midland Counties to use an umbrella. The one that belonged to him was a substantial concern, covered with oil-cloth or oil-silk, with a large ring at the top, by which it was hung up.

Having a reputation in the Society as a minister, he now and then paid visits to other meetings, but never very far from home; and considering himself connected with Phebe Howitt of Heanor, by the marriage of his stepson John to her aunt, felt it doubly incumbent to repair at times to that Derbyshire village. With Thomas and Phebe Howitt, the parents of my future husband, we had no personal acquaintance, merely a somewhat disagreeable association from his having obtained from them the plant asarabacca, which had caused my mother violent headaches and was the chief ingredient of his cephalic snuff.

In their society the simple, religious, and therefore the best side of his character was exhibited. He was consequently described to me in after years by my husband as a welcome guest, generally arriving at harvest-time, when he would employ himself in the pleasant field-labour, quoting beautiful and appropriate texts of Scripture as applicable to the scenes around him. This I can well understand, from a little occurrence in my childhood.

Rebecca Summerland, the daughter of my half-uncle John, had married, in 1801, a Friend named Joseph Burgess, of Grooby Lodge, near Leicester. She became the mother of a little boy – William – with whom, when staying at his grandparents', we were permitted to play. On one of these happy occasions, their rarity enhancing the delight, we were enjoying ourselves at aunt Summerland's when our grandfather unexpectedly arrived. Our parents were absent from home – probably at Quarterly Meeting – and he, wishful to look after us, had come to take us a walk. To refuse was not to be thought of. We very reluctantly left little William and started under his escort. But our grandfather was unusually kind and gentle, and to give us a treat, took us to see our father's small tillage farm at the distance of a couple of miles from home.

He talked about the trees and plants in Timber Lane, which, winding up from the town to the top of a hill, was hemmed in by steep mossy banks, luxuriant with wild flowers and ferns, and overarched by the boughs of the oak, hawthorn, and elder, having a clear little stream gurgling along one side. When we came out of the open breezy hill, with the high bushy banks of Needwood Forest extending before us in wooded promontories for many a mile, there were lambs and young calves in the fields, and primroses; and so as we went on our minds were calmed and interested. At length we reached the farm of eighteen acres, which we had last seen in autumnal desolation. Now all was beautifully green and fresh; the lower portion closed for hay, the upper filled with vigorous young vegetation; tender blades of wheat springing from the earth, green leaflets of the flax for our mother's spinning just visible; next, the plot reserved for turnips; the entire field being enclosed by a broad grassy headland, a perfect border of spring flowers, of which we had soon our hands full. Our grandfather showed us the tender, delicate flax, and contrasted it with the rougher growth of the turnip and the grass-like blades of wheat, and preached a little sermon about God making every plant and flower spring out of the dry, barren earth. As we listened the last shadow of discontent vanished. The walk back was all cheerfulness and sunshine, and we were taken to aunt Summerland's to finish the visit, happier than we had been on our arrival.

This walk gave my sister Anna her first taste for botany. She probably inherited from our grandfather her passionate love of flowers. She learnt from his copy of Miller's *Gardener's Dictionary*, which became her property after his death, to appreciate the wonderful beauty of the Linnaean system.[3]

It is impossible to give an adequate idea of the stillness and isolation of our lives as children. Our father's introverted character and naturally meditative turn of mind made him avoid social intercourse and restrict his participation in outward events to what was absolutely needful for the exact fulfilment of his professional and religious labours. Our dear mother's clear, intelligent mind, her culture and refinement, were chastened and subdued by her new spiritual convictions and by painful social surroundings, which were aggravated by the death of her sympathiser, Ann Shipley. Our nurse, Hannah Finney, was dull and melancholy, seeking to stifle an attachment which she had formed in the Forest of Dean for a handsome carpenter of dubious character and unconvinced of Friends' principles. Each of our reticent caretakers was subjected to severe inward ordeals, and incapable of infusing knowledge and brightness into our young minds. At four years of age little Anna had been unable to talk, and had therefore been sent daily to a cheerful old woman who kept a dame school, and in more lively surroundings had acquired the power of speech.

In fact, after we could both talk, being chiefly left to converse together, our ignorance of the true appellations for many ordinary sentiments and actions compelled us to coin and use words of our own. To sneeze was to us both *akisham* – the sound which one of our parents must have made in sneezing. Roman numerals, which we saw on the title-pages of most books, conveyed no other idea than the word *icklymicklydictines*. Italic printing was *softly* writing. Our parents often spoke together of dividends. This suggested to me some connection with the devil. I was grieved and perplexed to hear our good parents talk without hesitation or sense of impropriety of those wicked *dividends*. Had there been an open communicative spirit in the family, these strange expressions and misapprehensions would have either never arisen or been at once corrected.

Our mother must, however, have taught us early to read, for I cannot remember when we could not do so; but neither she nor our father ever gave or permitted us to receive religious tuition. Firmly adhering to the fundamental principles of George Fox, that Christ, the true inward light, sends to each individual interior inspirations as their guide of Christian faith, and that His Spirit, being free, does not submit to human learning and customs, they aimed to preserve us in unsullied innocence, consigning us to Him in lowly confidence for guidance and instruction. So fearful were they of interfering with His workings, that they did not even teach us the Lord's Prayer; nor do I remember that they ever intimated to us the duty of each morning and evening raising our hearts in praise and petition to God. Yet they gave us to commit to memory Robert Barclay's *Catechism and Confession of Faith*, a compilation of texts applied to the doctrines of Friends, and supposed 'to be fitted for the wisest and largest as well as the weakest and lowest capacities', but which left us in the state of the perplexed eunuch before Philip instructed him in the Holy Writ.[4]

It was the earnest desire of our father that our attention should be directed to Christ as the one great, all-sufficient sacrifice; yet, nevertheless, so entirely was the fundamental doctrine of the Saviour being the Incarnate God hidden from us, that we grew up to the age when opinions assert themselves to find that our minds had instinctively shaped themselves into the Unitarian belief, out of which we have both been brought by different means. As regards my sister Anna, she has said that she found in reading *Ecce Homo*[5] the exact counterpart of her own youthful views of Jesus, which had grown up in the unassisted soil of her mind ...

Let me describe our mother as she was in those days. Not handsome, but of a singularly intelligent countenance, well-cut features, clear grey eyes; the whole expression being that of a character strong and decisive, but not impulsive. She was of middle height; her dress always the same. The soft silk gowns of neutral tints of her wedding outfit were carefully folded away on the shelves of her wardrobe, for her husband disapproved of silk. She wore generally a mixture of silk and wool, called silkbine, of a dark colour, mostly some shade of brown. The dress, being made long, was worn, even in the house, usually drawn up on each side through the pocket-holes; the effect of which was good, and would have been really graceful if the material had been soft and pliable, but the thread of both silk and wool was spun with a close twist, which produced a stiff and harsh fabric. A thin double muslin handkerchief covered the bust. Her transparent white muslin cap of the ordinary Quaker make was raised somewhat behind, leaving the back hair visible rolled over a small pad.

In the November of the year 1806 a great event occurred – a baby sister was born, and called Emma. We had hitherto been two sisters; now we were three. Our astonishment and delight over the sweet little blue-eyed creature were unbounded.

In the following May our old grandfather quietly passed away, in his eighty-third year, and was laid to rest in the green graveyard by the silent Meeting-house.

A twelvemonth passed, and fresh surprises awaited us. One summer First-day, at the close of afternoon meeting, our parents were mysteriously summoned from the Meeting-house door to visit our father's old half-brother Joseph, whom, as he had been a confirmed invalid for many years, we children had never seen. An hour later we were fetched from home, and taken for the first time into a large, gloomy house, along mysterious passages into a dimly-lighted chamber. Our parents were sitting there in solemn silence on either side of an arm-chair, in which reclined a large-limbed, but fearfully emaciated, pallid old man. We were taken up to him. He spoke to us in a feeble, husky voice; then, like an aged patriarch, placed a trembling hand on each of our heads and blessed us. We were then quietly led away, our parents remaining with him.

The next morning we were told that our uncle Joseph had died in the night. Again, a few mornings later, on July 9, 1808, we were told that a little brother had been born to us in the preceding night. In the midst of our amazement and yet undeveloped joy arose the question within us, 'Will our parents like it?' for we had the impression that they never approved of boys. The doubt speedily vanished; their infant son, who was named Charles, was evidently their peculiar pride and delight. Under those circumstances, surely there was no family in the county that was happier than ours.

Anna and I almost lived in the nursery, for we were devoted to our sweet little sister Emma and our new treasure, baby Charles. The nursery, too, was one of the most cheerful rooms in the house, furnished with every suitable comfort and convenience. A light and rather low window looked over the whole neighbourhood; there we sat for hours. Rhoda, the highly respectable nurse who had been engaged for Charles, was a new and interesting character to us. Her parents dwelt in the market-place, and she told us she had seen the bull-baiting there every year. It was a horrid, cruel sight, which we should never have thought of witnessing, and our father had tried year after year to put a stop to it. But Rhoda's description was like a traveller's account of a bull-fight in Spain. You disapprove, but read the narrative. Then she had her own books, which she lent us, *The Shepherdess of the Alps*[6] and *The Arabian Nights*, over which, as a matter of course, we sat hour after hour reading with unwearying wonder and delight. We, in return as it were for her good offices, brought up into the nursery for her to read the best books we knew of, namely the *Life of Madame Guyon* and *Telemachus*.[7] The former work was our favourite, from the glimpses it gave us of what our father termed the 'dark ages of Popery'. I question whether Rhoda attempted either of them. Her head was full of private interviews with secret sweethearts. She wrote her love-letters, and we children must write ours.

I do not think that Anna, who was a year and half older than I, was bewitched by the sorceries of this dangerous young woman; but I was so far captivated by her talk, that I wrote a letter about love and marriage at her dictation. When I think of myself, the simple child of nine, brought up, as my parents believed, in perfect innocence, my soul so pure that an angel might inscribe upon it words direct from the Holy Spirit, I feel the most intense compassion for myself. Poor child! Nanny had already dimmed the brightness of my young spirit's innocence; now came another tempter, and whilst our parents slept, as it were, sowed the tares and the poison seed in the fruitful soil of my forlorn soul. *Madame Guyon* lay on a shelf in one of the nursery cupboards, and between the leaves Rhoda laid my unholy letter.

All this had wholly passed out of my mind, when one First-day, after dinner, my father inquired for the *Life of Madame Guyon*. It was immediately brought, and he, dear good man! sat down to read it before going to afternoon meeting.

My heart aches to think of the dismay and the astonishment of sorrow that must have filled his soul when he came upon the evil paper in my child's handwriting. He himself had taught me to write, and this was the fruit of that knowledge. What length of time elapsed after this painful discovery, he and my mother sitting together in grieved consternation, I cannot say. Summoned to their presence, I went down without fear or anticipation of evil. I was confounded by the revelation of my enormous ill-doing. Alas! poor father and mother, their sorrow was very great, yet not much was said. It was now time for afternoon meeting, and we must all go.

I suppose I felt something as our first parents did when God called to them in the garden. But, strange to say, I did not think I regarded my offence as the enormity my father and mother did. I was both ashamed and afraid; nevertheless, I had not written those evil, idle words out of my own heart, but at the dictation of another, and with small knowledge of what their meaning implied. A sad silence and solemnity lay on my parents' countenances; they did not, however, inflict any punishment. I was neither degraded nor humbled, only bitterly ashamed.

On the 24th of Tenth Month 1809, I being ten years of age, my sister a year and a half older, we left home for school, under our mother's escort. Perhaps our parents, in their unworldliness, had forgotten that on the morrow, the 25th of October, all England was to celebrate the fiftieth year of King George the Third's reign. Be it as it may, we children knew of the approaching festivity, and were thereby reconciled to the pain of leave-taking. We were glad we should be travelling, for in Uttoxeter we should have seen none or little of the rejoicings. The greatness of our curiosity made us eager to start; and as we drove through the outskirts of our town, by Tutbury and its castle to Ashby-de-la-Zouch, where we had a fresh postchaise, and then on to Grooby Lodge, where we spent the night, we had the delight of watching the busy preparations. Even our Quaker relatives, the Burgesses, we found in a mild state of excitement in anticipation of the morrow ...

We felt ourselves in a new world at Croydon. I do not remember that we were unhappy or had any longings for home. We were all in all to each other, and had been so through the whole of our lives, and could give to each other the comfort and sympathy we needed. But we very soon felt we were different from those amongst whom we were placed. Many indeed were the mortifications caused us as the children of rigidly plain Friends out of a remote midland county brought into the midst of London girls, all belonging to the same denomination, it is true, but whose quakerly attire and life-experience were less precise, were even different from ours. There were ten or twelve girls when we arrived. I believe the number was to be limited to sixteen. We were the youngest, peculiar, provincial, but I do not think in general knowledge we were behind the others. We seemed to them, however, to have come from the uttermost ends of the earth; the very word Uttoxeter was to them uncouth, and caused laughter.

Each girl had her fancy-work. We had none, but were expected by our mother to make in our leisure moments half-a-dozen linen shirts for our father, with all their back-stitching and button-holes complete. We had never learnt to net, nor had we ever seen before fine strips of coloured paper plaited into delicate patterns, or split straw worked into a pattern on coarse net. Each girl could do this kind of work. It was one of our characteristics that we could do whatever we had once seen done. We could haokle flax or spin a rope. We could drive a nail, put in a screw or draw it out. We knew the use of a glue-pot or how to paper a room. But fancy-work was quite beyond our experience. We soon, however, furnished ourselves with coloured paper for plaiting, and straw to split and weave into net; and I shall never forget my admiration of diamonds woven with strips of gold paper on a black ground. They were my first efforts at artistic work.

We had also the great happiness of being allowed at school our own little garden, which contained a fine holly-tree that belonged exclusively to ourselves. If my sister had a passionate love of flowers, I was equally endowed with a deep appreciation of trees. The Scotch firs in our garden at home, the spruce firs, arbor vitae, and Weymouth pine in a neighbour's; the group of tall poplars, which I never failed to see when sitting in our silent meeting, had been my dear familiar friends from infancy. It was splendid late autumn weather when we arrived at Croydon, and I do not remember any beginning of winter. It must, therefore, have been a fine season, enabling us to be much out of doors. What a new pleasure we had in finding skeleton ivy and holly-leaves under the alcove-shaped summer-house at the end of the general garden! This delight, however, was soon stopped, as Mary M., who had the character of being the black sheep of the flock, having spoken from the summer-house to some young cadets of Addiscombe College, that part of the garden was closed to one and all of us.

Brought south, and into proximity with the capital, we were met at every point by objects new to our small experience, whose beauty, grandeur, or perfect novelty stirred the very depths of my child-soul. We had both of us an intense love of nature and inborn taste for what was beautiful, poetical, or picturesque. Our souls were imbued with Staffordshire scenery: districts of retired farms, where no change came from age to age; tall old hedges surrounding quiet pastures; silent fields, dark woodlands, ancient parks, shaded by grey gnarled oaks and rugged, gashed old birch-trees; venerable ruins, shrouded by the dusky yew. The calm of this old-world and primitive scenery, together with the peculiar character of sunrise and sunset, and of each alternating season, had profoundly affected our feelings and imaginations. Now a fresh revelation came to both of us equally, but somewhat differently, so that I had best confine myself to my own recollections.

Much that was attractive in our new surroundings, at the same time, troubled me, filling my heart with indescribable sadness, and awakening within me an unappeasable longing for I knew not what. It was my first perception of the dignity and charm of culture. My impressionable mind had already yielded to the power of Nature; it was now to feel and accept the control of Art. Yet I was at the time, in my ugly, unusually plain Quaker garb, no better to look at than a little brown chrysalis, in the narrow cell of whose being, however, the first early sunbeam was awakening the germ of a higher existence.

The stately mansions, with all their latest appliances of luxury and ease – their sunshades, their balconies filled with flowers, the graceful creepers wreathing colonnades, heavy-branched cedar-trees, temple-like summer-houses half-concealed in bowery garden solitudes, distant waters, winding walks – belonged to a new, vast, and more beautiful world. No less interesting and impressive were the daily features of human life around us. A hatchment over a lofty doorway, a splendid equipage, with its attendant liveried servants, bowling in or out of heavy, ornamental park-gates, would marvellously allure my imagination. There was a breadth, fulness [sic], perfectedness around us, that strikingly contrasted with the restricted, common, prosaic surroundings of the Friends in Staffordshire.

In our home-life Christmas had been of no account. It was neither a season of religious regard nor yet of festivity. How astonished were we, then, to hear the London girls anticipating a great deal of pleasure and social enjoyment, with much talk of Christmas good-cheer! We were familiar with plum-pudding and mince-pies, but not with Twelfth cakes, of which much was said, and which were to be brought back with them after the holidays. To our astonishment, the school broke up for Christmas, all the pupils going home except Ann Lury of Bristol and ourselves. She received from her relatives a goodly present of chocolate, Spanish chestnuts, and oranges; we had no box of seasonable good things.

With the return of schoolgirls two new pupils arrived, who proved, to our surprise, our cousins Mary Ann and Maria Marriage, from Essex. Their mother and grandmother brought them; and we, sent for to the best parlour, dimly and with difficulty identified the little, dark-complexioned elderly Friend who most kindly invited us to spend the midsummer holidays at her house as the same who some years before had paid an afternoon visit to our father and mother. It was no other than the widow of our uncle, James Botham, and now Rebecca Marriage. On leaving she gave us half-a-crown, which was by no means an unwelcome present. During the new term great misery and discomfort was caused in the school by the teachers, Sarah Bevan and Anna Wooley, listening to the complaints of the London pupils against Mary M., usually called 'Mussy', also a Londoner. They allowed an open persecution to be carried on against her, and even rhythmical enumeration of the various Friends' schools from which it was reported that she had been expelled, to be chanted at every corner to catch her ear: 'Wandsworth, Plaistow, Tottenham, and Croydon' sounded through the house and garden. This aid and abetting on the part of our governesses was unjust to the girl, injurious to her companions, and a disgrace to themselves. ... Although the school management was extremely defective and the tuition imperfect, there was an excellent custom of making during fine weather long excursions of almost weekly recurrence. At about eleven the pupils, attended by one of the mistresses, set out, the train being ended by a stout serving-woman, who drew after her a light-tilted waggon containing abundant provisions for our midday meal. So through Croydon we went to the open country, to the Addington Hills, as far as Norwood – all no doubt now covered or scattered over with houses; up and down pleasant lanes where the clematis, which we only knew as a garden plant, wreathed the hedges. Now and then we rested on some breezy common with views opening far and wide. Sometimes we passed through extensive lavender-fields in which women were working, or came upon an encampment of gipsies, with their tents and tethered horses, looking to us more oriental than any similar encampment in our more northern lanes.

Surrey breathed to Anna and me beauty and poetry, London the majesty of history and civilisation. From the highest point of the Addington Hills we were shown St. Paul's in the distance. It sent a thrill through us. Even the visits sanctioned by our teachers to the confectioner's for the purchase of Chelsea buns and Parliament gingerbread enhanced our innocent enjoyment.

Our stay at Croydon was prematurely ended by the serious illness of our mother. After leaving us she had caught a severe cold during a dense fog in London, which brought on an illness that had lasted long ere danger was apprehended. Then we were sent for. The visit to our Essex relatives remained unpaid. We returned home in the care of James Dix of Leek, a Friend whom we had known from childhood. He was the Representative from the Cheshire and Staffordshire Quarterly Meeting to the Yearly Meeting in London, and took us

back with him after the great gathering had dispersed. Before our arrival at home
a favourable change in our dear mother's condition had occurred. We found her
weak, propped up in a large easy-chair with pillows, and suffering at times from
a violent cough. Still, she was advancing to an assured recovery.

In August 1810 my sister was sent to a Friends' school held in high repute
in Sheffield, but owing to an alarm of fever in the town, was recalled in the depth
of the winter. She then remained at home, whilst my mother took me to the same
school the following spring. It was conducted by Hannah Kilham, the widow of
Alexander Kilham, the founder of the New Methodist or Kilhamite Connection,
by her stepdaughter Sarah, and a niece named Ann Corbett of Manchester; all
Friends by convincement.

Hannah Kilham, an ever-helpful benefactress to the poor, devoted herself to
a life of active Christian charity. She treated me as one of the older girls, I being
tall for twelve, and often took me with her in her rounds. Once she sent me alone
to a woman whose destitute condition so awoke my compassion as to induce me
to bestow on her my last sixpence, with the hope uttered, 'May the Lord bless it!'
This was followed by self-questionings whether by my speech I had meant in my
heart that the Lord should bless the gift to the sufferer or to me – then penniless.
Another time, at nightfall, Hannah Kilham made me wait in a desolate region of
broken-up ground and half-built, ruinous houses while she visited some haunt of
squalor. It seems strange that a highly conscientious woman should leave a young
girl alone, even for a few minutes, in a low, disreputable suburb of a large town.
But she was on what she felt to be her Master's errand, and I doubt not had
committed me to His keeping; for whilst I was appalled by the darkness and
desolation around me, I saw the great comet of the autumn of 1811 majestically
careering through the heavens, and received an impression of Divine omnipotence
which no school teaching could have given me.

Among my fellow-scholars was Hannah West, from Uttoxeter ... She was
a warm-hearted girl, and reciprocated my good-will with passionate devotion. Her
delight was to sit with me in the twilight and imagine what we should do when we
were women. Her innocent, highest idea was, that we should live together,
something in the style of the Ladies of Llangollen,[8] though we had never heard of
them; dwell in a country place, have a beautiful garden, plenty of money, and be
able to travel.

I knew the idea to be absurd; yet, without being disloyal to my sister, I
enjoyed her affectionate romance, and can even recall the sort of intoxication of
fancy in which I indulged her day-dreams. When, however, we both returned
home, and I sat with my relatives in the upper part of the meeting, she with hers
in the lower, and no interchange of the commonest civility ever occurred, poor
Hannah's illusions were dispelled. She ended by marrying a journeyman butcher.

Sheffield never affected me as Croydon had done. The only point of
extraneous interest was the fact that the way to meeting led through the Hart's
Head and over the doorstep almost of the office of the *Iris* newspaper, making me
hope, but in vain, to catch a glimpse of the editor, James Montgomery.[9] He was

one of my heroes. Hannah Kilham had advocated with him the cause of the climbing-boys, as the juvenile, much-abused chimney-sweeps were then called; and we had in the school the complete set of his poems. I greatly admired them, particularly *The Wanderer in Switzerland*.

It was at Sheffield that I grew painfully conscious of my unsightly attire. The girls had, for fine summer Sundays, white frocks, and sometimes a plain silk spencer. I had nothing but my drab cotton frock and petticoat, a small Friends' bonnet and little shawl. On week-days, when they wore their printed frocks, I could bear it; but First-days were bitter days to me. There was no religion to me in that cross; and I rejoiced that the trying, humiliating day only came once a week, when I had to appear in the school-train, marching down to meeting, the one scarecrow, as it appeared to me, of the little party.

In 1812 I left this school, which was some years later discontinued ... Our father, however, was greatly dissatisfied with our attainments. Our spelling especially was found defective; and though Anna, at Croydon, when failing to spell 'soldier' correctly, had the spelling-book thrown in her face by the choleric Anna Woolley, yet it was I who offended most in this way at home. Thomas Goodall, the master of the only boys' school in the town, was engaged to teach us spelling, Latin, the globes, and indeed whatever else he could impart. He was a man of some learning, who in early life, when residing in London, had been brutally attacked in some lonely street or passage by a lawless band of ruffians, the Mohocks. His face still bore the marks of their violence, being scarred with deep wounds, as if made with daggers and knives.

Death having deprived us of this teacher, a young man-Friend of good birth and education was next employed to lead us into the higher branches of mathematics. He made himself, however, so objectionable to us by his personal attentions, that we very soon refused his instructions. Although we never revealed the reason, our father, perhaps surmising it, allowed us to have our own way, and being earnest students, we henceforth became our own educators.

We retained and perfected our rudimentary knowledge by instructing others. Our father fitted up a schoolroom for us in the stable-loft, where twice a week we were allowed to teach poor children. In this room, also, we instructed our dear little sister and brother. I had charge of Emma and Anna of Charles. Our father, in his beautiful handwriting, set them copies, texts of Scripture, such as he no doubt had found of a consolatory character. On one occasion, however, I set the copies, and well remember the tribulation I experienced in consequence. I always warred in my mind against the enforced gloom of our home, and having for my private reading at that time Young's *Night Thoughts*, came upon what seemed to me the very spirit of true religion, a cheerful heart gathering up the joyfulness of surrounding nature; on which the poet says –

'Tis impious in a good man to be sad.

How I rejoiced in this! – and thinking it a great fact which ought to be trumpeted abroad, wrote it down in my best hand as a copy. It fell under our father's eye, and sorely grieved he was at such a sentiment, and extremely angry with me as its promulgator.

When the summer days were fine and the evenings warm, we carried the school-benches into the garden, and thus did our teaching in the open air, on the grass plat, with borders of flowers and trees round us.

We were very busy girls, and had not through the day an idle moment. Our mother required us to be expert in all household matters, and we ourselves took a pride in the internal management being nicely ordered. Our home possessed a charm, a sense of repose, which we felt, but could not at the time define. It was caused by our father's correct, purified taste, that had led him to select oak for the furniture, quiet colours and small patterns for the low rooms. The houses of our neighbours displayed painted wood, flaming colours, and large designs on the floors and walls.

I feel a sort of tender pity for Anna and myself when I remember how we were always seeking and struggling after the beautiful, and after artistic production, though we knew nothing of art. I am thankful that we made no alm-baskets or hideous abortions of the kind. What we did was from the innate yearnings of our own souls for perfection in form and colour; and our accomplished work, though crude and poor, was the genuine outcome of our own individuality.

*Source*: Mary Howitt, *An Autobiography*, ed. Margaret Howitt, 2 vols (London: William Isbister, 1889).

## Notes

1. The Peace of Amiens was a treaty signed in 1802 between Great Britain, France, Spain and Holland, which caused a temporary lull in the Napoleonic Wars.

2. Andrew Bell (1753–1832) and Joseph Lancaster (1778–1838) pioneered the system of mass education by which 'monitors' (older children) taught vast numbers of other children by a method that became increasingly mechanical.

3. *The Gardener's and Florist's Dictionary, or a Complete System of Horticulture* (1724) by Philip Miller(1691–1771), foreman of the Chelsea Garden; the Linnaean system, which was the first to define and name species, was invented by the Swedish botanist Carl Linnaeus (1707–78), author of the *Systema Naturae* (1735) and *Species Plantarum* (1753).

4. Robert Barclay (1648–90), best known for his *Apology for the True Christian Divinity held by the Quakers* (1678), an early statement of Quaker doctrine.

5. A readable and human life of Jesus Christ (1865) by Sir John Robert Seeley (1834–95).

6. One of the *Contes Moraux* (1761) by Jean Francois Marmontel (1723–99), described as 'a very interesting, pathetic, and moral history'.

7. Madame Guyon (1648–1717), French quietist writer, whose ideas attracted Francois

de Selignac de la Mothe (1651–1715), author of *Telemaque* (1699) a political novel with a purpose, based on the story of Ulysses's son Telemachus. Howitt was probably reading *The Exemplary Life of the Pious Lady Guyon* (1775), translated from her own account. William Cowper translated Madame Guyon's *Life* in 1820.

8. Lady Eleanor Butler (1739–1829) and Sarah Ponsonby (1755–1831), two Irishwomen who lived together in a Gothic cottage at Plas Newydd, Llangollen, where, among others, they entertained De Quincey, Scott and Wordsworth.

9. James Montgomery (1771–1854), editor of the *Sheffield Iris* (which he owned after 1795), and author of *The Wanderer of Switzerland* (1806), a poem about the French conquest of Switzerland.

# 10

# Sara Coleridge

The incomplete 'Recollections of the early life of Sara Coleridge, Written by herself', were published in the *Memoir and Letters of Sara Coleridge* edited by her daughter Edith in 1873, and addressed to her in the form of a letter. Edith, however, omitted certain parts of the manuscript, especially a passage critical of the Wordsworths' untidy household. The full manuscript is held by the Harry Ransom Humanities Research Center at the University of Texas at Austin, and reprinted by Bradford Keyes Mudge in his *Sara Coleridge, A Victorian Daughter* (Yale University Press, 1989). Sara (1802–52), 'a poor little, delicate, low-spirited child', as she describes herself, was the youngest child of the poet Samuel Taylor Coleridge, born at a point when his marriage to Sara Fricker was already as good as over. Although she saw little of her father in childhood, she devoted much of her adult life to editing his work and safeguarding his reputation. He wrote of her in 1808: 'she has the sweetest Tongue in the world – she talks by the hour to me in bed' (Mudge, p. 261). Married to her cousin, Henry Nelson Coleridge (d. 1843) in 1829, she suffered recurrent bouts of nervous illness, exacerbated by constant pregnancies and the deaths of all but two of her children, Herbert and Edith. Even in this childhood memoir, she returns several times to her brothers' physical superiority to herself, as well as her own failure to meet with adult approval. At the same time she is proud of her delicate looks, her physical agility, and large blue eyes. She was, in fact, a precocious intellectual, who began her literary career helping her brother Derwent with difficult translation work from Latin and medieval French. Her own publications included *Pretty Lessons in Verse for Good Children* (1834) and *Phantasmion* (1837), a fairy tale with lyrics. She died of breast cancer which was allowed to develop without adequate treatment.

I shall divide my history into Childhood, Earlier and Later – Youth, Earlier and Later – Wedded Life ditto – Widowhood ditto – and I shall endeavour to state the chief Moral or Reflection suggested by each – some maxim which it specially illustrated, or truth which it exemplified, or warning which it suggested.

My Father has entered his marriage with my mother, and the births of my three brothers with some particularity in a family Bible, given him, as he also notes, by Joseph Cottle[1] on his marriage; the entry of my birth is in my dear Mother's handwriting, and this seems like an omen of our life-long separation; for I never lived with him for more than a few weeks at a time. He lived not much more, indeed, with his other children, but most of their infancy passed under his eye. Alas! more than any of them I inherited that uneasy health of his, which kept us apart. But I did not mean to begin with 'alas!' so soon, or so early to advert to the great misfortune of both our lives – want of bodily vigour adequate to the ordinary demands of life even under favourable circumstances.

I was born at Greta hall, near Keswick, December 23rd, 1802. My brother Hartley was then six years and three months, born Sep 19, 1796, at Bristol, Derwent, born Sep 14 1800, at Keswick, four [sic] years and three months old. My Father, married at Bristol Oct 4, 1795, was now 29 years of age, my mother 31 [;] their second child Berkeley, born at Nether Stowey, May 10th 1798, died while my Father was in Germany, February 10th, 1799, in consequence of a cold caught after inoculated small-pox, which brought on decline. Mama used to tell me mother's tales, which, however, were confirmed by my Aunt Lovell,[2] of this infant's noble and lovely style of beauty – his large, soft eyes of a London smoke colour, exquisite complexion, regular features, and goodly size. She said that my Father was very proud of him, and one day when he saw a neighbour approaching his little cottage at Stowey, snatched him away from the nurse half-drest, and with a broad smile of pride and delight, presented him to be admired. In her lively way, she mimicked the tones of satisfaction with which he uttered, 'This is my second son.' Yet, when the answer was: 'Well, this is something like a child', he felt affronted on behalf of his little darling Hartley.

... Mama used to tell me that as a young infant I was not so fine and flourishing as Berkeley who was of a taller make than any of her other children, or Derwent, though not quite so small as her oldest born. I was somewhat disfigured with red gum. In a few months however I became very presentable, and had my share of *adoration*. 'Little Grand Lamas', my Father used to call babes in arms, feeling doubtless all the while what a blessed contrivance of the Supreme Benignity it is, that man, in the very weakest stage of his existence, has power in that very weakness. Mere babyhood, even where attended with no special grace, has a certain loveliness of its own, and seems to be surrounded, as by a spell, in its attractions for the female heart, and for all hearts which partake of woman's tenderness, and whose tenderness is drawn by circumstances in that particular direction.

... Of this first stage of my life of course I have no remembrance, but something happened to me, when I was two years old, which was so striking as to leave an indelible trace on my memory. I fancy I can even now recall, though it may be but an echo or reflection of past remembrances, my coming dripping up the Forge field, after having fallen into the river between the rails of the high wooden bridge that crossed the Greta, which flowed behind the Greta hall Hill. The maid had my baby cousin Edith, 16 months younger than I, in her arms; I was rushing away from Derwent, who was fond of playing the elder brother, on the strength of his two years' seniority, when he was trying in some way to control me, and, in my hurry, slipped from the bridge into the current. Luckily for me young Richardson was still at work in his father's forge. He doffed his coat and rescued me from the water. I had fallen from a considerable height, but the strong current of the Greta received me safely. I remember nothing of this adventure but the walk home through the field. I was put between blankets on my return to the house; but my constitution had received a shock, and I became tender and delicate, having before been a thriving child, & called by my Uncle Southey 'fat Sall'. As an infant I had been nervous & insomnolent. My mother has often told me how seldom I would sleep in the cradle – how I required to be in her arms before I could settle into sound sleep. This weakness has accompanied me through life.

One other glimpse of early childhood my mind retains. I can just remember sitting by my Aunt Lovell in her little downstairs wing room, and exclaiming in a piteous tone 'I'se miseral!' A poor little delicate, low-spirited child I doubtless was, with my original nervous tendencies, after that escape from the Greta. 'Yes, and you will be miserable,' Aunt Lovell compassionately broke out, as mama has told me, 'if your mother doesn't put you on a cap.' The hint was taken, and I wore a cap till I was 8 years old. I appear in a cap, playing with a doll, in a little miniature taken of me at that age by the sister of Sir William Betham,[3] who also made portraits in the same style of my Uncle and Aunt Southey, my mother, Aunt Lovell and cousins Edith and Herbert.

I cannot leave this period of my existence without some little [allusion] to my brother Derwent's sweet childhood. I often heard from mama what a fine, fair, broad chested little fellow he was at two years old, and how he got the name of Stumpy Canary, when he wore a yellow frock, which made him look like one of these feathery bundles in colour & form. I fancy I see him now, as my mother's description brought him before me, racing from kitchen to parlour, & parlour to kitchen, just putting in his head at the door, with roguish smile to catch notice, then off again, shaking his little sides with laughter. Mr. Lamb and his sister, who paid a visit of three weeks to my parents, in the summer of 1802, were charmed with the little fellow, and much struck with the quickness of eye and of memory that he displayed in naming the subjects of prints in books which he was acquainted with. 'Pi-pos, – Pot-pos', were his names for the striped and spotted opossum, and these he would utter with a nonchalant air, as much as to say of course I know it all as pat as possible. 'David Lesly, Deneral of the Cock Army', was another of his familiars.[4] Mr. Lamb calls him Pi-pos in letters to Greta hall, after his visit to the Lakes.

[*She quotes a letter from her mother describing a trip to Bristol and Nether Stowey.*]

I was in my fifth year during this visit to the South, and my remembrances of it are partial and indistinct – glimpses of memory, islanded amid the sea of non remembrance. I recollect more of Derwent than of Hartley & have an image of his stout build, and of his resolute, managing way, as we played together at Bristol. I remember Mrs. Perkins, with her gentle Madonna countenance, and walking round the Square with her daughter, who gave me currants when we came round to a certain point. I have faint recollections too of Stowey and of staying at the Kosters at Liverpool. At this time I was fond of reading the original Poems of the Miss Taylors[5] & used to repeat some of them by heart to friends of mama. Aunt Martha I thought a fine lady on our first arrival at College Street. She wore a white veil, so it seems to my remembrance, when I first saw her. I can but just remember Aunt Eliza, then at Mrs. Watson's, and that there was an old lady, very invalidish, at College Street, Mrs Fricker, my mother's mother. At this time I could not eat meat, except bacon.

My brothers were allowed to amuse themselves with the noble art of painting, which they practised in the way of daubing with one or two colours, I think chiefly scarlet, over any bit of a print or engraving in vol., or out of it, that was abandoned to their clutches. It was said of Derwent, that upon one of those pictorial occasions, after diligently plying his brush for some time, he exclaimed, with a slow, solemn, half-pitying, half self-complacent air, 'Thethe little minute thingth are very difficult!! but they *mutht* be done!! ethpethially *thaitheth*! [chaises].' This '*mutht be done*' conveyed an awful impression of resistless necessity, the mighty force of a principled submission to duty, with a hint of the exhausting struggles and trials of life.

Talking of struggles and trials of life, my mother's two unmarried sisters were maintaining themselves at this time by their own labours. Aunt Martha, the elder, a plain, but lively pleasing woman, about five feet high or little more, was earning her bread as a dress-maker. She had lived a good deal with a farmer, in the country, Uncle Hendry, who married Edith Fricker, her father's sister; but not liking a female farmer mode of life, came to Bristol, and fitted herself for the business. Uncle Hendry left her a small sum of money – some hundreds – and would have done more doubtless had she remained by him. [George] Burnet[6] offered marriage to my Aunt Martha during the agitation of the Pantisocracy scheme. She refused him scornfully, seeing that he only wanted a *wife in a hurry*, not her individually of all the world.

Aunt Eliza, a year or 20 months younger, about the same height, or but a barleycorn above it, was thought pretty in youth from her innocent blue eyes, ingenuous florid countenance fine light-brown hair, and easy light motions. She was not nearly so handsome in face, however, as my mother & Aunt Lovell, & had not my Aunt Southey's fine figure and quietly commanding air. Her face was too broad, therefore she looked best in a bonnet, her mouth too small, and no feature was really fine. Yet, on the whole, she was very pleasing, feminine, and attractive. Both sisters sang, but had never learned music artistically.

Such were my Aunts Martha and Elizabeth Fricker in youth; but they had sterling qualities, which gave their characters a high respectability. Without talent, except of an ordinary kind, without powerful connexions, by life long perseverance, fortitude, and determination, by prudence, patience, and punctuality, they not only maintained themselves, but, with a little aid from kind friends, whom their merits won, laid by a comfortable competency for their old age. They asked few favours, accepted few obligations, and were most scrupulous in returning such as they did accept, as soon as possible. They united caution and discretion with perfect honesty & truth, strict frugality and self control, with the disposition to be kind & charitable, and even liberal, as soon as ever it was in their power. Their chief faults were pride & irritability of temper. Upon the whole, they were admirable women. I say *were*, but one, Aunt E F still survives, in the Isle of Man. Aunt M died of paralysis, at the Isle of Man, September 26, 1850, at 73. Aunt Eliza is ailing; she must be 73 I believe now – or 72 [d. 1868].

Our return to Greta Hall has left an image in my mind, and a pleasant one. I can just remember entering the parlour, seeing the urn on the table, and tea-things laid out, and a little girl, very fair, with thick yellow hair, and round, rosy cheeks, seated, I think, on a stool near the fire. This was my cousin Edith, and I thought her quite a beauty. She looked very shy at first, but ere long we were sociably travelling round the room together on one stool, our joint vessel, and our childish noises soon required to be moderated. I was five years old the Christmas after this return, which I believe was latish in autumn. I remember how Mr. Dequincey jested with me on the journey, and declared I was to be his wife, which I partly believed. I thought he behaved faithlessly in not claiming my hand.

*[A lengthy description of Greta Hall is omitted.]*

My young life is almost a blank in memory from that well remembered evening of my return from our series of Southern visits, till the time of my visit to Allan Bank, when I was six years old. That journey to Grasmere gleams before me as a shadow of a shade. Some goings on of my stay there I remember more clearly. Allan Bank is a large house on a hill overlooking Easedale on one side and Grasmere Lake on the other. Dorothy, Mr. Wordsworth's only daughter, was at this time very picturesque in her appearance, with her long thick yellow locks, which were never cut, but curled with papers, a thing which seems much out of keeping with the poetic simplicity of the household. I remember being asked by my father and Miss Wordsworth, the Poet's sister, if I did not think her very pretty. No, said I bluntly; for which I [met a] rebuff which made me feel as if I was a culprit.

My Father's wish it was to have me for a month with him at Grasmere, where he was domesticated with the Wordsworths. He insisted on it that I became rosier and hardier during my absence from mama. She did not much like to part with me, and I think my Father's motive at bottom must have been a wish to fasten my affections on him. I slept with him and he would tell me fairy stories, when he came to bed at 12 or one o'clock. I remember his telling me a witch tale too in his study, and my trying to repeat it to the maids afterwards.

I have no doubt there was much enjoyment in my young life at that time but some of my recollections are tinged with pain. I think my dear Father was anxious that I should learn to love him and the Wordsworths & their children, and not cling so exclusively to my mother and all around me at home. He was therefore much annoyed when on my mother's coming to Allan Bank I flew to her and wished not to be separated from her any more. I remember his showing displeasure with me, and accusing me of want of affection. I could not understand why. The young Wordsworths came in and caressed him. I sate benumbed; for truly nothing does so freeze affection as the breath of Jealousy. The sense that you have done very wrong, or at least given great offence, you know not how or why – that you are dunned for some payment of love or feeling which you know not how to produce or demonstrate on a sudden – chills the heart & fills it with perplexity and bitterness. My Father reproached me & contrasted my coldness with the childish caresses of the little Wordsworths – who felt but slightly, and easily adopted any ways of affection that were required with lively but not deep feeling.[7] I slunk away & hid myself in the wood behind the house, and there my friend John [Wordsworth], whom at that time I called my future husband, came to seek me. How much more vividly we remember the painful than the pleasurable

...

It was during this stay at Allan Bank that I used to see my father and Mr. Dequincey pace up and down the room in conversation. I understood not, nor listened to a word they said, but used to note the handkerchief hanging out of the pocket behind, and long to clutch it. Mr. Wordsworth too must have been one of the room-walkers. How gravely & earnestly used S TC and WW, & my Uncle Southey also, to discuss the affairs of the nation, as if it all came home to their business & bosoms – as if it were their private concern. Men do not canvass these matters now-a-days, I think, quite in the same tone: domestic concerns absorb their deeper feelings – national ones are treated more as things aloof,– the speculative rather than the practical.

My Father used to talk to me with much admiration and affection of Sarah [sic] Hutchinson, Mrs. Wordsworth's sister, who resided partly with the Wordsworths, partly with her own brothers. At this time she used to act as my Father's amanuensis. She wrote out great parts of The Friend to his dictation.[8] She had fine long light brown hair, I think her only beauty except a fair skin, for her features were plain & contracted, her figure dumpy& devoid of grace & dignity. She was a plump woman of little more than five foot. I remember my Father talking to me admiringly of her long light locks, and saying how mildly she bore it when the baby pulled them hard in play.

Miss Wordsworth, Mr. W's beloved sister, of most poetic eye and temper, took a great part with the children. She told us once a pretty story of a primrose,

I think, which she spied by the way side when she went to see me soon after my birth, though that was at Christmas, and how this same primrose was still blooming when she went back to Grasmere.

Our dear friends, the Wordsworths, were rather rough & rustic in their management of children; there was a greater care and refinement in these matters at my own home, though nothing like the delicacy and softness of the present day. I remember how we children sometimes left our beds at 4 o'clock & roamed about the kitchen barefoot before there was any one to dress us. But this may have been only once. I have a dim vision too of being washed in a tub in the kitchen, in an exposed sort of way, and of some men or man coming in & out during the operation.

The Wordsworths and my Father boasted that I was rosier after a month's stay at Grasmere than I had been at Keswick. But I have not a comfortable remembrance [of] nursery arrangements and accommodations. Nursery indeed if I recollect rightly, there was none of any regular description. I remember telling my cousin Edith, with childlike ingratitude, or rather incapability of seeing & feeling, that there was aught to be grateful for, that I had suffered a deal of '*miserality*' at Grasmere. Long afterwards I heard from Miss Crump at Allan Bank a scornful account of the untidy tenancy of the Ws – the horrid smoke, which indeed I remember, the dirt, the irregular Scotchy ways, the mischief inflicted on the walls by the children, who were chid & cuffed freely enough, yet far from kept in good order. The extreme order, cleanness and neatness of Rydal Mount presented a strange contrast to former W residences to those who remembered them in the Grasmere hut, in this for them too large & roomy mansion, and again in the shabby once Vicarage house near the church. At Alfoxden, there were but two – the Poet and his Sister, no wife children or sister-in-law, and a single but united pair *can* live rustically & simply without such disorder and uncleanness as are sure to appear, where there is a numerous family, and no well considered arrangements and provisions made for their comfort. A single lady keeps herself neat without servant's aid, if she be well trained & handy; so does a man. But children are sure to be dirty untidy & riotous unless time and trouble of grown persons are bestowed in keeping them clean & neat & quiet and cheerful contented.

My Father had particular feelings and fancies about dress, as had my Uncle Southey & Mr. Wordsworth also. He could not abide the scarlet socks which Edith and I wore at one time. I remember going to him when mama had just drest me in a new stuff frock. He took me up and set me down again without a caress. I thought he disliked the dress – perhaps he was in an uneasy mood. He much liked everything feminine and domestic, pretty and becoming, but *not* fine ladyish. My Uncle Southey was all for gay bright cheerful colours & even declared he had a taste for the *grand*, in half jest. Mr. W. loved all that was rich and picturesque, light & free in clothing. A deep Prussian blue or purple was one of his favourite colours for a silk dress. He wished that white dresses were banished, & that our peasantry wore blue and scarlet and other warm colours instead of sombre, dingy black, which converts a crowd that might be ornamental in the landscape, into a swarm of magnified ants. I remember his saying how much better young girls looked of an evening in bare arms even if the arms themselves were not very lovely – it gave such a lightness to their general air. I think he was looking at Dora when he said this. White dresses he thought cold – a blot and disharmony in any picture, in door or out door. My Father admired white clothing, because he looked at [it] in reference to woman as expressive of her delicacy & purity, not merely as a component part of a general picture.

My Father liked my wearing a cap. He thought it looked girlish & domestic. Dora and I must have been a curious contrast – she with her wild eyes, impetuous movements, and fine long floating yellow hair – I with my timid large blue eyes slender form & little fair delicate face muffled up in lace border & muslin. But I thought little of looks then; only I fancied Edith S on first seeing her most beautiful.

I attained my sixth year on the Christmas after this my first Grasmere visit. It must have been the next summer that I made my first appearance at the dancing school, of which more hereafter. All I can remember of this first entrance into public is that our good humoured able but rustical dancing-master, Mr. Yewdale, tried to make me dance a minuet with Charlie Denton, the youngest of our worthy Pastor's home flock – (he had ten children, 7 boys & 3 girls) – a very pretty rosy-cheeked large black eyed compact little laddikin. But I was not *quite* up to the business. I think my beau was a year older. At all events, it was I who broke down, & Mr. Y after a little impatience, gave the matter up. All teaching is wearisome, but to teach dancing of all teaching the wearisomest.

The last event of my earlier childhood which abides with me is a visit to Allonby, when I was 9 years old, with Mrs. Calvert – I think this was Mr. Calvert's doing.[9] I remember the ugliness & meanness of Allonby, the town, a cluster of red-looking houses, as far as I recollect, and being laughed at at home for describing it as a 'pretty place', which I did conventionally, according to the usual practice, as I conceived, of elegant letter writers. The sands are really fine in their way, so unbroken & extensive, capital for galloping over on poney-back; I recollect the pleasures of these sands, and of the seaside animation and vegetation; the little close white Scotch roses, the shells, the crabs of every size, from Lilliputian to Brobdignagian, crawling in the pools, the sea anemones, with their flower-like appendages, which we kept in jugs of salt water, delighted to see them draw in their petals or expand them by a sudden blossoming, the sea weed with its ugly berries, of which we made hideous necklaces. All these things I recollect but not what I should most regard now, the fine forms of the Scotch hills on the opposite coast, sublime in the distance, and the splendid sunsets which give to this sort of outline a gorgeous furnishing.

Of the party, beside John & Raisley Calvert, and Mary their sister, who was two years younger than I were Tom & William Maude, two sons of Mrs. Calvert's handsome portly eldest sister, Mrs. Maude. We used to gallop up & down the wide sands on two little ponies, a dark one called Sancho, and a light one called Airey behind the boys. Mary and I sometimes quarreled with the boys and of course, in a trial of strength, got the worst of it. I remember Raisley & the rest bursting angrily into our bedroom, & flinging a pebble at Mary, enraged at our having dared to put crumbs into their porridge & not content with which inroad & onslaught, they put mustard into ours next morning, the sun gone down upon their boyish wrath without quenching it. One of them said 'It was all that little vixen, Sara Coleridge; Mary was quiet enough by herself.'

... I had a leaven of malice I suppose in me, for I remember being on hostile terms with some little old woman, who lived by herself in a hut, and took offence at something I did, as it struck me, unnecessarily. She repaired to Mrs. Calvert to complain & the kend & kind of her accusation was, 'That'un' (meaning me) 'ran up & down the mound before [my] door.' Mrs. C thought this no heinous offence, but it was done by me, no doubt, with an air of derision. The crone was one of those morose ugly withered, ill-conditioned ignorant creatures, who, in earlier times, were persecuted as witches, and tried to be such. Still I ought to have been gently corrected for my behaviour, and told of the duty of bearing with the ill temper of the poor & ignorant and afflicted. At this time, on coming to Allonby, I was rather delicate. I remember that Mrs. Calvert gave me a glass of port wine daily, which she did not give to the other children.

Oh me! How rough those young Calverts & Maudes were; and yet they had a certain respect for me mingled with a contrary feeling, or at least with great rudeness. I was honoured among them for my extreme agility – my power of running & leaping. They called me 'Cheshire Cat' because I grinned. 'Almost as pretty as Miss Cheshire', said T Maude to me one day of some admired little girl.

Such are the chief *historical* events of my little life, up to nine years of age. But can I in any degree retrace what being I was then – what relation my then being held to my maturer self? Can I draw any useful reflection from my childish experience, or found any useful maxim upon it?

*What* was I? In person very slender and delicate, not habitually colourless, but often enough pallid and feeble looking. Strangers used to exclaim about my eyes, & I remember remarks made upon their large size both by my Uncle S[outhey] and Mr. W[ordsworth]. I suppose the thinness of my face, & the smallness of the other features, with the muffling close cap increased the apparent size of the eye, for only artists, since I have grown up, speak of my eyes as large & full. They were bluer too in my early years than now.

I had great muscular activity, which I cultivated into agility: great were my feats in the way of jumping, climbing and race-running.

My health alternated as it has done all my life, till the last ten or twelve years when it has been unchangeably depressed, between delicacy and a very easy comfortable condition. I remember well that nervous sensitiveness and morbid imaginativeness had set in with me very early. During my Grasmere visit I used to feel frightened at night, on account of the darkness. I then was a stranger to the whole host of night-agitators – ghosts, goblins, demons, devils, boggles, burglarists, elves and witches. Horrid ghastly tales & ballads, of which crowds afterwards came in my way, had not yet cast their shadows over my mind. And yet I was terrified in the dark, and used to think of lions the only form of terror which my dark-engendered agitation would take. My next bugbear was the Ghost in Hamlet. Then the picture of Death at Hellgate in an old edition of Par[adise] Lost, the delight of my girlhood – last & worst came my Uncle Southey's ballad horrors, above all the Old Woman of Berkeley. Oh the agonies I have endured between nine & twelve at night, before mama joined me in bed in presence of that hideous assemblage of images: – the horse with eyes of flame! Oh! I dare not, even now, rehearse these particulars for fear of calling up some of the old feeling, which indeed I have never in my life been quite free from. What made the matter worse was, that like all other nervous sufferings, it could not be understood by the inexperienced and consequently subjected the sufferer to ridicule and censure. My Uncle S laughed heartily at my agonies. I mean at the cause – he did not enter into the agonies. Even mama scolded me for creeping out of bed after an hour's torture and stealing down to her in the Parlour, saying I could bear the loneliness and the night fears no longer. But my Father understood the case better. He insisted that a lighted candle should be left in my room, in the interval between my retiring to bed & mama's joining me. From that time forth my sufferings ceased. I believe they would have destroyed my health had they continued. I preferred sleeping with Miss Hutchinson at Allan Bank to sharing my Father's bed because he was late in joining me.

Yet I was a most fearless child by daylight – ever ready to take the difficult mountain path and outgo my companions' daring in tree-climbing. In those early days we used to spend much of our summer time in trees, greatly to the horror of Mrs. Rickman[10] and some of our London visitors.

On reviewing my earlier childhood I find the predominant reflection ...

[*Her 'Recollections' break off here unfinished.*]

*Source*: 'Recollections of the early life of Sara Coleridge. Written by herself', manuscript from the Harry Ransom Humanities Research Center, the University of Texas at Austin. The abridged version appears in *Memoir and Letters of Sara Coleridge Edited by Her Daughter*, 2 vols (London: Henry S. King and Co., 1873); full text based on manuscript in Bradford Keyes Mudge, *Sara Coleridge, A Victorian Daughter: Her Life and Essays* (New Haven and London: Yale University Press, 1989).

**Notes**

1.   Joseph Cottle (1770–1853), a Bristol bookseller and poet, who was the original publisher of *Lyrical Ballads* (1798).
2.   Mary Lovell (née Fricker), a sister of Mrs Southey and Mrs Coleridge, and married

to Robert Lovell, one of the founding members of the Pantisocracy scheme.

3.  Mary Matilda Betham (1776–1852), poet and portrait miniaturist, who became friendly with Coleridge and Southey. Her brother William became Ulster King-of-Arms.

4.  David Lesly: probably David Leslie (1601–82), 1st Baron Newark, military commander of the Scots (mispronounced 'Cock'?) during the English Civil War. He fought with Cromwell at the Battle of Marston Moor in 1644, and subsequently for Charles II after the restoration. there was, however, an Hon. David Leslie, who was a Lieutenant-Colonel in Ireland (and subsequently Major-General) at the time of Derwent's childhood (1796–1801; 1804–6).

5.  Ann (1782–1866) and Jane (1783–1824), writers of poems for children, including *Original Poems for Infant Minds* (1804–1805).

6.  George Burnett (1776?–1811), a friend of Southey's from Balliol College, Oxford. The Pantisocracy scheme, planned by Coleridge and Southey in 1794, was to establish an ideal community on the banks of the Susquehanna river in America. Although the scheme was abandoned it involved them in marriage to the two Fricker sisters, Edith, who married Southey, and Sara, who married Coleridge.

7.  This unflattering sentence was omitted from Edith's version, as were the other comments on the roughness of the Wordsworth household.

8.  Coleridge dictated the *Friend* ('A Literary, Moral, and Political Weekly Paper') to Sara Hutchinson in twenty-eight numbers from 1809–10 at Allan Bank.

9.  Mary Calvert, later Mrs Joshua Stranger, became a close friend of Sara Coleridge. Her father William Calvert (1771–1829) was a friend of Coleridge, and the family lived at Keswick.

10.  Wife of John Rickman (1771–1840), economist and statistician, and friend of Southey's.

# 11

# Harriet Martineau

Harriet Martineau (1802–76), best known as a popularizer of political economy, was born in Norwich, the sixth child of Thomas Martineau (1764–1826), manufacturer of bombazines, and his wife Elizabeth (née Rankin) (1771–1848) of Newcastle. The family were Unitarians, and strongly committed to educating their daughters as highly as their sons. Intellectual from childhood, Harriet was first taught at home by her older brother and sister before attending a co-educational day-school in Norwich, and then her aunt's boarding-school in Bristol. She was passionately attached to her younger brother, James (1805–1900), the Unitarian theologian, and to their youngest sister, Ellen (1811–89), but according to her *Autobiography* (1877) had a difficult relationship with her sister Rachel (1800–1878) and her mother, whom she blames for her undemonstrativeness: a view James strongly contested after her death. By the time their father's business failed in 1825, Harriet had already begun her literary career, writing short articles for the Unitarian *Monthly Repository.* Her deafness precluded her from earning her living by teaching, and her one and only love affair ended in 1827 with the death of her fiancé, a college friend of James's. Martineau regarded the family's financial ruin as providential: it saved her from being a genteel young lady with nothing to do, and the death of her fiancé left her free to enjoy an active professional life as a writer.

Martineau shot to fame in 1832 with the success of her *Illustrations of Political Economy*, a series of twenty-four short tales showing the operation of economic laws in specific communities. When the series was completed, she spent two years in America, and became an expert on the state of American society and politics. A committed abolitionist, she wrote regularly against the southern slave-holders in her journalism of the 1850s and 1860s. Proving exceptionally versatile, Martineau wrote a novel, *Deerbrook* (1839) which in many ways prefigures the concerns of George Eliot's *Middlemarch* (1871–72); she wrote on tourism, Ireland, the Middle East, Birmingham manufactories and Lake District smallholdings. When she became ill in 1839 and was allegedly cured by mesmerism, she wrote about that. She also broke with her Unitarian faith and split with her once beloved brother, James. Moving away from London, where she had gone to live in 1832, Martineau built a house in Ambleside in the Lake District, where she wrote her *Autobiography* in three months in 1855, convinced she was about to die from heart disease. In fact, Martineau survived for another twenty-one years, but she added nothing to her *Autobiography*, which remained unpublished until after her death. Its freshness and vitality are especially evident in the opening sections, where she recalls her vivid sensory impressions as a young child.

*First Period: Section I*

My first recollections are of some infantine impressions which were in abeyance for a long course of years, and then revived in an inexplicable way, – as by a flash of lightning over a far horizon in the night. There is no doubt of the genuineness of the remembrance, as the facts could not have been told me by any one else. I remember standing on the threshold of a cottage, holding fast by the doorpost, and putting my foot down, in repeated attempts to reach the ground. Having accomplished the step, I toddled (I remember the uncertain feeling) to a tree before the door, and tried to clasp and get round it; but the rough bark hurt my hands. At night of the same day, in bed, I was disconcerted by the coarse feel of the sheets, – so much less smooth and cold than those at home; and I was alarmed by the creaking of the bedstead when I moved. It was a turn-up bedstead in a cottage, or small farm-house at Carleton, where I was sent for my health, being a delicate child. My mother's account of things was that I was all but starved to death in the first weeks of my life, – the wetnurse being very poor, and holding on to her good place after her milk was going or gone. The discovery was made when I was three months old, and when I was fast sinking under diarrhoea. My bad health during my whole childhood and youth, and even my deafness, was always ascribed by my mother to this. However it might be about that, my health certainly was very bad till I was nearer thirty than twenty years of age; and never was poor mortal cursed with a more beggarly nervous system. The long years of indigestion by day and night-mare terrors are mournful to think of now. – Milk has radically disagreed with me, all my life: but when I was a child, it was a thing unheard of for children not to be fed on milk: so, till I was old enough to have tea at breakfast, I went on having a horrid lump at my throat for hours of every morning, and the most terrific oppressions in the night. Sometimes the dim light of the windows in the night seemed to advance till it pressed upon my eyeballs, and then the windows would seem to recede to an infinite distance. If I laid my hand under my head on the pillow, the hand seemed to vanish almost to a point, while the head grew as big as a mountain. Sometimes I was panic struck at the head of the stairs, and was sure I could never get down; and I could never cross the yard to the garden without flying and panting, and fearing to look behind, because a wild beast was after me. The star-light sky was the worst; it was always coming down, to stifle and crush me, and rest upon my head. I do not remember any dread of thieves or ghosts in particular; but things as I actually saw them were dreadful to me; and it now appears to me that I had scarcely any respite from the terror. My fear of persons was as great as any other. To the best of my belief, the first person I was ever not afraid of was Aunt Kentish,[1] who won my heart and my confidence when I was sixteen. My heart was ready enough to flow out; and it often did: but I always repented of such expansion, the next time I dreaded to meet a human face. – It now occurs to me, and it may be worth while to note it, – what the extremest terror of all was about. We were often sent to walk on the Castle Hill at Norwich. In the wide area below, the residents were wont to expose their feather-beds, and to beat them with a stick. That sound, – a dull shock, – used to make my heart stand still: and it was no use my standing at the rails above, and seeing the process. The striking of the blow and the arrival of the sound did not correspond; and this made matters worse. I hated that walk; and I believe for that reason. My parents knew nothing of all this. It never occurred to me to speak of any thing I felt most: and I doubt whether they ever had the slightest idea of my miseries. It seems to me now that a little closer observation would have shown them the causes of the bad health and fitful temper which gave them so much anxiety on my account; and I am sure that a little more of the cheerful tenderness which was in those days thought bad for children, would have saved me from my worst faults, and from a world of suffering.

My hostess and nurse at the above-mentioned cottage was a Mrs Merton, who was, as was her husband, a Methodist or melancholy Calvinist of some sort. The family story about me was that I came home the absurdest little preacher of my years (between two and three) that ever was. I used to nod my head emphatically, and say 'Never ky for tyfles': 'Dooty fust, and pleasure afterwards', and so forth: and I sometimes got courage to edge up to strangers, and ask them to give me – 'a maxim'. Almost before I could join letters, I got some sheets of paper, and folded them into a little square book, and wrote, in double lines, two or three in a page, my beloved maxims. I believe this was my first effort at book-making. It was probably what I picked up at Carleton that made me so intensely religious as I certainly was from a very early age. The religion was of a bad sort enough, as might be expected from the urgency of my needs; but I doubt whether I could have got through without it. I pampered my vain-glorious propensities by dreams of divine favour, to make up for my utter deficiency of self-respect; and I got rid of otherwise incessant remorse by a most convenient confession and repentance, which relieved my nerves without at all, I suspect, improving my conduct.

To revert to my earliest recollections: – I certainly could hardly walk alone when our nursemaid took us, – including my sister Elizabeth, who was eight years older than myself, – an unusual walk; through a lane, (afterwards called by us the 'Spinster's Lane') where some Miss Taskers, acquaintances of Elizabeth's and her seniors, were lodging, in a cottage which had a fir grove behind it. Somebody set me down at the foot of a fir, where I was distressed by the slight rising of the ground at the root, and by the long grass, which seemed a terrible entanglement. I looked up the tree, and was scared at its height, and at that of so many others. I was comforted with a fir-cone; and then one of the Miss Taskers caught me up in her arms and kissed me; and I was too frightened to cry till we got away. – I was not more than two years old when an impression of touch occurred to me which remains vivid to this day. It seems indeed as if impressions of touch were at that age more striking than those from the other senses. I say this from observation of others besides myself; for my own case is peculiar in that matter. Sight, hearing and touch were perfectly good in early childhood; but I never had the sense of smell; and that of taste was therefore exceedingly imperfect. – On the occasion I refer to, I was carried down a flight of steep back stairs, and Rachel (a year and half older than I) clung to the nursemaid's gown, and Elizabeth was going before (still quite a little girl) when I put down my finger ends to feel a flat velvet button on the top of Rachel's bonnet. The rapture of the sensation was really monstrous, as I remember it now. Those were our mourning bonnets for a near relation; and this marks the date, proving me to have been only two years old.

I was under three when my brother James was born. That day was another of the distinct impressions which flashed upon me in after years. I found myself within the door of the best bedroom, – an impressive place from being seldom used, from its having a dark, polished floor, and from the awful large gay figures of the chintz bed hangings. That day the curtains were drawn, the window blinds were down, and an unknown old woman, in a mob cap, was at the fire, with a bundle of flannel in her arms. She beckoned to me, and I tried to go, though it seemed impossible to cross the slippery floor. I seem to hear now the pattering of my feet. When I arrived at her knee, the nurse pushed out with her foot a tiny chair, used as a foot-stool, made me sit down on it, laid the bundle of flannel across my knees, and opened it so that I saw the little red face of the baby. I then found out that there was somebody in the bed, – seeing a nightcap on the pillow. This was on the 21st of April, 1805. I have a distinct recollection of some incidents of that summer. My mother did not recover well from her confinement, and was sent to the sea, at Yarmouth. On our arrival there, my father took me along the old jetty, – little knowing what terror I suffered. I remember the strong grasp of his large hand being some comfort; but there were holes in the planking of the jetty quite big enough to let my foot through; and they disclosed the horrible sight of waves flowing and receding below, and great tufts of green weeds swaying to and fro. I remember the sitting-room at our lodgings, and my mother's dress as she sat picking shrimps, and letting me try to help her. – Of all my many fancies, perhaps none was so terrible as a dream that I had at four years old. The impression is as fresh as possible now; but I cannot at all understand what the fright was about. I know nothing more strange than this power of re-entering, as it were, into the narrow mind of an infant, so as to compare it with that of maturity; and therefore it may be worth while to record that piece of precious nonsense, – my dream at four years old. I imagine I was learning my letters then from cards, where each letter had its picture, – as a stag for S. I dreamed that we children were taking our walk with our nursemaid out of St. Austin's Gate (the nearest bit of country to our house). Out of the public-house there came a stag, with prodigious antlers. Passing the pump, it crossed the road to us, and made a polite bow, with its head on one side, and with a scrape of one foot, after which it pointed with its foot to the public-house, and spoke to me, inviting me in. The maid declined, and turned to go home. Then came the terrible part. By the time we were at our own door, it was dusk, and we went up the steps in the dark; but in the kitchen it was bright sunshine. My mother was standing at the dresser, breaking sugar; and she lifted me up, and set me in the sun, and gave me a bit of sugar. Such was the dream which froze me with horror! Who shall say why? – But my panics were really unaccountable. They were a matter of pure sensation, without any intellectual justification whatever, even of the wildest kind. A magic-lantern was exhibited to us on Christmas-day, and once or twice in the year besides. I used to see it cleaned by daylight, and to handle all its parts, – understanding its whole structure; yet, such was my terror of the white circle on the wall, and of the moving slides, that, to speak the plain truth, the first apparition always brought on bowel-complaint; and, at the age of thirteen, when I was pretending to take care of little children during the exhibition, I could never look at it without having the back of a chair to grasp, or hurting myself, to carry off the intolerable sensation. My bitter shame may be conceived; but then, I was always in a state of shame about something or other. I was afraid to walk in the town, for some years, if I remember right, for fear of meeting two people. One was an unknown old lady who very properly rebuked me one day for turning her off the very narrow pavement of London Lane, telling me, in an awful way, that little people should make way for their elders. The other was an unknown farmer, in whose field we had been gleaning (among other trespassers) before the shocks were carried. This man left the field after us, and followed us into the city, – no doubt, as I thought, to tell the Mayor, and send the constable after us. I wonder how long it was before I left off expecting that constable. There were certain little imps, however, more alarming still. Our house was in a narrow street; and all its windows, except two or three at the back, looked eastwards. It had no sun in the front rooms, except before breakfast in summer. One summer morning, I went into the drawing-room, which was not much used in those days, and saw a sight which made me hide my face in a chair, and scream with terror. The drops of the lustres on the mantle-piece, on which the sun was shining, were somehow set in motion, and the prismatic colours danced vehemently on the walls. I thought they were alive, – imps of some sort; and I never dared go into that room alone in the morning, from that time forward. I am afraid I must own that my heart has beat, all my life long, at the dancing of prismatic colours on the wall.

I was getting some comfort, however, from religion by this time. The Sundays began to be marked days, and pleasantly marked, on the whole. I do not know why crocuses were particularly associated with Sunday at that time; but probably my mother might have walked in the garden with us, some early spring Sunday. My idea of Heaven was of a place gay with yellow and lilac crocuses. My love of gay colours was very strong. When I was sent with the keys to a certain bureau in my mother's room, to fetch miniatures of my father and grandfather, to be shown to visitors, I used to stay an unconscionable time, though dreading punishment for it, but utterly unable to resist the fascination of a certain watch-ribbon kept in a drawer there. This ribbon had a pattern in floss silk, gay and beautifully shaded; and I used to look at it till I was sent for, to be questioned as to what I had been about. The young wild parsley and other weeds in the hedges used to make me sick with their luscious green in spring. One crimson and purple sunrise I well remember, when James could hardly walk alone, and I could not therefore have been more than five. I awoke very early, that summer morning, and saw the maid sound asleep in her bed, and 'the baby' in his crib. The room was at the top of the house; and some rising ground beyond the city could be seen over the opposite roofs. I crept out of bed, saw James's pink toes showing themselves invitingly through the rails of his crib, and gently pinched them, to wake him. With a world of trouble I got him over the side, and helped him to the window, and upon a chair there. I wickedly opened the window, and the cool air blew in; and yet the maid did not wake. Our arms were smutted with the blacks on the window-sill, and our bare feet were corded with the impression of the rush-bottomed chair; but we were not found out. The sky was gorgeous, and I talked very religiously to the child. I remember the mood, and the pleasure of expressing it, but nothing of what I said.

I must have been a remarkably religious child, for the only support and pleasure I remember having from a very early age was from that source. I was just seven when the grand event of my childhood took place, – a journey to Newcastle to spend the summer (my mother and four of her children) at my grandfather's; and I am certain that I cared more for religion before and during that summer than for anything else. It was after our return, when Ann Turner, daughter of the Unitarian minister there,[2] was with us, that my piety first took a practical character; but it was familiar to me as an indulgence long before. While I was afraid of everybody I saw, I was not in the least afraid of God. Being usually very unhappy, I was constantly longing for heaven, and seriously, and very frequently planning suicide in order to get there. I was sure that suicide would not stand in the way of my getting there. I knew it was considered a crime; but I did not feel it so. I had a devouring passion for justice; – justice, first to my own precious self, and then to other oppressed people. Justice was precisely what was least understood in our house, in regard to servants and children. Now and then I desperately poured out my complaints; but in general I brooded over my injuries, and those of others who dared not speak; and then the temptation to suicide was very strong. No doubt, there was much vindictiveness in it. I gloated over the thought that I would make somebody care about me in some sort of way at last: and, as to my reception in the other world, I felt sure that God could not be very angry with me for making haste to him when nobody else cared for me, and so many people plagued me. One day I went to the kitchen to get the great carving knife, to cut my throat; but the servants were at dinner; and this put it off for that time. By degrees, the design dwindled down into running away. I used to lean out of the window, and look up and down the street, and wonder how far I could go without being caught. I had no doubt at all that if I once got into a farm-house, and wore a woollen petticoat, and milked the cows, I should be safe, and that nobody would inquire about me any more. – It is evident enough that my temper must have been very bad. It seems to me now that it was downright devilish, except for a placability which used to annoy me sadly. My temper might have been early made a thoroughly good one, by the slightest indulgence shown to my natural affections, and any rational dealing with my faults: but I was almost the youngest of a large family, and subject, not only to the rule of severity to which all were liable, but also to the rough and contemptuous treatment of the elder children, who meant no harm, but injured me irreparably. I had no self-respect, and an unbounded need of approbation and affection. My capacity for jealousy was something frightful. When we were little more than infants, Mr. Thomas Watson, son of my father's partner, one day came into the yard, took Rachel up in his arms, gave her some grapes off the vine, and carried her home, across the street, to give her *Gay's Fables*, bound in red and gold.[3] I stood with a bursting heart, beating my hoop, and hating every body in the world. I always hated *Gay's Fables*, and for long could not abide a red book. Nobody dreamed of all this; and the 'taking down' system was pursued with me as with the rest, issuing in the assumed doggedness and wilfulness which made me desperately disagreeable during my youth, to every body at home. The least word or tone of kindness melted me instantly, in spite of the strongest predeterminations to be hard and offensive. Two occasions stand out especially in my memory, as indeed almost the only instances of the enjoyment of tenderness manifested to myself individually.

When I was four or five years old, we were taken to a lecture of Mr. Drummond's, for the sake, no doubt, of the pretty shows we were to see, – the chief of which was the Phantasmagoria of which we had heard, as a fine sort of magic-lantern. I did not like the darkness, to begin with; and when Minerva appeared, in a red dress, at first extremely small, and then approaching, till her owl seemed coming directly upon me, it was so like my nightmare dreams that I shrieked aloud. I remember my own shriek. A pretty lady who sat next us, took me on her lap, and let me hide my face in her bosom, and held me fast. How intensely I loved her, without at all knowing who she was! From that time we knew her, and she filled a large space in my life; and above forty years after, I had the honour of having her for my guest in my own house. She was Mrs. Lewis Cooper, then the very young mother of two girls of the ages of Rachel and myself, of whom I shall have to say more presently. – The other occasion was when I had a terrible ear-ache one Sunday. The rest went to chapel in the afternoon; and my pain grew worse. Instead of going into the kitchen to the cook, I wandered into a lumber room at the top of the house. I laid my aching ear against the cold iron screw of a bedstead, and howled with pain; but nobody came to me. At last, I heard the family come home from chapel. I heard them go into the parlour, one after another, and I knew they were sitting round the fire in the dusk. I stole down to the door, and stood on the mat, and heard them talking and laughing merrily. I stole in, thinking they would not observe me, and got into a dark corner. Presently my mother called to me, and asked what I was doing there. Then I burst out, – that my ear ached so I did not know *what* to do! Then she and my father both called me tenderly, and she took me on her lap, and laid the ear on her warm bosom. I was afraid of spoiling her starched muslin handkerchief with the tears which *would* come; but I was very happy, and wished that I need never move again. Then of course came remorse for all my naughtiness; but I was always suffering that, though never, I believe, in my whole childhood, being known to own myself wrong. I must have been an intolerable child: but I need not have been so.

I was certainly fond of going to chapel before that Newcastle era which divided my childhood into two equal portions: but my besetting troubles followed me even there. My passion for justice was baulked there, as much as any where. The duties preached were those of inferiors to superiors, while the *per contra* was not insisted on with any equality of treatment at all. Parents were to bring up their children 'in the nurture and admonition of the Lord',[4] and to pay servants due wages; but not a word was ever preached about the justice due from the stronger to the weaker. I used to thirst to hear some notice of the oppression which servants and children had (as I supposed universally) to endure, in regard to their feelings, while duly clothed, fed, and taught: but nothing of the sort ever came; but instead, a doctrine of passive obedience which only made me remorseful and miserable. I was abundantly obedient in act; for I never dreamed of being otherwise; but the interior rebellion kept my conscience in a state of perpetual torture. As far as I remember, my conscience was never of the least use to me; for I always concluded myself wrong about every thing, while pretending entire complacency and assurance. My moral discernment was almost wholly obscured by fear and mortification. – Another misery at chapel was that I could not attend to the service, nor refrain from indulging in the most absurd vain-glorious dreams, which I was ashamed of, all the while. The Octagon Chapel at Norwich has some curious windows in the roof; – not skylights, but letting in light indirectly. I used to sit staring up at those windows, and looking for angels to come for me, and take me to heaven, in sight of all the congregation, – the end of the world being sure to happen while we were at chapel. I was thinking of this, and of the hymns, the whole of the time, it now seems to me. It was very shocking to me that I could not pray at chapel. I believe that I never did in my life. I prayed abundantly when I was alone; but it was impossible to me to do it in any other way; and the hypocrisy of appearing to do so was a long and sore trouble to me. – All this is very painful; but I really remember little that was not painful at that time of my life. – To be sure, there was Nurse Ayton, who used to come, one or two days in the week, to sew. She was kind to me, and I was fond of her. She told us long stories about her family; and she taught me to sew. She certainly held the family impression of my abilities, – that I was a dull, unobservant, slow, awkward child. In teaching me to sew, she used to say (and I quite acquiesced) that 'slow and sure' was the maxim for me, and 'quick and well' was the maxim for Rachel. I was not jealous about this, – it seemed to me so undeniable. On one occasion only I thought Nurse Ayton unkind. The back of a ricketty old nursing-chair came off when I was a playing on it; and I was sure she could save me from being scolded by sewing it on again. I insisted that she could sew *anything*. This made my mother laugh when she came up; and so I forgave nurse: and I believe that was our only quarrel.

My first political interest was the death of Nelson. I was then four years old.[5] My father came in from the counting-house at an unusual hour, and told my mother, who cried heartily. I certainly had some conception of a battle, and of a great man being a public loss. It always rent my heart-strings (to the last day of her life), to see and hear my mother cry; and in this case it was clearly connected with the death of a great man. I had my own notions of Bonaparte too. One day, at dessert, when my father was talking anxiously to my mother about the expected invasion, for which preparations were being made all along the Norfolk coast, I saw them exchange a glance, because I was standing staring, twitching my pinafore with terror. My father called me to him, and took me on his knee, and I said 'But, papa, what will you do if Boney comes?' 'What will I do?' said he, cheerfully, 'Why, I will ask him to take a glass of Port with me', – helping himself to a glass as he spoke. That wise reply was of immense service to me. From the moment I knew that 'Boney' was a creature who could take a glass of wine, I dreaded him no more. Such was my induction into the department of foreign affairs. As to social matters, – my passion for justice was cruelly crossed, from the earliest time I can remember, by the imposition of passive obedience and silence on servants and tradespeople, who met with a rather old-fashioned treatment in our house. We children were enough in the kitchen to know how the maids avenged themselves for scoldings in the parlour, before the family and visitors, to which they must not reply; and for being forbidden to wear white gowns, silk gowns, or any thing but what strict housewives approved. One of my chief miseries was being sent with insulting messages to the maids, – e.g., to 'bid them not be so like cart-horses overhead', and the like. On the one hand, it was a fearful sin to alter a message; and, on the other, it was impossible to give such an one as that: so I used to linger and delay to the last moment, and then deliver something civil, with all imaginable sheepishness, so that the maids used to look at one another and laugh. Yet, one of my most heartfelt sins was towards a servant who was really a friend of my mother's, and infinitely respected, and a good deal loved, by us children, – Susan Ormsby, who came to live with us just before James was born, and staid till that memorable Newcastle journey, above four years afterwards. When she was waiting at dinner one day, I stuck my knife upright, in listening to something, so that the point cut her arm. I saw her afterwards washing it at the pump; and she shook her head at me in tender reproach. My heart was bursting; but I dared not tell her how sorry I was. I never got over it, or was happy with her again; and when we were to part, the night before our journey, and she was kissing us with tears, it was in dumb grief and indignation that I heard her tell my mother that children do not feel things as grown people do, and that they could not think of any thing else when they were going a journey.

One more fact takes its place before that journey, – the awakening of a love of money in me. I suspect I have had a very narrow escape of being an eminent miser. A little more, or a little less difficulty, or another mode of getting money would easily have made me a miser. The first step, as far as I remember, was when we played cards, one winter evening, at our uncle Martineau's, when I was told that I had won twopence. The pavement hardly seemed solid when we walked home, – so elated was I. I remember equal delight when Mrs. Meadows Taylor[6] gave us children twopence when we expected only a halfpenny, to buy string for a top: but in this last case it was not the true *amor nummi*,[7] as in the other. The same avarice was excited in the same way, a few years later, when I won eighteen-pence at cards, on a visit. The very sight of silver and copper was transporting to me, without any thought of its use. I stood and looked long at money, as it lay in my hand. Yet, I do not remember that this passion ever interfered with my giving away money, though it certainly did with my spending it otherwise. I certainly was very close, all my childhood and youth. I may as well mention here that I made rules and kept them, in regard to my expenditure, from the time I had an allowance. I believe we gave away something out of our first allowance of a penny a week. When we had twopence, I gave away half. The next advance was to half-a-guinea a quarter, to buy gloves and sashes: then to ten pounds a year (with help) for clothes; then fifteen, and finally twenty, without avowed help. I sewed indefatigably all those years, – being in truth excessively fond of sewing, with the amusement of either gossiping, or learning poetry by heart, from a book, lying open under my work. I never had the slightest difficulty in learning any amount of verse; and I knew enough to have furnished me for a wandering reciter, – if there had been such a calling in our time, – as I used to wish there was. While thus busy, I made literally all my clothes, as I grew up, except stays and shoes. I platted bonnets at one time, knitted stockings as I read aloud, covered silk shoes for dances, and made all my garments. Thus I squeezed something out of the smaller allowance, and out of the fifteen pounds, I never spent more than twelve in dress; and never more than fifteen pounds out of the twenty. The rest I gave away, except a little which I spent in books. The amount of time spent in sewing now appears frightful; but it was the way in those days, among people like ourselves. There was some saving in our practice of reading aloud, and in mine of learning poetry in such mass: but the censorious gossip which was the bane of our youth drove prose and verse out of the field, and wasted more of our precious youthful powers and dispositions than any repentance and amendment in after life could repair. This sort of occupation, the sewing, however, was less unfitting than might now appear, considering that the fortunes of manufacturers, like my father, were placed in jeopardy by the war, and that there was barely a chance for my father ever being able to provide fortunes for his daughters. He and my mother exercised every kind of self-denial to bring us up qualified to take care of ourselves. They pinched themselves in luxuries to provide their girls, as well as their boys, with masters and schooling; and they brought us up to an industry like their own; – the boys in study and business, and the girls in study and household cares. Thus was I saved from being a literary lady who could not sew; and when, in after years, I have been wont to explain, for my mother's sake, that I could make shirts and puddings, and iron and mend, and get my bread by my needle, if necessary, – (as it once was necessary, for a few months), before I won a better place and occupation with my pen.

## Section II

But it is time to set out on the second period of my childhood, – beginning with that memorable Newcastle journey. That period was memorable, not only from the enlarging of a child's ideas which ensues upon a first long journey, but because I date from it my becoming what is commonly called 'a responsible being'. On my return home I began to take moral charge of myself. I had before, and from my earliest recollections, been subject to a haunting, wretched, useless remorse; but from the time of our return from Newcastle, bringing Ann Turner with us, I became practically religious with all my strength. Ann was, I think, fourteen, when I was seven; and that she made herself my friend at all was a great thing for me; and it fell out all the more easily for her tendencies being exclusively religious, while I was only waiting for some influence to determine my life in that direction.

Travelling was no easy matter in those days. My mother, our dear, pretty, gentle aunt Margaret,[8] sister Elizabeth, aged fifteen, Rachel, myself, and little James, aged four, and in nankeen frocks, were all crammed into a post-chaise, for a journey of three or four days. Almost every incident of those days is still fresh: but I will report only one, which is curious from showing how little aware we children were of our own value. I really think, if I had once conceived that any body cared for me, nearly all the sins and sorrow of my anxious childhood would have been spared me; and I remember well that it was Ann Turner who first conveyed the cheering truth to me. She asked me why my mother sat sewing so diligently for us children, and sat up at night to mend my stockings, if she did not care for me; and I was convinced at once; – only too happy to believe it, and being unable to resist such evidence as the stocking-mending at night, when we children were asleep. Well: on our second day's journey, we stopped at Burleigh House, and the three elders of the party went in, to see the picture gallery. – Children were excluded ; so we three little ones were left, to play among the haymakers on the lawn. After what seemed a long time, it suddenly struck us that the elders must have forgotten us, and gone on to Newcastle without us. I, for my part, was entirely persuaded that we should never be missed, or remembered more by any body; and we set up a terrible lamentation. A good-natured haymaker, a sunburnt woman whose dialect we could not understand, took us in hand, and led us to the great door, where we were soon comforted by my mother's appearance. I remember wondering why she and aunt Margaret laughed aside when they led us back to the chaise.

Of course it was difficult to amuse little children so cooped up for so long. There was a little quiet romping, I remember, and a great deal of story telling by dear aunty: but the finest device was setting us to guess what we should find standing in the middle of grandpapa's garden. As it was something we had never seen or known about, there was no end to the guessing. When we arrived at the gates of the Forth (my grandfather's house) the old folks and their daughters came out to meet us, all tearful and agitated: and I, loathing myself for the selfishness, *could not* wait, but called out, – 'I want to see what that thing is in the garden.' After an enlightening hint, and without any rebuke, our youngest aunt took me by the hand, and led me to face the mystery. I could make nothing of it when I saw it. It was a large, heavy, stone sundial. That dial is worth this much mention, for it was of immeasurable value to me. I could see its face only by raising myself on tiptoe on its step: and there, with my eyes on a level with the plate, did I watch and ponder, day by day, painfully forming my first clear conceptions of Time, amidst a bright confusion of notions of day and night, and of the seasons, and of the weather. I loved that dial with a sort of superstition; and when, nearly forty years after, I built a house for myself at Ambleside, my strong wish was to have this very dial for the platform below the terrace: but it was not to be had. It had been once removed already, – when the railway cut through the old garden; and the stone mass was too heavy, and far too much fractured and crumbled for a second removal. So a dear friend set up for me a beautiful new dial; and I can only hope that it may possibly render as great a service to some child of a future generation as my grandfather's did for me.

It seems to me now that I seldom asked questions in those days. I went on for years together in a puzzle, for want of its ever occurring to me to ask questions. For instance, no accounts of a spring-gun answered to my conception of it; – that it was a pea-green musket, only used in spring! This absurdity at length lay by unnoticed in my mind till I was twenty! Even so! At that age, I was staying at Birmingham; and we were returning from a country walk in the dusk of the evening, when my host warned us not to cross a little wood, for fear of spring-guns; and he found and showed us the wire of one. I was truly confounded when the sense of the old mistake, dormant in my mind till now, came upon me. Thus it was with a piece of mystification imposed on me by my grandfather's barber in 1809. One morning, while the shaving-pot was heating, the barber took me on his knee, and pretended to tell me why he was late that morning. Had I ever heard of a falling star? Yes, I had. Well: a star had fallen in the night; and it fell in the Forth lane, which it completely blocked up, beside Mr. Somebody's orchard. It was quite round, and of the beautifullest and clearest crystal. 'Was it there still?' O yes, – or most of it: but some of the crystal was shivered off, and people were carrying it away when he arrived at the spot. He had to go round by Something Street; and it was that which made him late. 'Would there be any left by the time we went for our walk?' He hoped there might. I got through my lessons in a fever of eagerness that morning, and engaged the nurse maid to take us through that lane. There was the orchard, with the appletree stretching over the wall: but not a single spike of the crystal was left. I thought it odd; but it never occurred to me to doubt the story, or to speak to any body about it, except the barber. I lay in wait for him the next morning; and very sorry he professed to be; – so sorry that he had not just picked up some crystals for me while there were so many; but no doubt I should come in the way of a fallen star myself, some day. We kept this up till October, when we bade him good bye: and my early notions of astronomy were cruelly bewildered by that man's rhodomontade. I dare not say how many years it was before I got quite clear of it.

There is little that is pleasant to say of the rest of that absence from home. There was a naughty boy staying at my grandfather's, who caused us to be insulted by imputations of stealing the green fruit, and to be shut out of the garden, where we had never dreamed of touching a gooseberry: and he led little James into mischief; and then canted and made his own part good. Our hearts swelled under the injuries he caused us. Then, we were injudiciously fed, and my nightmare miseries were intolerable. The best event was that my theological life began to take form. I had a prodigious awe of clergymen and ministers, and a strong yearning towards them for notice. No doubt there was much vanity in this; but it was also one investment of the religious sentiment, as I know by my being at times conscious of a remnant of the feeling now, while radically convinced that the intellectual and moral judgment of priests of all persuasions is inferior to that of any other order of men. The first of the order who took any direct notice of me was, as far as I know, good Mr. Turner of Newcastle, my mother's pastor and friend before her marriage. At Newcastle, we usually went to tea at his house on Sunday evenings; and it was then that we began the excellent practice of writing recollections of one of the sermons of the day. When the minister preaches what children can understand, this practice is of the highest use in fixing their attention, and in disclosing to their parents the character and imperfections of their ideas on the most important class of subjects. On occasion of our first attempt, – Rachel's and mine, – I felt very triumphant before hand. I remembered the text; and it seemed to me that my head was full of thoughts from the sermon. I scrawled over the whole of a large slate, and was not a little mortified when I found that all I had written came into seven or eight lines of my mother's handwriting. I made sure that I had not been cheated, and then fell into discouragement at finding that my grand 'sermon' came to nothing more. However, my attempt was approved; I was allowed to 'sit up to supper,' and the Sunday practice was begun which continued till I grew too deaf to keep up my attention successfully. For some years of that long period, our success was small, because Mr. Madge's, (our minister's)[9] sermons conveyed few clear ideas to children, though much sweet and solemn impression. Dr. Carpenter's[10] were the best I ever listened to for the purpose: – so good that I have known him carry a 'recollection' written by a cousin of mine at the age of sixteen, to Mrs. Carpenter, as a curiosity, – not a single sentence of his sermon being altogether absent from the hearer's version of it. – Another religious impression that we children brought from Newcastle is very charming to me still. Our gentle, delicate aunt Mary, whom I remember so well in her white gown, with her pink colour, thin silky brown hair, and tender manner towards us, used to get us round her knees as she sat in the window-seat at the Forth, where the westerly sun shone in, and teach us to sing Milton's hymn 'Let us with a gladsome mind'. It is the very hymn for children, set to his own simple tune; and I always, to this day, hear aunt Mary's weak, earnest voice in it. That was the gentle hymn. The woe-breathing one was the German Evening Hymn. The heroic one, which never failed to rouse my whole being, was 'Awake, my soul; stretch every nerve', sung to Artaxerxes. – In those days, we learned Mrs. Barbauld's Prose Hymns[11] by heart; and there were parts of them which I dearly loved: but other parts made me shiver with awe. I did not know what 'shaking bogs' were, and was alarmed at that mysterious being 'Child of Mortality'. On the whole, however, religion was a great comfort and pleasure to me; and I studied the New Testament very heartily and profitably, from the time that Ann Turner went south with us, and encouraged me to confession and morning and nightly prayer.

*Second Period: Section I*

I think it could not have been long after that time that I took up a project which was of extraordinary use to me. My mind, considered dull and unobservant and unwieldy by my family, was desperately methodical. Every thing must be made tabular that would at all admit of it. Thus, I adopted in an immense hurry Dr. Franklin's youthful and absurd plan of pricking down his day's virtues and vices under heads.[12] I found at once the difficulty of mapping out moral qualities, and had to give it up, – as I presume he had too. But I tried after something quite as foolish, and with immense perseverance. I thought it would be a fine thing to distribute scripture instructions under the heads of the virtues and vices, so as to have encouragement or rebuke always ready at hand. So I made (as on so many other occasions) a paper book, ruled and duly headed. With the Old Testament, I got on very well; but I was amazed at the difficulty of the New. I knew it to be of so much more value and importance than the Old, that I could not account for the small number of cut and dry commands. I twisted meanings and wordings, and made figurative things into precepts, at an unconscionable rate, before I would give up: but, after rivalling any old puritan preacher in my free use of scripture, I was obliged to own that I could not construct the system I wanted. Thus it was that I made out that great step in the process of thought and knowledge, – that whereas Judaism was a preceptive religion, Christianity was mainly a religion of principles, – or assumed to be so ...

My religious belief, up to the age of twenty, was briefly this. I believed in a God, milder and more beneficent and passionless than the God of the orthodox inasmuch as he would not doom any of his creatures to eternal torment. I did not at any time, I think, believe in the Devil, but understood the Scriptures to speak of Sin under that name, and of eternal detriment under the name of eternal punishment. I believed in inestimable and eternal rewards of holiness; but I am confident that I never in my life did a right thing, or abstained from a wrong one from any consideration of reward or punishment. To the best of my recollection, I always feared sin and remorse extremely, and punishment not at all; but, on the contrary, desired punishment or any thing else that would give me the one good that I pined for in vain, – ease of conscience. The doctrine of forgiveness on repentance never availed me much, because forgiveness for the past was nothing without safety in the future; and my sins were not curable, I felt, by any single remission of their consequences, – if such remission were possible. If I prayed and wept, and might hope that I was pardoned at night, it was small comfort, because I knew I should be in a state of remorse again before the next noon. I do not remember the time when the forgiveness clause in the Lord's Prayer was not a perplexity and a stumbling-block to me. I did not care about being let off from penalty. I wanted to be at ease in conscience; and that could only be by growing good, whereas I hated and despised myself ever day. My belief in Christ was that he was the purest of all beings, under God; and his sufferings for the sake of mankind made him as sublime in my view and my affections as any being could possibly be. The Holy Ghost was a mere fiction to me. I took all the miracles for facts, and contrived to worship the letter of the Scriptures long after I had, as desired, given up portions as 'spurious', 'interpolations', and so forth. I believed in a future life as a continuation of the present, and not as a new method of existence; and, from the time when I saw that the resurrection of the body and the immortality of the soul could not both be true, I adhered to the former, – after St. Paul. I was uncomfortably disturbed that Christianity had done so little for the redemption of the race: but the perplexity was not so serious as it would have been if I had believed in the perdition of the majority of men; and, for the rest, I contrived to fix my view pretty exclusively on Christendom itself, – which Christians in general find a grand resource in their difficulties. In this way, and by the help of public worship, and of sacred music, and Milton, and the Pilgrim's Progress, I found religion my best resource, even in its first inconsistent and unsatisfactory form, till I wrought my way to something better, as I shall tell by and by.[13]

When I was seven years old, – the winter after our return from Newcastle, – I was kept from chapel one Sunday afternoon by some ailment or other. When the house door closed behind the chapel-goers, I looked at the books on the table. The ugliest-looking of them was turned down open; and my turning it up was one of the leading incidents of my life. That plain, clumsy, calf-bound volume was *Paradise Lost*; and the common blueish paper, with its old-fashioned type, became as a scroll out of heaven to me. The first thing I saw was 'Argument', which I took to mean a dispute, and supposed to be stupid enough: but there was something about Satan cleaving Chaos, which made me turn to the poetry; and my mental destiny was fixed for the next seven years. That volume was henceforth never to be found but by asking me for it, till a young acquaintance made me a present of a little Milton of my own. In a few months, I believe there was hardly a line in Paradise Lost that I could not have instantly turned to. I sent myself to sleep by repeating it: and when my curtains were drawn back in the morning, descriptions of heavenly light rushed into my memory. I think this must have been my first experience of moral relief through intellectual resource. I am sure I must have been somewhat happier from that time forward; though one fact of which I am perfectly certain shows that the improvement must have been little enough. From the time when Ann Turner and her religious training of me put me, as it were, into my own moral charge, I was ashamed of my habit of misery, – and especially of crying. I tried for a long course of years, – I should think from about eight to fourteen, – to pass a single day without crying. I was a persevering child; and I know I tried hard: but I failed. I gave up at last; and during all those years, I never did pass a day without crying. Of course, my temper and habit of mind must have been excessively bad. I have no doubt I was an insufferable child for gloom, obstinacy and crossness. Still, when I remember my own placability, – my weakness of yielding every thing to the first word or tone of tenderness, I cannot but believe that there was grievous mistake in the case, and that even a little more sympathy and moral support would have spared me and others a hideous amount of fault and suffering.

How I found my way out we shall see hereafter: meantime, one small incident, which occurred when I was eleven years old, may foreshadow my release. Our eldest brother, Thomas, was seven years older than myself. He was silent and reserved generally, and somewhat strict to us younger ones, to whom he taught our Latin grammar. We revered and loved him intensely, in the midst of our awe of him: but once in my childhood I made him laugh against his will, by a pun in my Latin lesson (which was a great triumph) and once I ventured to confide in him a real difficulty, – without result. I found myself by his side during a summer evening walk, when something gave me courage to ask him – (the man of eighteen!) – the question which I had long been secretly revolving: – how, if God foreknew every thing, we could be blamed or rewarded for our conduct, which was thus absolutely settled for us beforehand. He considered for a moment, and then told me, in a kind voice, that this was a thing which I could not understand at present, nor for a long time to come. I dared not remonstrate; but I was disappointed: and I felt that if I could feel the difficulty, I had a right to the solution. No doubt, this refusal of a reply helped to fix the question in my mind.

I have said that by this time I had begun to take moral or spiritual charge of myself. I did try hard to improve; but I fear I made little progress. Every night, I reviewed the thoughts and actions of the day, and tried to repent; but I could seldom comfort myself about any amendment. All the while, however, circumstances were doing for me what I could not do for myself, – as I have since found to be incessantly happening. The first great wholesome discipline of my life set in (unrecognised as such) when I was about eight years old. The kind lady who took me upon her lap at Mr. Drummond's lecture had two little girls, just the ages of Rachel and myself: and, after that incident, we children became acquainted, and very soon, (when the family came to live close beside us in Magdalen Street) as intimate as possible. I remember being at their house in the Market Place when I was seven years old; and little E[mily]. could not stand, nor even sit, to see the magic-lantern, but was held in her papa's arms, because she was so very lame. Before the year was out, she lost her leg. Being a quiet-tempered child, and the limb being exceedingly wasted by disease, she probably did not suffer very much under the operation. However that might be, she met the occasion with great courage, and went through it with remarkable composure, so that she was the talk of the whole city. I was naturally very deeply impressed by the affair. It turned my imagination far too much on bodily suffering, and on the peculiar glory attending fortitude in that direction. I am sure that my nervous system was seriously injured, and especially that my subsequent deafness was partly occasioned by the exciting and vain-glorious dreams that I indulged in for many years after my friend E. lost her leg. All manner of deaths at the stake and on the scaffold, I went through in imagination, in the low sense in which St. Theresa craved martyrdom; and night after night, I lay bathed in cold perspiration till I sank into the sleep of exhaustion. All this is detestable to think of now; but it is a duty to relate the truth, because parents are apt to know far too little of what is passing in their children's imaginations, unless they win the confidence of the little creatures about that on which they are shyest of all, – their aspirations. The good side of this wretched extravagance of mine was that it occasioned or strengthened a power of patience under pain and privation which was not to be looked for in a child so sensitive and irritable by nature. Fortitude was in truth my favourite virtue; and the power of bearing quietly a very unusual amount of bodily pain in childhood was the poor recompense I enjoyed for the enormous detriment I suffered from the turn my imagination had taken.

This, however, is not the discipline I referred to as arising from my companionship with E. In such a case as hers, all the world acquiesces in the parents' view and method of action: and in that case the parents made a sad mistake. They enormously increased their daughter's suffering from her infirmity by covering up the fact in an unnatural silence. E.'s lameness was never mentioned, nor recognised in any way, within my remembrance, till she, full late, did it herself. It was taken for granted that she was like other children; and the delusion was kept up in play-hours at my expense. I might almost say that from the time E. and I grew intimate, I never more had any play. Now, I was fond of play, – given to romp; and I really wonder now when I look back upon the many long years during which I stood, with cold feet and a longing mind, with E. leaning on my arm, looking on while other children were at play. It was a terrible uneasiness to me to go walks with her, – shy child as I was, – fancying everybody in the streets staring at us, on account of E.'s extreme difficulty in walking. But the long self-denial which I never thought of refusing or grumbling at, must have been morally good for me, if I may judge by the pain caused by two incidents; – pain which seems to me now to swallow up all that issued from mere privation. – the fatigue of walking with E. was very great, from her extreme need of support, and from its being always on the same side. I was never very strong; and when growing fast, I was found to be growing sadly crooked, from E.'s constant tugging at one arm. I cannot at all understand how my mother could put it upon me to tell E.'s mother that I must not walk with her, because it made me crooked: but this ungracious message I was compelled to carry; and it cost me more pain than long years of privation of play. The hint was instantly taken; but I suffered the shame and regret over again every time that I saw E. assigned to any one else; and I had infinitely rather have grown crooked than have escaped it by such a struggle. – The other incident was this. We children were to have a birthday party; and my father gave us the rare and precious liberty to play hide-and-seek in the warehouse, among the packing-cases and pigeon-holes where the bombasines were stored. For weeks I had counted the days and hours till this birthday and this play; but E. could not play hide-and-seek; and there we stood, looking at the rest, – I being cold and fidgetty, and at last uncontrollably worried at the thought that the hours were passing away, and I had not had one bit of play. I did the fatal thing which has been a thorn in my mind ever since. I asked E. if she would much mind having some one else with her for a minute while I hid once, – just once. O no, – she did not mind; so I sent somebody else to her, and ran off, with a feeling of self-detestation which is fresh at this day. I had no presence-of-mind for the game, – was caught in a minute; and came back to E. damaged in self-respect, for the whole remaining course of our friendship. However, I owe her a great deal; and she and her misfortune were among the most favourable influences I had the benefit of after taking myself in hand for self-government. I have much pleasure in adding that nothing could be finer than her temper in after life, when she had taken her own case in hand, and put an end, as far as it lay with her to do so, to the silence about her infirmity. After I wrote my 'Letter to the Deaf' [1834], we seemed to be brought nearer together by our companionship in infirmity. Years after that, when I had written *The Crofton Boys*,[14] and was uneasy lest my evident knowledge of such a case should jar upon her feelings, – always so tenderly considered, – I wrote her a confession of my uneasiness, and had in rely a most charming letter, – free, cheerful, magnanimous; – such a letter as has encouraged me to write as I have now done.

The year 1811 was a marked one to me, – first by my being sent into the country for my health, for the whole summer and autumn; and next, for the birth of the best-loved member of my family, – my sister Ellen. – It was not a genuine country life in a farm-house, that summer, but a most constrained and conventional one, in the abode of a rich lawyer, – a cousin of my father's, who sent a daughter of his to our house for the advantage of city masters, in exchange for me, who went for health. I was not, on the whole, happy there: – indeed, it is pretty clear by this time that I was not happy anywhere. The old fancy for running away came back strongly upon me, and I was on the very point of attempting it when a few words of concession and kindness upset my purpose, as usual. I detested the governess, – and with abundant reason. The very first day, she shut me up and punished me because I, a town-bred child, did not know what a copse was. 'Near yonder copse', &c.[15] She insisted that every body must know what a copse is, and that therefore I was obstinate and a liar. After such a beginning, it will be easily conceived that our relations could not be cordial or profitable. She presently showed herself jealous of my being in advance of her pupils in school-room knowledge; and she daily outraged my sense of justice, expressly, and in the most purpose-like manner. She was thoroughly vulgar; and in a few weeks she was sent away. – One annoyance that I remember at that place was (what now appears very strange) the whispers I overheard about myself, as I sat on a little stool in a corner of the dining-room, reading. My hostess, who might have said anything in her ordinary voice without my attending to her, used to whisper to her morning visitors about my wonderful love of reading, – that I never heard anything that was said while I sat reading, and that I had written a wonderful sermon. All the while, she pretended to disguise it, winking and nudging, and saying '*We* never hear any thing when we are reading.' '*We* have written a sermon which is really quite wonderful at *our* age', &c.&c. I wished that sermon at Jericho a hundred times; for in truth, I was heartily ashamed of it. It was merely a narrative of St. Paul's adventures, out of the Acts; and I knew it was no more a sermon than a string of parables out of the Gospels would have been.

There were some sweet country pleasures that summer. I never see chesnuts [sic] bursting from their sheaths, and lying among the autumn leaves, without remembering the old Manor-house where we children picked up chesnuts in the avenue, while my hostess made her call at the house. I have always loved orchards and apple-gatherings since, and blossomy lanes. The truth is, my remembrances of that summer may be found in 'Deerbrook', [16] though I now finally, (as often before), declare that the characters are not real. More or less suggestion from real characters there certainly is; but there is not one, except the hero, (who is not English), that any person is justified in pointing out as 'from the life'. Of the scenery too, there is more from Great Marlow than from that bleak Norfolk district; but the fresh country impressions are certainly derived from the latter. It was there that I had that precious morsel of experience which I have elsewhere detailed;[17] – the first putting my hand in among the operations of Nature, to modify them. After a morning walk, we children brought in some wild strawberry roots, to plant in our gardens. My plant was sadly withered by the time we got home; and it was then hot noon, – the soil of my garden was warm and parched, and there seemed no chance for my root. I planted it, grieved over its flabby leaves, watered it, got a little child's chair, which I put over it for shelter, and stopped up the holes in the chair with grass. When I went at sunset to look at it, the plant was perfectly fresh; and after that, it grew very well. My surprise and pleasure must have been very great, by my remembering such a trifle so long; and I am persuaded that I looked upon Nature with other eyes from the moment that I found I had power to modify her processes.

In November came the news which I had been told to expect. My sister Rachel had been with us in the country for a fortnight; and we knew that there was to be a baby at home before we went back; and I remember pressing so earnestly, by letter, to know the baby's name as to get a rebuff. I was told to wait till there was a baby. At last, the carrier brought us a letter one evening which told us that we had a little sister. I still longed to know the name, but dared not ask again. Our host saw what was in my mind. He went over to Norwich a day or two after, and on his return told me that he hoped I should like the baby's name now that she had got one; – 'Beersheba'. I did not know whether to believe him or not; and I had set my mind on 'Rose'. 'Ellen', however, satisfied me very well. – Homesick before, I now grew downright ill with longing. I was sure that all old troubles were wholly my fault, and fully resolved that there should be no more. Now, as so often afterwards, (as often as I left home) I was destined to disappointment. I scarcely felt myself at home before the well-remembered bickerings began; – not with me, but from the boys being troublesome, James being naughty; and our eldest sister angry and scolding. I then and there resolved that I would look for my happiness to the new little sister, and that she should never want for the tenderness which I had never found. This resolution turned out more of a prophecy than such decisions, born of a momentary emotion, usually do. That child was henceforth a new life to me. I did lavish love and tenderness on her; and I could almost say that she has never caused me a moment's pain but by her own sorrows. There has been much suffering in her life; and in it I have suffered with her: but such sympathetic pain is bliss in comparison with such feelings as she has *not* excited in me during our close friendship of above forty years. When I first saw her it was as she was lifted out of her crib, at a fortnight old, asleep, to be shown to my late hostess, who had brought Rachel and me home. The passionate fondness I felt for her from that moment has been unlike any thing else I have felt in life, – though I have made idols of not a few nephews and nieces. But she was a pursuit to me, no less than an attachment. I remember telling a young lady at the Gate-House Concert, (a weekly undress concert) the next night, that I should now see the growth of a human mind from the very beginning. I told her this because I was very communicative to all who showed me sympathy in any degree. Years after, I found that she was so struck by such a speech from a child of nine that she had repeated it till it had spread all over the city, and people said somebody had put it into my head; but it was perfectly genuine. My curiosity *was* intense; and all my spare minutes were spent in the nursery, watching, – literally watching, – the baby. This was a great stimulus to me in my lessons, to which I gave my whole power, in order to get leisure the sooner. That was the time when I took it into my head to cut up the Bible into a rule of life, as I have already told; and it was in the nursery chiefly that I did it, – sitting on a stool opposite the nursemaid and baby, and getting up from my notes to devour the child with kisses. There were bitter moments and hours, – as when she was vaccinated or had her little illnesses. My heart then felt bursting, and I went to my room, and locked the door, and prayed long and desperately. I knew then what the Puritans meant by 'wrestling in prayer.' – One abiding anxiety which pressed upon me for two years or more was lest this child should be dumb: and if not, what an awful amount of labour was before the little creature! I had no other idea than that she must learn to speak at all as I had now to learn French, – each word by an express effort: and if I, at ten and eleven, found my vocabulary so hard, how could this infant learn the whole English language? The dread went off in amazement when I found that she sported new words every day, without much teaching at first, and then without any. I was as happy to see her spared the labour as amused at her use of words in her pretty prattle.

For nearly two years after our return from that country visit, Rachel and I were taught at home. Our eldest brother taught us Latin, and the next brother, Henry, writing and arithmetic: and our sister, French, reading and exercises. We did not get on well, except with the Latin. Our sister expected too much from us, both morally and intellectually; and she had not been herself carried on so far as to have much resource as a teacher. We owed to her however a thoroughgoing grounding in our French grammar (especially the verbs) which was of excellent service to us afterwards at school, as was a similar grounding in the Latin grammar, obtained from our brother. As for Henry, he made our lessons in arithmetic, &c. his funny time of day; and sorely did his practical jokes and ludicrous severity afflict us. He meant no harm; but he was too young to play schoolmaster; and we improved less than we should have done under less head-ache and heart-ache from his droll system of torture. I should say, on their behalf, that I, for one, must have seemed a most unpromising pupil, – my wits were so completely scattered by fear and shyness. I could never give a definition, for want of presence of mind. I lost my place in class for every thing but lessons that could be prepared beforehand. I was always saying what I did not mean. The worst waste of time, energy, money and expectation was about my music. Nature made me a musician in every sense. I was never known to sing out of tune. I believe all who knew me when I was twenty would give a good account of my playing. There was no music that I ever attempted that I did not understand, and that I could not execute, – under the one indispensable condition, that nobody heard me. Much money was spent in instruction; and I dislike thinking of the amount of time lost in copying music. My mother loved music, and, I know, looked to me for much gratification in this way which she never had. My deafness put an end to all expectation of the kind at last; but long before that, my music was a misery to me, – while yet in another sense, my dearest pleasure. My master was Mr. Beckwith, organist of Norwich Cathedral;[18] – an admirable musician; but of so irritable a temper as to be the worst of masters to a shy girl like me. It was known that he had been dismissed from one house for rapping his pupils' knuckles; and that he had been compelled to apologize for insufferable scolding. Neither of these things happened at our house; but really I wondered sometimes that they did not, – so very badly did I play and sing when he was at my elbow. My fingers stuck together as in cramp, and my voice was as husky as if I had cotton-wool in my throat. Now and then he complimented my ear; but he oftener told me that I had no more mind than the music-book, – no more feeling than the lid of the piano, – no more heart than the chimney-piece; and that it was no manner of use trying to teach me any thing. All this while, if the room-door happened to be open without my observing it when I was singing Handel by myself, my mother would be found dropping tears over her work, and used myself as I may now own, to feel fairly transported. Heaven opened before me at the sound of my own voice when I believed myself alone; – that voice which my singing-master assuredly never heard. It was in his case that I first fully and suddenly learned the extent of the mischief caused by my shyness. He came twice a week. On those days it was an effort to rise in the morning, – to enter upon a day of misery; and nothing could have carried me through the morning but the thought of the evening, when he would be gone, – out of my way for three days, or even four. The hours grew heavier: my heart fluttered more and more: I could not eat my dinner; and his impatient loud knock was worse to me than sitting down in the dentist's chair. Two days per week of such feelings, strengthened by the bliss of the evenings after he was gone, might account for the catastrophe, which however did not shock me the less for that. Mr. Beckwith grew more and more cross, thinner and thinner, so that his hair and beard looked blacker and blacker, as the holidays approached, when he was wont to leave home for a week or two. One day when somebody was dining with us, and I sat beside my father at the bottom of the table, he said to my mother, 'By the way, my dear, there is a piece of news which will not surprise you much, I fancy. Poor John Beckwith is gone. He died yesterday.' Once more, that name made my heart jump into my mouth; but this time, it was with a dreadful joy. While the rest went on very quietly saying how ill he had looked for some time, and 'who would have thought he would never come back?' – and discussing how Mrs. B. and the children were provided for, and wondering who would be organist at the Cathedral, my spirits were dancing in secret rapture. The worst of my besetting terrors was over for ever! All days of the week would henceforth be alike, as far as that knock at the door was concerned. Of course, my remorse at this glee was great; and thus it was that I learned how morally injured I was by the debasing fear I was wholly unable to surmount.

Next to fear, laziness was my worst enemy. I was idle about brushing my hair, – late in the morning, – much afflicted to have to go down to the apple-closet in winter; and even about my lessons I was indolent. I learned any thing by heart very easily, and I therefore did it well: but I was shamefully lazy about using the dictionary, and went on, in full anticipation of rebuke, translating *la rosee* the rose, *tomber* to bury, and so on. This shows that there must have been plenty of provocation on my side, whatever mistakes there may have been on that of my teachers. I was sick and weary of the eternal 'Telemachus',[19] and could not go through the labours of the dictionary for a book I cared so little about. This difficulty soon came to an end; for in 1813 Rachel and I went to a good day-school for two years, where our time was thoroughly well spent; and there we enjoyed the acquisition of knowledge so much as not to care for the requisite toil.

Before entering on that grand new period, I may as well advert to a few noticeable points. – I was certainly familiar with the idea of death before that time. The death of Nelson, when I was four years old, was probably the earliest association in my mind of mournful feelings with death. When I was eight or nine, an aunt died whom I had been in the constant habit of seeing. She was old-fashioned in her dress, and peculiar in her manners. Her lean arms were visible between the elbow-ruffles and the long mits she wore; and she usually had an apron on, and a muslin handkerchief crossed on her bosom. She fell into absent-fits which puzzled and awed us children: but we heard her so highly praised (as she richly deserved) that she was a very impressive personage to us. One morning when I came down, I found the servants at breakfast unusually early: they looked very gloomy; bade me make no noise; but would not explain what it was all about. The shutters were half-closed; and when my mother came down, she looked so altered by her weeping that I hardly knew whether it was she. She called us to her, and told us that aunt Martineau had died very suddenly, of a disease of the heart. The whispers which were not meant for us somehow reached our ears all that week. We heard how my father and mother had been sent for in the middle of the night by the terrified servants, and how they had heard our poor uncle's voice of mourning before they had reached the house; and how she looked in her coffin, and all about the funeral: and we were old enough to be moved by the sermon in her praise at chapel, and especially by the anthem composed for the occasion, with the words from Job, – 'When the ear heard that then it blessed her,' &c.[20] My uncle's gloomy face and unpowdered hair were awful to us; and, during the single year of his widowhood, he occasionally took us children with him in the carriage, when he went to visit country patients. These drives came to an end with the year of widowhood; but he gave us something infinitely better than any other gift or pleasure in his second wife, whose only child was destined to fill a large space in our hearts and our lives.[21] – Soon after that funeral, I somehow learned that our globe swims in space, and that there is sky all round it. I told this to James; and we made a grand scheme which we never for a moment doubted about executing. We had each a little garden, under the north wall of our garden. The soil was less than two feet deep; and below it was a mass of rubbish, – broken bricks, flints, pottery, &c. We did not know this; and our plan was to dig completely through the globe, till we came out at the other side. I fully expected to do this, and had an idea of an extremely deep hole, the darkness of which at the bottom would be lighted up by the passage of stars, slowly traversing the hole. When we found our little spades would not dig through the globe, nor even through the brickbats, we altered our scheme. We lengthened the hole to our own length, having an extreme desire to know what dying was like. We lay down alternately in this grave, and shut our eyes, and fancied ourselves dead, and told one another our feelings when we came out again. As far as I can remember, we fully believed that we now knew all about it.

A prominent event of my childhood happened in 1812, when we went to Cromer for the sake of the baby's health. I had seen the sea, as I mentioned, when under three years old, as it swayed under the old jetty at Yarmouth: and I had seen it again at Tynemouth, when I was seven: but now it was like a wholly new spectacle; and I doubt whether I ever received a stronger impression than when from the rising ground above Cromer, we caught sight of the sparkling expanse. At Tynemouth, that singular incident took place which I have elsewhere narrated,[22] – that I was shown the sea, immediately below my feet, at the foot of the very slope on which I was standing, and could see it. The rest of the party must have thought me crazy or telling a lie; but the distress of being unable to see what I had so earnestly expected, was real enough; and so was the amazement when I at last perceived the fluctuating tide. All this had gone out of my mind when we went to Cromer; and the spectacle seemed a wholly new one. That was a marvellous month that the nursemaid and we children spent there. When we were not down on the sands, or on the cliffs, I was always perched on a bank in the garden whence I could see that straight blue line, or those sparkles which had such a charm for me. It was much that I was happy for à whole month; but I also obtained many new ideas, and much development; – the last chiefly, I think, in a religious direction.

In the preceding year another instance had occurred, – a most mortifying one to me, – of that strange inability to see what one is looking for (no doubt because one looks wrongly) of which the Tynemouth sea-gazing was a strong illustration.[23] When the great comet of 1811 was attracting all eyes, my star-gazing was just as ineffectual. Night after night, the whole family of us went up to the long windows at the top of my father's warehouse; and the exclamations on all hands about the comet perfectly exasperated me, – because I could not see it! 'Why, there it is!' 'It is as big as a saucer.' 'It is as big as a cheese-plate.' 'Nonsense; – you might as well pretend not to see the moon.' Such were the mortifying comments on my grudging admission that I could not see the comet. And I never did see it. Such is the fact; and philosophers may make of it what they may, – remembering that I was then nine years old, and with remarkably good eyes.

*Section II*

I was eleven when that delectable schooling began which I always recur to with clear satisfaction and pleasure. There was much talk in 1813 among the Norwich Unitarians of the conversion of an orthodox dissenting minister, the Rev. Isaac Perry, to Unitarianism. Mr. Perry had been minister of the Cherry Lane Chapel, and kept a large and flourishing boys' school. Of course, he lost his pulpit, and the chief part of his school. As a preacher he was wofully [sic] dull; and he was far too simple and gullible for a boys' schoolmaster. The wonder was that his school kept up so long, considering how completely he was at the mercy of naughty boys. But he was made to be a girls' schoolmaster. Gentlemanly, honourable, well provided for his work, and extremely fond of it, he was a true blessing to the children who were under him. – Rachel and I certainly had some preconception of our approaching change, when my father and mother were considering it; for we flew to an upper window one day to catch a sight of this Mr. Perry and our minister, Mr. Madge, before they turned the corner. That was my first sight of the black coat and grey pantaloons, and powdered hair, and pointing and see-sawing fore-finger, which I afterwards became so familiar with.

We were horribly nervous, the first day we went to school. It was a very large vaulted room, white-washed, and with a platform for the master and his desk; and below, rows of desks and benches, of wood painted red, and carved all over with idle boys' devices. Some good many boys remained for a time; but the girls had the front row of desks, and could see nothing of the boys but by looking behind them. The thorough way in which the boys did their lessons, however, spread its influence over us, and we worked as heartily as if we had worked together. I remember being somewhat oppressed by the length of the first morning, – from nine till twelve, and dreading a similar strain in the afternoon, and twice every day: but in a very few days, I got into all the pleasure of it; and a new state of happiness had fairly set in. I have never since felt more deeply and thoroughly the sense of progression than I now began to do. As far as I remember, we never failed in our lessons, more or less. Our making even a mistake was very rare; and yet we got on fast. This shows how good the teaching must have been. We learned Latin from the old Eton grammar, which I therefore, and against all reason, cling to, – remembering the repetition-days (Saturdays) when we recited all that Latin, prose and verse, which occupied us four hours. Two other girls, besides Rachel and myself, formed the class; and we certainly attained a capability of enjoying some of the classics, even before the two years were over. Cicero, Virgil, and a little of Horace were our main reading then: and afterwards I took great delight in Tacitus. I believe it was a genuine understanding and pleasure, because I got into the habit of thinking in Latin, and had something of the same pleasure in sending myself to sleep with Lain as with English poetry. Moreover, we stood the test of verse-making, in which I do not remember that we ever got any disgrace, while we certainly obtained, now and then, considerable praise. When Mr. Perry was gone, and we were put under Mr. Banfather, one of the masters at the Grammar School, for Latin, Mr. B. one day took a little book out of his pocket, and translated from it a passage which he desired us to turn into Latin verse. My version was precisely the same as the original, except one word (*annosa* for *antiqua*) and the passage was from the Eneid [sic]. Tests like these seem to show that we really were well taught, and that our attainment was sound, as far as it went. Quite as much care was bestowed on our French, the grammar of which we learned thoroughly, while the pronunciation was scarcely so barbarous as in most schools during the war, as there was a French lady engaged for the greater part of the time. Mr. Perry prided himself, I believe, on his process of composition being exceedingly methodical; and he enjoyed above every thing initiating us into the mystery. The method and mystery were more appropriate in our lessons in school than in his sermons in chapel; – at least, the sermons were fearfully dull; whereas the lessons were highly interesting and profitable. The only interest we could feel in his preaching was when he first brought the familiar fore-finger into play, and then built up his subject on the scaffolding which we knew so well. There was the Proposition, to begin with: then the Reason, and the Rule; then the Example, ancient and modern; then the Confirmation; and finally, the Conclusion. This may be a curious method (not altogether apostolic) of preaching the gospel; but it was a capital way of introducing some order into the chaos of girls' thoughts. One piece of our experience which I remember is highly illustrative of this. In a fit of poetic fervour one day we asked leave for once to choose our own subject for a theme, – the whole class having agreed before-hand what the subject should be. Of course, leave was granted; and we blurted out that we wanted to write 'on Music.' Mr. Perry pointed out that this was not definite enough to be called a subject. It might be on the Uses of Psalmody, or on the effect of melody in certain situations, or of martial music, or of patriotic songs, &c. &c.: but he feared there would be some vagueness if so large a subject were taken, without circumscription. However, we were bent on our own way, and he wisely let us have it. The result may easily be foreseen. We were all floating away on our own clouds, and what a space we drifted over may be imagined. We came up to Mr. P's desk all elate with the consciousness of our sensibility and eloquence; and we left it prodigiously crest-fallen. As one theme after another was read, – no two agreeing even so far as the Proposition, our folly became more and more apparent; and the master's few, mild, respectful words at the end were not necessary to impress the lesson we had gained. Up went the fore-finger, with 'You perceive, ladies' … and we saw it all; and thenceforth we were thankful to be guided, or dictated to, in the choice of our topics. Composition was my favourite exercise; and I got credit by my themes, I believe. Mr Perry told me so, in 1834, when I had just completed the publication of my *Political Economy* Tales, and when I had the pleasure of making my acknowledgments to him as my master in composition, and probably the cause of my mind being turned so decidedly in that direction. That was a gratifying meeting, after my old master and I had lost sight of one another for so many years. It was our last. If I remember right, we met on the eve of my sailing for America; and he was dead before my return.

Next to Composition, I think arithmetic was my favourite study. My pleasure in the working of numbers is something inexplicable to me, – as much as any pleasure of sensation. I used to spend my play hours in covering my slate with sums, washing them out, and covering the slate again. The fact is, however, that we had no lessons that were not pleasant. That was the season of my entrance upon an intellectual life. In an intellectual life I found then, as I have found since, refuge from moral suffering, and an always unexhausted spring of moral strength and enjoyment.

Even then, and in that happy school, I found the need of a refuge from trouble. Even there, under the care of our just and kind master, I found my passion for justice liable to disappointment as elsewhere. Some of our school-fellows brought a trumpery charge, out of school, against Rachel and me; and our dismay was great at finding that Mrs. Perry, and therefore, no doubt, Mr. Perry believed us capable of a dirty trick. We could not establish our innocence; and we had to bear the knowledge that we were considered guilty of the offence in the first place, and of telling a lie to conceal it in the next. How vehemently I used to determine that I would never, in all my life, believe people to be guilty of any offence, where disproof was impossible, and they asserted their innocence. – Another incident made a great impression on me. It happened before the boys took their final departure; and it helped to make me very glad when we girls (to the number of sixteen) were left to ourselves.

Mr. Perry was one day called out, to a visitor who was sure to detain him for some time. On such occasions, the school was left in charge of the usher, whose desk was at the farther end of the great room. On this particular day, the boys would not let the girls learn their lessons. Somehow, they got the most absurd masks within the sphere of our vision; and they said things that we could not help laughing at, and made soft bow-wows, cooings, bleatings, &c., like a juvenile House of Commons, but so as not to be heard by the distant usher. While we girls laughed, we were really angry, because we wanted to learn our lessons. It was proposed by somebody, and carried unanimously, that complaint should be made to the usher. I believe I was the youngest; and I know I was asked by the rest to convey the complaint. Quite innocently I did what I was asked. The consequence, – truly appalling to me, – was that coming up the school-room again was like running the gauntlet. O! that hiss! 'S-s-s – tell-tale – tell-tale!' greeted me all the way up: but there was worse at the end. The girls who had sent me said I was served quite right, and they would have nothing to do with a tell-tale. Even Rachel went against me. And was I really that horrible thing called a tell-tale? I never meant it; yet not the less was it even so! When Mr. Perry came back, the usher's voice was heard from the lower regions – 'Sir!' and then came the whole story, with the names of all the boys in the first class. Mr. Perry was generally the mildest of men; but when he went into a rage, he did the thing thoroughly. He became as white as his powdered hair, and the ominous fore-finger shook: and never more than on this occasion. J.D., as being usually 'correct', was sentenced to learn only thirty lines of Greek, after school. (He died not long after, much beloved.) W.D., his brother, less 'correct' in character, had fifty. Several more had from thirty to fifty; and R.S. (now, I believe, the leading innkeeper in old Norwich) – 'R.S., always foremost in mischief, must now meet the consequences.

R.S. shall learn SEVENTY lines of Greek before he goes home.' How glad should I have been to learn any thing within the compass of human knowledge to buy off those boys! They probably thought I enjoyed seeing them punished. But I was almost as horror-struck at their fate as at finding that one could be a delinquent, all in a moment, with the most harmless intentions.

An incident which occurred before Mr. Perry's departure from Norwich startled me at the time, and perhaps startles me even more now, as showing how ineffectual the conscience becomes when the moral nature of the a child is too much depressed. – All was going on perfectly well at school, as far as we knew, when Mr. Perry one day called, and requested a private interview with my father or mother. My mother and he were talking so long in the drawing-room, that dinner was delayed above half-an-hour, during which time I was growing sick with apprehension. I had no doubt whatever that we had done something wrong, and that Mr. Perry had come to complain of us. This was always my way, so accustomed was I to censure, and to stiffen myself under it, right or wrong; so that all clear sense of right and wrong was lost. I believe that, at bottom, I always concluded myself wrong. In this case it made no difference that I had no conception what it was all about. When my mother appeared, she was very grave: the mood spread, and the dinner was silent and gloomy, – father, brothers and all. My mother had in her heart a little of the old-fashioned liking for scenes: and now we had one, – memorable enough to me! 'My dear,' said she to my father, when the dessert was on the table, and the servant was gone, 'Mr. Perry has been here.' 'So I find, my love.' 'He had some very important things to say. He had something to say about – Rachel – and – Harriet.' I had been picking at the fringe of my doily; and now my heart sank, and I felt quite faint. 'Ah! here it comes', thought I, expecting to hear of some grand delinquency. My mother went on, very solemnly. 'Mr. Perry says that he has never had a fault to find with Rachel and Harriet; and that if he had a school full of such girls, he should be the happiest man alive.' The revulsion was tremendous. I cried desperately, I remember, amidst the rush of congratulations. But what a moral state it was, when my conscience was of no more use to me than this! The story carries its own moral.

What Mr. Perry came to say was, however, dismal enough. He was no man of the world; and his wife was no manager: and they were in debt and difficulty. Their friends paid their debts (my father taking a generous share) and they moved to Ipswich. It was the bitterest of my young griefs, I believe, – their departure. Our two years' schooling seemed like a lifetime to look back upon: and to this day it fills a disproportionate space in the retrospect of my existence, – so inestimable was its importance. When we had to bid our good master farewell, I was deputed to utter the thanks and good wishes of the pupils: but I could not get on for tears, and he accepted our grief as his best tribute. He went round, and shook hands with us all, with gracious and solemn words, and sent us home passionately mourning. – Though this seemed like the close of one period of my life, it was in fact the opening of its chief phase, – of that intellectual existence which my life has continued to be, more than any thing else, through its whole course.

After his departure, and before I was sent to Bristol, our mode of life was this. We had lessons in Latin and French, and I in music, from masters; and we read aloud in family a good deal of history, biography, and critical literature. The immense quantity of needlework and music-copying that I did remains a marvel to me; and so does the extraordinary bodily indolence. The difficulty I had in getting up in the morning, the detestation of the daily walk, and of all visiting, and of every break in the monotony that I have always loved, seem scarcely credible to me now, – active as my habits have since become. My health was bad, however, and my mind ill at ease. It was a depressed and wrangling life; and I have no doubt I was as disagreeable as possible. The great calamity of my deafness was now opening upon me; and that would have been quite enough for youthful fortitude, without the constant indigestion, languor and muscular weakness which made life a burden to me. My religion was a partial comfort to me; and books and music were a great resource: but they left a large margin over for wretchedness. My beloved hour of the day was when the cloth was drawn, and I stole away from the dessert, and read Shakspere [sic] by firelight in winter in the drawing-room. My mother was kind enough to allow this breach of good family manners; and again at a subsequent time when I took to newspaper reading very heartily. I have often thanked her for this forbearance since. I was conscious of my bad manners in keeping the newspaper on my chair all dinner-time, and stealing away with it as soon as grace was said; and of sticking to my Shakspere, happen what might, till the tea was poured out: but I could not forego those indulgences, and I went on to enjoy them uneasily. Our newspaper was the *Globe*, in its best days, when, without ever mentioning Political Economy, it taught it, and viewed public affairs in its light. This was not quite my first attraction to political economy (which I did not know by name till five or six years later); for I remember when at Mr. Perry's fastening upon the part of our geography book (I forget what it was) which treated of the National Debt, and the various departments of the Funds.[24] This was fixed in my memory by the unintelligible raillery of my brothers and other companions, who would ask me with mock deference to inform them of the state of the Debt, or would set me, as a forfeit at Christmas Games, to make every person present understand the operation of the Sinking Fund. I now recal Mr. Malthus's[25] amusement, twenty years later, when I told him I was sick of his name before I was fifteen. His work was talked about then, as it has been since, very eloquently and forcibly, by persons who never saw so much as the outside of the book. It seems to me that I heard and read an enormous deal against him and his supposed doctrines; whereas when, at a later time, I came to inquire, I could never find any body who had read his book. In a poor little struggling Unitarian periodical, the *Monthly Repository*, in which I made my first appearance in print,[26] a youth, named Thomas Noon Talfourd, was about this time making *his* first attempts at authorship.[27] Among his earliest papers, I believe, was one 'On the System of

Malthus', which had nothing in fact to do with the real Malthus and his system, but was a sentimental vindication of long engagements. It was prodigiously admired by very young people: not by me, for it was rather too luscious for my taste, – but by some of my family, who read it, and lived on it for awhile: but it served to mislead me about Malthus, and helped to sicken me of his name, as I told him long afterwards. In spite of this, however, I was all the while becoming a political economist without knowing it, and, at the same time, a sort of walking Concordance of Milton and Shakspere.

The first distinct recognition of my being deaf, more or less, was when I was at Mr. Perry's, – when I was about twelve years old. It was a very slight, scarcely perceptible hardness of hearing at that time; and the recognition was merely this; – that in that great vaulted school-room before-mentioned, where there was a large space between the class and the master's desk or the fire, I was excused from taking places in class, and desired to sit always at the top, because it was somewhat nearer the master, whom I could not always hear further off. When Mr. Perry changed his abode, and we were in a smaller school-room, I again took places with the rest. I remember no other difficulty about hearing at that time. I certainly heard perfectly well at chapel, and all public speaking (I remember Wilberforce in our vast St. Andrew's Hall) and general conversation everywhere: but before I was sixteen, it had become very noticeable, very inconvenient, and excessively painful to myself. I did once think of writing down the whole dreary story of the loss of a main sense, like hearing; and I would not now shrink from inflicting the pain of it on others, and on myself, if any adequate benefit could be obtained by it. But, really, I do not see that there could. It is true, – the sufferers rarely receive the comfort of adequate, or even intelligent sympathy: but there is no saying that an elaborate account of the woe would create the sympathy, for practical purposes. Perhaps what I have said in the 'Letter to the Deaf', which I published in 1834, will serve as well as anything I could say here to those who are able to sympathise at all; and I will therefore offer no elaborate description of the daily and hourly trials which attend the gradual exclusion from the world of sound.

Some suggestions and conclusions, however, it is right to offer. – I have never seen a deaf child's education well managed at home, or at any ordinary school. It does not seem to be ever considered by parents and teachers how much more is learned by oral intercourse than in any other way; and, for want of this consideration, they find too late, and to their consternation, that the deaf pupil turns out deficient in sense, in manners, and in the knowledge of things so ordinary that they seem to be matters of instinct rather than information. Too often, also, the deaf are sly and tricky, selfish and egotistical; and the dislike which attends them is the sin of the parent's ignorance visited upon the children. These worst cases are of those who are deaf from the outset, or from a very early age; and in as far as I was exempt from them, it was chiefly because my education was considerably advanced before my hearing began to go. In such a case as mine, the usual evil (far less serious) is that the sufferer is inquisitive, – *will* know every thing that is said, and becomes a bore to all the world. From this I was saved (or it helped to save me) by a kind word from my eldest brother. (From how much would a few more such words have saved me?) He had dined in company with an elderly single lady, – a sort of provincial blue-stocking in her time, – who was growing deaf, rapidly, and so sorely against her will that she tried to ignore the fact to the last possible moment. At that dinner-party, this lady sat next to her old acquaintance, William Taylor of Norwich,[28] who never knew very well how to deal with ladies (except, to his honour be it spoken, his blind mother); and Miss N – teased him to tell her all that every body said till he grew quite testy and rude. My brother told me, with tenderness in his voice, that he thought of me while blushing, as every body present did, for Miss N –; and that he hoped that if ever I should grow as deaf as she, I should never be seen making myself so irksome and absurd. This helped me to a resolution which I made and never broke, – never to ask what was said. Amidst remonstrance, kind and testy, and every sort of provocation, I have adhered to this resolution, – confident in its soundness. I think now, as I have thought always, that it is impossible for the deaf to divine what is worth asking for and what is not; and that one's friends may always be trusted, if left unmolested, to tell one whatever is essential, or really worth hearing ...

I believe my family would have made almost any sacrifice to save me from my misfortune; but not the less did they aggravate it terribly by their way of treating it. First, and for long, they insisted that it was all my own fault, – that I was so absent, – that I never cared to attend to any thing that was said, – that I ought to listen this way, or that, or the other; and even (while my heart was breaking) they told me that 'none are so deaf as those that won't hear'. When it became too bad for this, they blamed me for not doing what I was sorely tempted to do, – inquiring of them about every thing that was said, and not managing in *their* way, which would have made all right. This was hard discipline; but it was most useful to me in the end. It showed me that I must take my case into my own hands; and with me, dependent as I was upon the opinion of others, this was redemption from probable destruction. Instead of drifting helplessly as hitherto, I gathered myself up for a gallant breasting of my destiny; and in time I reached the rocks where I could take a firm stand. I felt that here was an enterprise; and the spirit of enterprise was roused in me; animating me to sure success, with many sinkings and much lapse by the way. While about it, I took my temper in hand, – in this way. I was young enough for vows, – was, indeed, at the very age of vows; – and I made a vow of patience about this infirmity; – that I would smile in every moment of anguish from it; and that I would never lose temper at any consequences from it, – from losing public worship (then the greatest conceivable privation) to the spoiling of my cap-borders by the use of the trumpet I foresaw I must arrive at. With such a temper as mine was then, an infliction so worrying, so unintermitting, so mortifying, so isolating as loss of hearing must 'kill or cure'. In time, it acted with me as a cure, (in comparison with what my temper was in my youth): but it took a long time to effect the cure; and it was so far from being evident, or even at all perceptible when I was fifteen, that my parents were determined by medical advice to send me from home for a considerable time, in hope of improving my health, nerves and temper by a complete and prolonged change of scene and objects.

Before entering upon that new chapter of my life, however, I must say another word about this matter of treatment of personal infirmity. We had a distant relation, in her young woman-hood when I was a child, who, living in the country, came into Norwich sometimes on market days, and occasionally called at our house. She had become deaf in infancy, – very very deaf; and her misfortune had been mismanaged. Truth to speak, she was far from agreeable: but it was less for that than on account of the trouble of her deafness that she was spoken of as I used to hear, long before I ever dreamed of being deaf myself. When it was announced by any child at the window that — was passing, there was an exclamation of annoyance; and if she came up the steps, it grew into lamentation. 'What *shall* we do?' 'We shall be as hoarse as ravens all day.' 'We shall be completely worn out', and so forth. Sometimes she was wished well at Jericho. When I was growing deaf, all this came back upon me; and one of my self-questionings was – 'Shall *I* put people to flight as — does? Shall *I* be dreaded and disliked in that way all my life?' The lot did indeed seem at times too hard to be borne. Yet here I am now, on the borders of the grave, at the end of a busy life, confident that this same deafness is about the best thing that ever happened to me; – the best, in a selfish view, as the grandest impulse to self-mastery; and the best in a higher view, as my most peculiar opportunity of helping others, who suffer the same misfortune without equal stimulus to surmount the false shame, and other unspeakable miseries which attend it.

By this time, the battle of Waterloo had been fought [1815]. I suppose most children were politicians during the war. I was a great one. I remember Mr. Perry's extreme amusement at my breaking through my shyness, one day, and stopping him as he was leaving the school-room, to ask, with much agitation, whether he believed in the claims of one of the many Louis XVII.'s who have turned up in my time. It must be considered that my mother remembered the first French Revolution. Her sympathies were with the royal family; and the poor little Dauphin was an object of romantic interest to all English children who knew anything of the story at all. The pretence that he was found set thousands of imaginations on fire, whenever it was raised; and among many other wonderful effects, it emboldened me to speak to Mr. Perry about other things than lessons. Since the present war[29] (of 1854) broke out, it has amused me to find myself so like my old self of forty years before, in regard to telling the servants the news. In the old days, I used to fly into the kitchen, and tell my father's servants how sure 'Boney' was to be caught, – how impossible it was that he should escape, – how his army was being driven back through the Pyrenees, – or how he had driven back the allies here or there. Then, I wanted sympathy, and liked the importance and the sensation of carrying news. Now, the way has been to summon my own servants after the evening post, and bid them get the map, or come with me to the globe, and explain to them the state of the war, and give them the latest news, probably with some of the old associations lingering in my mind; but certainly with the dominant desire to give these intelligent girls an interest in the interests of freedom, and a clear knowledge of the position and duties of England in regard to the war. I remember my father's bringing in the news of some of the Peninsular victories, and what his face was like when he told my mother of the increase of the Income-tax to ten per cent., and again, of the removal of the Income-tax. I remember the proclamation of peace in 1814, and our all going to see the illuminations; those abominable transparencies, among the rest, which represented Bonaparte (always in green coat, white breeches and boots) as carried to hell by devils, pitch-forked in the fiery lake by the same attendants, or haunted by the Duc d'Enghien.[30] I well remember the awful moment when Mr. Drummond (of the chemical lectures) looked in at the back door (on his way from the counting-house) and telling my mother that 'Boney' had escaped from Elba, and was actually in France. This impressed me more than the subsequent hot Midsummer morning when somebody (I forget whether father or brother) burst in with the news of the Waterloo slaughter. It was the slaughter that was uppermost with us, I believe, though we never had a relative, nor, as far as I know, even an acquaintance, in either army or navy.

I was more impressed still with the disappointment about the effects of the peace, at the end of the first year of it. The country was overrun with disbanded soldiers, and robbery and murder were frightfully frequent and desperate. The Workhouse Boards were under a pressure of pauperism which they could not have managed if the Guardians had been better informed than they were in those days; and one of my political panics (of which I underwent a constant succession) was that the country would become bankrupt through its poor-law. Another panic was about revolution, – our idea of revolution being, of course, of guillotines in the streets, and all that sort of thing. Those were Cobbett's grand days, and the days of Castlereagh and Sidmouth spy-systems and conspiracies.[31] Our pastor was a great radical; and he used to show us the caricatures of the day (Hone's, I think)[32] in which Castlereagh was always flogging Irishmen, and Canning spouting forth, and the Regent insulting his wife. And the hungry, haggard multitude praying for vengeance on the Court and the Ministers; and every Sunday night, after supper, when he and two or three other bachelor friends were with us, the talk was of the absolute certainty of a dire revolution. When, on my return from Bristol in 1819, I ventured to say what my conscience bade me say, and what I had been led to see by a dear aunt, that it was wrong to catch up and believe and spread reports injurious to the royal family, who could not reply to slander like other people, I was met by a shout of derision first, and then by a serious reprimand for my immorality in making more allowance for royal sinners than for others. Between my dread of this worldliness, and my sense that they had a worse chance than other people, and my further feeling that respect should be shown them on account of their function first, and their defenceless position afterwards, I was in what the Americans would call 'a fix'. The conscientious uncertainty I was in was a real difficulty and trouble to me; and this probably helped to fix my attention upon the principles of politics and the characteristics of parties, with an earnestness not very common at that age. Still, – how astonished should I have been if any one had then foretold to me that, of all the people in England, I should be the one to write the 'History of the Peace!'[33]

One important consequence of the peace was the interest with which foreigners were suddenly invested, in the homes of the middle classes, where the rising generation had seen no foreigners except old *emigrés*, – powdered old Frenchmen, and ladies with outlandish bonnets and high-heeled shoes. About this time there came to Norwich a foreigner who excited an unaccountable interest in our house, – considering what exceedingly proper people we were, and how sharp a look-out we kept on the morals of our neighbours. It was poor Polidori, well known afterwards as Lord Byron's physician, as the author of 'the Vampire', and as having committed suicide under gambling difficulties.[34] When we knew him, he was a handsome, harum-scarum young man, – taken up by William Taylor as William Taylor did take up harum-scarum young men, – and so introduced into the best society the place afforded, while his being a Catholic, or passing for such, ensured him a welcome in some of the most aristocratic of the country houses. He was a foolish rattle, – with no sense, scarcely any knowledge, and no principle; but we took for granted in him much that he had not, and admired whatever he had. For his part, he was an avowed admirer of our eldest sister, (who however escaped fancy-free); and he was for ever at our house. We younger ones romanced amazingly about him, – drew his remarkable profile on the backs of all our letters, dreamed of him, listened to all his marvellous stories, and, when he got a concussion of the brain by driving his gig against a tree in Lord Stafford's park, were inconsolable. If he had (happily) died then, he would have remained a hero in our imaginations. The few following years, (which were very possibly all the wilder for that concussion of the brain) disabused every body of all expectation of good from him; but yet when he died, frantic under gaming debts, the shock was great, and the impression, on my mind at least, deep and lasting. My eldest sister, then in a happy home of her own, felt it far more. I was then in the height of my religious fanaticism; and I remember putting away all doubts about the theological propriety of what I was doing, for the sake of the relief of praying for his soul. Many times a day, and with my whole heart, did I pray for his soul.

*Section III*

As I have said, it was the state of my health and temper which caused me to be sent from home when I was in my sixteenth year. So many causes of unhappiness had arisen, and my temper was so thoroughly ajar, that nothing else would have done any effectual good. Every thing was a misery to me, and was therefore done with a bad grace; and hence had sprung up a habit of domestic criticism which ought never to have been allowed, in regard to any one member of the family, and least of all towards one of the youngest, and certainly the most suffering of all. My mother received and administered a check now and then, which did good for the time; but the family habit was strong; and it was a wise measure to institute an entire change. Two or three anecdotes will suffice to give an idea of what had to be surmounted.

I was too shy ever to ask to be taught any thing, – except, indeed, of good-natured strangers. I have mentioned that we were well practiced in some matters of domestic management. We could sew, iron, make sweets, gingerbread and pastry, and keep order generally throughout the house. But I did not know, – what nobody can know without being taught, – how to purchase stores, or to set out a table, or to deal with the butcher and fishmonger. It is inconceivable what a trouble this was to me for many years. I was always in terror at that great mountain of duty before me, and wondering what was to become of me if my mother left home, or if I should marry. Never once did it occur to me to go to my mother, and ask to be taught: and it was not pride but fear which so incapacitated me. I liked that sort of occupation, and had great pleasure in doing what I could do in that way; insomuch that I have sometimes felt myself what General F.[35] called his wife, – 'a good housemaid spoilt'. My 'Guides to Service', ('The Maid-of-all-Work', 'Housemaid,' 'Lady's Maid' and 'Dress-maker,') written twenty years afterwards, may show something of this.[36] Meantime, never was poor creature more dismally awkward than I was when domestic eyes were upon me: and this made me a most vexatious member of the family. I remember once upsetting a basin of moist sugar into a giblet-pie. (I remember nothing else quite so bad.) I never could find any thing I was sent for, though I could lay my hands in the dark on any thing I myself wanted. On one occasion, when a workwoman was making mourning in the midst of us, I was desired to take the keys, and fetch a set of cravats for marking, out of a certain drawer. My heart sank at the order, and already the inevitable sentence rung in my ears, – that I was more trouble than I was worth; which I sincerely believed. The drawer was large, and crammed. I could not see one thing from another; and in no way could I see any cravats. Slowly and fearfully I came back to say so. Of course, I was sent again, and desired not to come back without them. That time, and again the next, I took every thing out of the drawer; and still found no cravats. My eldest sister tried next; and great was my consolation when she returned crest-fallen, – having found no cravats. My mother snatched the keys, under a strong sense of the hardship of having to do every thing herself, when Rachel suggested another place where they might have been put. There they were found; and my heart was swelling with vindictive pleasure when my mother, by a few noble words, turned the tide of feeling completely. In the presence of the workwoman, she laid her hand on my arm, kissed me, and said, 'And now, my dear, I have to beg *your* pardon.' I answered only by tears; but the words supported me for long after.

I look back upon another scene with horror at my own audacity, and wonder that my family could endure me at all. At Mr. Perry's, one of our school-fellows was a clever, mischievous girl, – so clever, and so much older than myself as to have great influence over me when she chose to try her power, though I disapproved her ways very heartily. She one day asked me, in a corner, in a mysterious sort of way, whether I did not perceive that Rachel was the favourite at home, and treated with manifest partiality. Every body else, she said, observed it. This had never distinctly occurred to me. Rachel was handy and useful, and not paralysed by fear, as I was; and, very naturally, our busy mother resorted to her for help, and put trust in her about matters of business, not noticing the growth of an equally natural habit in Rachel of quizzing or snubbing me, as the elder ones did. From the day of this mischievous speech of my school-fellow, I was on the watch, and with the usual result to the jealous. Months – perhaps a year or two – passed on while I was brooding over this, without a word to any one; and then came the explosion, one winter evening after tea, when my eldest sister was absent, and my mother, Rachel and I were sitting at work.

Rachel criticised something that I said, in which I happened to be right. After once defending myself, I sat silent. My mother remarked on my 'obstinacy', saying that I was 'not a bit convinced'. I replied that nothing convincing had been said. My mother declared that she agreed with Rachel, and that I ought to yield. Then I passed the verge, and got wrong. A sudden force of daring entering my mind, I said, in the most provoking way possible, that this was nothing new, as she always did agree with Rachel against me. My mother put down her work, and asked me what I meant by that. I looked her full in the face, and said that what I meant was that every thing that Rachel said and did was right, and every thing that I said and did was wrong. Rachel burst into an insulting laugh, and was sharply bidden to 'be quiet'. I saw by this that I had gained some ground; and this was made clearer by my mother sternly desiring me to practise my music. I saw that she wanted to gain time. The question now was how I should get through. My hands were clammy and tremulous: my fingers stuck to each other; my eyes were dim, and there was a roaring in my ears. I could easily have fainted; and it might have done no harm if I had. But I made a tremendous effort to appear calm. I opened the piano, lighted a candle with a steady hand, began, and derived strength from the first chords. I believe I never played better in my life. Then the question was – how was I ever to leave off? On I went for what seemed to me an immense time, till my mother sternly called to me to leave off and go to bed. With my candle in my hand, I said, 'Good night.' My mother laid down her work, and said, 'Harriet, I am more displeased with you to-night than ever I have been in your life.' Thought I, 'I don't care: I have got it out, and it is all true.' 'Go and say your prayers,' my mother continued; 'and ask God to forgive you for your conduct to-night; for I don't know that I can. Go to your prayers.' Thought I, – 'No, I shan't.'

And I did not: and that was the only night from my infancy to mature womanhood that I did not pray. I detected misgiving in my mother's forced manner; and I triumphed. If the right was on my side (as I entirely believed) the power was on hers; and what the next morning was to be I could not conceive. I slept little, and went down sick with dread. Not a word was said, however, then or ever, of the scene of the preceding night; but henceforth, a most scrupulous impartiality between Rachel and me was shown. If the occasion had been better used still, – if my mother had but bethought herself of saying to me, 'My child, I never dreamed that these terrible thoughts were in your mind. I am your mother. Why do you not tell me every thing that makes you unhappy?' I believe this would have wrought in a moment that cure which it took years to effect, amidst reserve and silence.

It has been a difficulty with me all my life (and its being a difficulty shows some deep-seated fault in me) how to reconcile sincerity with peace and good manners in such matters as other people's little mistakes of fact. As an example of what I mean, – a school-fellow spelled Shakspere as I spell it here. Mr. Perry put in an *a*, observing that the name was never spelt in print without an *a*. I ventured to doubt this; but he repeated his assertion. At afternoon school, I showed him a volume of the edition we had at home, which proved him wrong. He received the correction with so indifferent a grace that I was puzzled as to whether I had done right or wrong, – whether sincerity required me to set my master right before the face of his scholars. Of course, if I had been older, I should have done it more privately. But this is a specimen of the difficulties of that class that I have struggled with almost ever since. The difficulty was immensely increased by the family habit of requiring an answer from me, and calling me obstinate if the reply was not an unconditional yielding. I have always wondered to see the ease and success with which very good people humour and manage the aged, the sick and the weak, and sometimes every body about them. I could never attempt this; for it always seemed to me such contemptuous treatment of those whom I was at the moment respecting more than ever, on account of their weakness. But I was always quite in the opposite extreme; – far too solemn, too rigid, and prone to exaggeration of differences and to obstinacy at the same time. It was actually not till I was near forty that I saw how the matter should really be, – saw it through a perfect example of an union of absolute sincerity with all possible cheerfulness, sweetness, modesty and deference for all, in proportion to their claims. I have never attained righteous good-manners, to this day; but I have understood what they are since the beauties of J.S.'s character and manners were revealed to me under circumstances of remarkable trial.

While organised, it seems to me, for sincerity, and being generally truthful, except for the exaggeration which is apt to beset persons of repressed faculties, I feel compelled to state here (what belongs to this part of my life) that towards one person I was habitually untruthful, from fear. To my mother I would in my childhood assert or deny any thing that would bring me through most easily. I remember denying various harmless things, – playing a game at battledore, for one; and often without any apparent reason: and this was so exclusively to one person that, though there was remonstrance and punishment, I believe I was never regarded as a liar in the family. It seems now all very strange: but it was a temporary and very brief phase. When I left home, all temptation to untruth ceased, and there was henceforth nothing more than the habit of exaggeration and strong expression to struggle with.

Before I went to Bristol, I was the prey of three griefs, – prominent among many. I cannot help laughing while I write them. They were my bad hand-writing, my deafness, and the state of my hair. Such a trio of miseries! I was the first of my family who failed in the matter of hand-writing; and why I did remains unexplained. I am sure I tried hard; but I wrote a vulgar, cramped, untidy scrawl till I was past twenty; – till authorship made me forget manner in matter, and gave freedom to my hand. After that, I did very well, being praised by compositors for legibleness first, and in course of time, for other qualities. But it was a severe mortification while it lasted; and many bitter tears I shed over the reflections that my awkward hand called forth. It was a terrible penance to me to write letters home from Bristol; and the day of the week when it was to be done was very like the Beckwith music-lesson days. If any one had told me then how many reams of paper I should cover in the course of my life, life would have seemed a sort of purgatory to me. – As to my deafness, I got no relief about that at Bristol. It was worse when I returned in weak health. – The third misery, which really plagued me seriously, was cured presently after I left home. I made my dear aunt Kentish the depositary of my confidence in all matters; and this, of course, among the rest. She induced me to consult a friend of hers, who had remarkably beautiful hair; and then it came out that I had been combing overmuch, and that there was nothing the matter with my hair, if I would be content with brushing it. So that grief was annihilated, and there was an end of one of those trifles which 'make up the sum of human things.'[37]

And now the hour was at hand when I was to find, for the first time, a human being whom I was not afraid of. That blessed being was my dear aunt Kentish, who stands distinguished in my mind by that from all other persons whom I have ever known.

I did not understand the facts about my leaving home till I had been absent some months; and when I did, I was deeply and effectually moved by my mother's consideration for my feelings. I had somehow been brought up in a supreme contempt of boarding-schools: and I was therefore truly amazed when my mother sounded me, in the spring of 1817, about going for a year or two to a Miss Somebody's school at Yarmouth. She talked of the sea, of the pleasantness of change, and of how happy L. T – , an excessively silly girl of our acquaintance, was there: but I made such a joke of L. and her studies, and of the attainments of the young ladies, as we had heard of them, that my mother gave up the notion of a scheme which never could have answered. It would have been ruin to a temper like mine at that crisis to have sent me among silly and ignorant people, to have my 'manners formed', after the most ordinary boarding-school fashion. My mother did much better in sending me among people so superior to myself as to improve me morally and intellectually, though the experiment failed in regard to health. A brother of my mother's had been unfortunate in business at Bristol, and had not health to retrieve his affairs; and his able and accomplished wife, and clever young daughters opened a school. Of the daughters, one was within a few weeks of my own age; and we have been intimate friends from that time (the beginning of 1818) till this hour. Another was two years younger; another, two years older; while the eldest had reached womanhood. Of these clever cousins we had heard much, for many years, without having seen any of them. At the opening of the year 1818, a letter arrived from my aunt to my mother, saying that it was time the young people should be becoming acquainted; that her girls were all occupied in the school, for the routine of which Rachel was somewhat too old; but that if Harriet would go, and spend some time with them, and take the run of the school, she would be a welcome guest, &c.&c. This pleased me much, and I heard with joy that I was to go when my father took his next journey to Bristol, – early in February. My notion was of a stay of a few weeks; and I was rather taken aback when my mother spoke of my absence as likely to last a year or more. It never entered my head that I was going to a boarding-school; and when I discovered, long after, that the Bristol family understood that I was, I was not (as I once might have been) angry at having been tricked into it, but profoundly contrite for the temper which made such management necessary, and touched by the trouble my mother took to spare my silly pride, and consider my troublesome feelings.

I was, on the whole, happy during the fifteen months I spent in Bristol, though home-sickness spoiled the last half of the time. My home affections seem to have been all the stronger for having been repressed and baulked. Certainly, I passionately loved my family, each and all, from the very hour that parted us; and I was physically ill with expectation when their letters became due; – letters which I could hardly read when they came, between my dread of something wrong, and the beating heart and swimming eyes with which I received letters in those days. There were some family anxieties during the latter part of the time; and there was one grand event, – the engagement of my eldest sister, who had virtually ceased to belong to us by the time I returned home.[38]

I found my cousins even more wonderfully clever than I had expected; and they must have been somewhat surprised at my striking inferiority in knowledge, and in the power of acquiring it. I still think that I never met with a family to compare with theirs for power of acquisition, or effective use of knowledge. They would learn a new language at odd minutes; get through a tough philosophical book by taking turns in the court for air; write down an entire lecture or sermon, without missing a sentence; get round the piano after a concert, and play and sing over every new piece that had been performed.. Ability like this was a novel spectacle to me; and it gave me the pure pleasure of unmixed admiration; for I was certainly not conscious of any ability whatever at that time. I had no great deal to do in the school, being older than every girl there but one; and I believe I got no particular credit in such classes as I did join. For one thing, my deafness was now bad enough to be a disadvantage; but it was a worse disqualification that my memory, always obedient to my own command, was otherwise disobedient. I could remember whatever I had learned in my own way, but was quite unable to answer in class, like far younger girls, about any thing just communicated. My chief intellectual improvement during that important period was derived from private study. I read some analytical books, on logic and rhetoric, with singular satisfaction; and I lost nothing afterwards that I obtained in this way. I read a good deal of History too, and revelled in poetry, – a new world of which was opened to me by my cousins. The love of natural scenery was a good deal developed in me by the beauty around Bristol. One circumstance makes me think that I had become rather suddenly awakened to it not long before, – though my delight in the sea at Cromer dated some years earlier. Mr. Perry tried upon us the reading of 'L'Allegro' and 'Il Penseroso';[39] and it failed utterly. I did not feel any thing whatever, though I supposed I understood what I heard. Not long after he was gone, I read both pieces in the nursery one day; and straightway went into a transport, as if I had discovered myself in possession of a new sense. Thus it was again now, when I was transferred from flat, bleak Norfolk to the fine scenery about Bristol. Even the humble beauty of our most frequent walk, by the Logwood Mills, was charming to me, – the clear running water, with its weedy channel, and the meadow walk on the brink: and about Leigh woods, Kingsweston, and the Downs, my rapture knew no bounds.

Far more important, however, was the growth of kindly affections in me at this time, caused by the free and full tenderness of my dear aunt Kentish, and of all my other relations then surrounding me. My heart warmed and opened, my habitual fear began to melt away. I have since been told that, on the day of my arrival, when some of the school-girls asked my cousin M. what I was like, (as she came out of the parlour where I was) she said that I looked as if I was cross; but that she knew I was not; and that I looked unhappy. When I left Bristol, I was as pale as a ghost, and as thin as possible; and still very frowning and repulsive-looking; but yet with a comparatively open countenance. The counteracting influence to dear aunt Kentish's was one which visited me very strongly at the same time, – that of a timid superstition. She was herself, then and always, very religious; but she had a remarkable faculty of making her religion suggest and sanction whatever she liked: and, as she liked whatever was pure, amiable, unselfish and unspoiling, this tendency did her no harm. Matters were otherwise with me. My religion too took the character of my mind; and it was harsh, severe and mournful accordingly. There was a great furor among the Bristol Unitarians at that time about Dr. Carpenter, who had recently become their pastor. He was a very devoted Minister, and a very earnest pietist: superficial in his knowledge, scanty in ability, narrow in his conceptions, and thoroughly priestly in his temper.

He was exactly the dissenting minister to be worshipped by his people, (and especially by the young) and to be spoiled by that worship. He was worshipped by the young, and by none more than by me; and his power was unbounded while his pupils continued young: but, as his instructions and his scholars were not bound together by any bond of essential Christian doctrine, every thing fell to pieces as soon as the merely personal influence was withdrawn. A more extraordinary diversity of religious opinion than existed among his pupils when they became men and women could not be seen. They might be found at the extremes of catholicism and atheism, and every where between. As for me, his devout and devoted Catechumen, he made me desperately superstitious, – living wholly in and for religion, and fiercely fanatical about it. I returned home raving about my pastor and teacher, remembering every word he had ever spoken to me, – with his instructions burnt in, as it were, upon my heart and conscience, and with an abominable spiritual rigidity and a truly respectable force of conscience curiously mingled together, so as to procure for me the no less curiously mingled ridicule and respect of my family. My little sister, then learning to sew on her stool at my mother's knee, has since told me what she perceived, with the penetrating eyes and heart of childhood. Whenever I left the room my mother and elder sisters used to begin to quiz my fanaticism, – which was indeed quizzical enough; but the little one saw a sort of respect for me underlying the mockery, which gave her her first clear sense of moral obligation, and the nature of obedience to it.

The results of the Bristol experiment were thus good on the whole. My health was rather worse than better, through wear and tear of nerves, – home-sickness, religious emotions, overmuch study (so my aunt said, against my conviction) and medical mismanagement. I had learned a good deal, and had got into a good way of learning more. My domestic affections were regenerated; and I had become sincerely and heartily religious, with some improvement in temper in consequence, and not a little in courage, hope, and conscientiousness. The fanaticism was a stage which I should probably have had to pass through at any rate, – and by the same phase of pastor-worship, – whoever the pastor might have been.

*Source*: *Harriet Martineau's Autobiography* (3 vols, 1877 incl. *Memorials* by Maria Weston Chapman; repr. without *Memorials*, London: Virago, 1983, ed. Gaby Weiner).

**Notes**

1. Ann Cole (1780–1840), married Martineau's maternal uncle, Robert Rankin. Martineau spent 15 months at her school in Bristol in 1818–19.

2. Revd William Turner (1761–1859), minister from 1782 to the Unitarian congregation at Hanover Square, Newcastle, is now best remembered as founder of the Literary and Philosophical Society in Newcastle in 1793. Ann Turner (1796–1850) was the youngest of his seven children, whose mother had died in 1797. Martineau's visit to Newcastle and her links with Turner's family are described by Stephen Harbottle in his *The Reverend William Turner:Dissent and Reform in Georgian Newcastle upon Tyne* (Northern Universities Press, 1997).

3. John Gay (1685–1732), author of *The Beggars' Opera*, also published two volumes of *Fables* in 1727 and 1738, illustrating moral themes, often using satirical techniques. They were frequently reissued in new editions.

4. *Epistle to the Ephesians*, 6:4.

5. She was actually three when Nelson died on 21 October 1805.

6. Elizabeth (née Dyson) (d.1845), wife of Meadows Taylor (1755–1838) of Diss, Norfolk: one of the prominent Taylor family of Norwich connected with the Martineaus by marriage.

7. Latin for love of money.

8. Her father's sister, Margaret (1756–1840), Mrs James Lee, who later lived with Harriet and her mother, first in Norwich and then in London.

9. Thomas Madge (1786–1870), from 1811 co-pastor, and 1812–25 sole pastor of the Octagon Chapel, Norwich.

10. Lant Carpenter (1780–1840), Minister at Lewin's Mead Chapel, Bristol, where Harriet Martineau became his 'devout and devoted Catechumen ... living wholly in and for religion, and fiercely fanatical about it' (p. 155). She suggested that James attend his school.

11. *Hymns in Prose for Children* (1781) by Anna Laetitia Barbauld (1743–1825).

12. Benjamin Franklin (1706–90), American scientist, writer and self-made man, describes his 'bold and arduous project of arriving at moral perfection' in Part II of his *Autobiography* (1817–18). He listed thirteen virtues in tabular form in a ruled book, marking down every fault he found to have been committed against each virtue every day. Franklin believed that he became 'by the endeavour, a better and a happier man' than he otherwise would have been (*Autobiography, and Other Pieces*, ed. Dennis Welland: Oxford University Press, 1970, pp. 77–85.

13. Martineau later describes the process by which she gradually lost her religious faith and became 'a free rover on the broad, bright breezy common of the universe' (I, 116).

14. *The Crofton Boys* was one of Martineau's tales for children in her *Playfellow* series (1841). It tells the story of Hugh Proctor, a schoolboy who has his foot amputated after an accident. George Eliot had 'some delightful crying over it' (*GE Letters*, I, 192: 25 May 1845).

15. Oliver Goldsmith's poem 'The Deserted Village' (1770) describes the village preacher's 'modest mansion' as being 'Near yonder copse, where once the garden smil'd' (line 137).

16. Martineau's novel of 1839, which tells of two Birmingham sisters who go to stay with their relatives in the country, and meet their future husbands.

17. Martineau's own footnote here cites her *Household Education* (1849), p. 152.

18. John Christmas Beckwith (1750–1809), organist at Norwich Cathedral since 1808, died of a stroke on 3 June 1809. According to the *Dictionary of National Biography* (1885) 'as an organist he took very high rank in his day' (IV, 90).

19. Fenelon's *Télémaque* (1699), a didactic romance, recounted the imaginary adventures of Odysseus's son Telemachus in his search for his father.

20. *Job* 29: 11.

21. Martineau describes the death of Elizabeth Martineau (née Humphrey) (1760–1810), who was the first wife of her father's older brother, Philip Meadows Martineau (1752–1829), surgeon, of Bracondale Lodge, Norwich. His second wife was a widow, Ann Dorothy Clarke (1772–1851), and their only daughter was Frances Anne (Fanny) (1812–77).

22. Martineau's footnote reads: 'Letters on the Laws of Man's Nature and Development, p. 161.' This was the book she wrote in conjunction with the phrenologist, Henry George Atkinson, and published in 1851. It was adversely reviewed by her brother James in the *Prospective Review*, finalizing the breach between them.

23. A second footnote of Martineau's refers the reader to her *Letters on the Laws*, p. 161.

24. Government stock.

25. Thomas Robert Malthus (1766–1834), economist best known for his *Essay on the Principle of Population* (1798), which argued that population increased at a faster rate than the means of sustaining it. Martineau was vilified by the press in the 1830s for allegedly espousing Malthusian ideas – thought particularly improper for an unmarried woman.

26. This was her pair of linked articles, 'Female Writers on Practical Divinity,' published under the pseudonym 'Discipulus' in the *Monthly Repository*, edited by Robert Aspland, in 1822. The journal, founded in 1806, was more important than Martineau implies. Particularly under the editorship of W.J. Fox, who was Martineau's particular mentor, it attracted some significant contributors, including John Stuart Mill and Robert Browning. Martineau became a regular contributor of reviews, essays and poems in the later 1820s and early 1830s.

27. Thomas Noon Talfourd (1795–1854), lawyer and judge, who wrote blank verse tragedies such as *Ion* (1836). He was elected MP for Reading three times between 1835 and 1847, during which time he introduced a Copyright Bill (1837). He is now probably best remembered for the Parliamentary assistance he gave Caroline Norton in her campaign for child custody rights in 1839.

28. William Taylor (1765–1836), man of letters who translated Burger's *Lenore* into English ballad metre (1790), was friendly with Southey, wrote literary criticism for the *Monthly Review*, and co-authored a memoir of Martineau's medical uncle, Philip Meadows Martineau (1831). He is a favourite butt of humour in the *Autobiography*.

29. The Crimean War (1854–56), between Russia on the one hand, and Great Britain, France and Turkey, broke out when Russia claimed the right to intervene in the affairs of Turkey, 'the sick man of Europe,' as Nicholas I of Russia called the country at the heart of the long-running 'Eastern Question'.

30.  When Louis Antoine Henri de Bourbon-Conde, Duc d'Enghien (1772–1804), was falsely accused of being involved in a conspiracy against France, and shot, there was widespread condemnation of Napoleon's behaviour in the case. The classic comment, attributed to Talleyrand, was 'C'est plus qu'un crime, c'est une faute' (it's more than a crime, it's a mistake).

31.  William Cobbett (1763–1835), radical journalist, whose *Political Register* (begun 1802) became a vehicle for working-class agitation for political and social reform. Cobbett's work had become so controversial after the 1815 peace that he fled to America for two years (1817–19). Robert Stewart, 2nd Marquess of Londonderry, better known as Viscount Castlereagh (1769–1822), played a key role in the peace negotiations and reconstruction of Europe after the Napoleonic Wars, but he was associated at home with the repressive regime of the Home Secretary from 1812–21, Henry Addington, 1st Viscount Sidmouth (1757–1844). Sidmouth responded to the widespread social and political unrest after the peace by prohibiting large public meetings and other kinds of political agitation. The Six Acts of 1819 were especially repressive. Sidmouth was also unpopular with radicals for using police spies to report on their activities.

32.  William Hone (1780–1842), political satirist, whose *Reformer's Register* (1817) criticized state abuses. Some of his later political parodies were illustrated by George Cruickshank. His political satires included *The Political House that Jack Built* (1819), and *The Queen's Matrimonial Ladder* (1820) which supported Queen Caroline in her fight to be crowned alongside her estranged husband, George IV.

33.  Her *History of England during the Thirty Years' Peace 1816–1846*, was published in two volumes in 1849–50.

34.  John William Polidori, uncle of Dante Gabriel and Christina Rossetti, and doctor and companion of Lord Byron from 1816. He took part in the famous competition between Byron, the Shelleys and himself at the Villa Diodati in Geneva in June 1816 to write a supernatural tale, which produced Mary Shelley's *Frankenstein*. His novel, *The Vampyre*, an adaptation of one of Byron's tales, was published in1819. Having parted company with Byron, he committed suicide in 1821.

35.  Unidentified.

36.  Martineau's *Guides to Service* were published in 1838–39.

37.  From Hannah More's poem 'Sensibility':

> Since trifles make the sum of human things,
> And half our misery from our foibles springs.

38.  The eldest Martineau daughter Elizabeth (1794–1850) married a Newcastle doctor, Thomas Michael Greenhow (1792–1881), in 1820. They were to be important in HM's later life when she became ill for five years with a prolapsed uterus and ovarian cyst, which she claimed had been relieved by mesmerism. Though Greenhow was her doctor, and had introduced her to her first mesmerist, relations between the two sisters deteriorated as Martineau came to prefer mesmerism to conventional medical treatment and diagnosis. Martineau also disapproved of Greenhow's publishing a report of her condition (*Medical Report of the Case of Miss H—*, 1845) in English rather than in Latin, so that everyone could read it.

39. Early (c. 1631) paired poems by John Milton celebrating the contrasting states of mirth and melancholy.

# 12

# Fanny Kemble

Frances Anne Kemble was born in 1809 into an established theatrical family, and made her acting debut as Juliet opposite her father's Mercutio and her mother's Lady Capulet in 1829. Her father was Charles Kemble (1775–1854), who managed Covent Garden, as well as being an actor; her mother was Marie Therese De Camp (1774–1838); her younger sister Adelaide Sartoris (1816–79) became a singer; and her aunt was Sarah Siddons. She became an actress to save her parents from having to sell Covent Garden, though she protests in her autobiography that she had no inclination for the stage. When her father took her on tour to America in 1833, she met and married an American planter, Pierce Butler (d. 1867), with whom she had two daughters, Fanny and Sarah. The marriage soon ran into difficulties, however, especially over slavery, which she abhorred. After their divorce in 1848, she returned to the stage and gave readings of Shakespeare, but continued living in America (Lennox, Massachusetts) to be near her daughters. She also embarked on a long autobiographical project, beginning with *Record of a Girlhood* (2 vols, 1878), and continuing with *Records of Later Life* (3 vols, 1882) and *Further Records 1848–1883* (1890). Together with her travel books, such as *Journal of a Residence on a Georgian Plantation in 1838–9* (1863), these provide an extensive response to a controversial way of life. She died in London in 1893. The following extract from *Records of a Girlhood*, which was designed primarily to be entertaining, begins when Fanny was about four years old.

At this period of my life, I have been informed, I began, after the manner of most clever children, to be exceedingly troublesome and unmanageable, my principal crime being a general audacious contempt for all authority, which, coupled with a sweet-tempered, cheerful indifference to all punishment, made it extremely difficult to know how to obtain of me the minimum quantity of obedience indispensable in the relations of a tailless monkey of four years and its elders. I never cried, I never sulked, I never resented, lamented, or repented either my ill-doings or their ill-consequences, but accepted them alike with a philosophical buoyancy of spirit which was the despair of my poor bewildered trainers.

Being hideously decorated once with a fool's cap of vast dimensions, and advised to hide, not my 'diminished head', but my horrible disgrace, from all beholders, I took the earliest opportunity of dancing down the carriage-drive to meet the postman, a great friend of mine, and attract his observation and admiration to my 'helmet', which I called aloud upon all wayfarers also to contemplate, until removed from an elevated bank I had selected for this public exhibition of myself and my penal costume, which was beginning to attract a small group of passers-by.

My next malefactions were met with an infliction of bread and water, which I joyfully accepted, observing, 'Now I am like those poor dear French prisoners, that everybody pities so.' Mrs. Siddons at that time lived next door to us; she came in one day when I had committed some of my daily offences against manners or morals, and I was led, nothing daunted, into her awful presence, to be admonished by her.

Melpomene[1] took me upon her lap, and, bending upon me her 'controlling frown', discoursed to me of my evil ways, in those accents which curdled the blood of the poor shopman, of whom she demanded if the printed calico she purchased of him 'would wash'. The tragic tones pausing, in the midst of the impressed and impressive silence of the assembled family, I tinkled forth, 'What beautiful eyes you have!' all my small faculties having been absorbed in the steadfast upward gaze I fixed upon those magnificent orbs. Mrs. Siddons set me down with a smothered laugh, and I trotted off, apparently uninjured by my great-aunt's solemn moral suasion.

A dangerous appeal, of a higher order, being made to me by my aunt's most intimate friend, Mrs. F——, a not very judicious person, to the effect, 'Fanny, why don't you pray to God to make you better?' immediately received the conclusive reply, 'So I do, and He makes me worse and worse.' Parents and guardians should be chary of handling the deep chords upon whose truth and strength the highest harmonies of the fully developed soul are to depend.

In short, I was as hopelessly philosophical a subject as Madame Roland, when, at six years old, receiving her penal bread and water with the comment, 'Bon pour la digestion!' and the retributive stripes which this drew upon her, with the further observation, 'Bon pour la circulation!' In spite of my 'wickedness', as Topsy[2] would say, I appear to have been not a little spoiled by my parents, and an especial pet and favourite of all their friends, among whom, though I do not remember him at this early period of our acquaintance, I know was Charles Young,[3] that most kindly good man, and pleasant gentleman, one of whose many amiable qualities was a genuine love for little children. He was an intimate friend of Mrs. Siddons and her brothers, and came frequently to our house; if the elders were not at home, he invariably made his way to the nursery, where, according to the amusing description he has often since given me of our early intercourse, one of his great diversions was to make me fold my fat little arms, – not an easy performance for small muscles, – and with a portentous frown, which puckered up my mouth even more than my eyebrows, receive from him certain awfully unintelligible passages from Macbeth; replying to them, with a lisp that must have greatly heightened the tragic effect of this terrible dialogue, '*My handth are of oo tolour*' (My hands are of your colour). Years – how many! – after this first lesson in declamation, dear Charles Young was acting Macbeth for the last time in London, and I was his 'wicked wife'; and while I stood at the side scenes, painting my hands and arms with the vile red stuff that confirmed the bloody-minded woman's words, he said to me with a smile, '*Ah ha! My handth are of oo tolour*'.

... To Miss B— I was indebted for the first doll I remember possessing – a gorgeous wax personage, in white muslin and cherry-coloured ribbons, who by desire of the donor was to be called Philippa, in honour of my uncle.[4] I never loved or liked dolls, though I remember taking some pride in the splendour of this, my firstborn. They always affected me with a grim sense of being a mockery of the humanity they were supposed to represent; there was something uncanny, not to say ghastly, in the doll existence and its mimicry of babyhood to me, and I had a nervous dislike, not unmixed with fear, of the smiling simulacra that girls are all supposed to love with a species of prophetic maternal instinct.

... About this time [1811 ] it was determined that I should be sent to school in France. My father was extremely anxious to give me every advantage that he could, and Boulogne, which was not then the British Alsatia it afterwards became, and where there was a girl's school of some reputation, was chosen as not too far from home to send a mite seven years old, to acquire the French language and begin her education. And so to Boulogne I went, to a school in the oddly named 'Rue tant perd tant paie', in the old town, kept by a rather sallow and grim, but still vivacious old Madame Faudier, with the assistance of her daughter, Mademoiselle Flore, a bouncing, blooming beauty of a discreet age, whose florid complexion, prominent black eyes, plaited and profusely pomatumed black hair, and full, commanding figure, attired for fete days in salmon-coloured merino, have remained vividly impressed upon my memory. What I learned here, except French (which I could not help learning), I know not. I was taught music, dancing, and Italian, the latter by a Signor Mazzochetti, an object of special detestation to me, whose union with Mademoiselle Flore caused a temporary fit of rejoicing in the school. The small seven-year-old beginnings of such particular humanities I mastered with tolerable success, but if I may judge from the frequency of my *penitences*, humanity in general was not instilled into me without considerable trouble. I was a sore torment, no doubt, to poor Madame Faudier, who, on being once informed by some alarmed passers in the street that one of her 'demoiselles' was perambulating the house roof, is reported to have exclaimed, in a paroxysm of rage and terror, 'Ah, ce ne peut etre que cette *diable* de Kemble!' and sure enough it was I. Having committed I know not what crime, I had been thrust for chastisement into a lonely garret, where, having nothing earthly to do but look about me, I discovered (like a prince in the *Arabian Nights*) a ladder leading to a trap-door, and presently was out on a sort of stone coping, which ran round the steep roof of the high, old-fashioned house, surveying with serene satisfaction the extensive prospect landward and seaward, unconscious that I was at the same time an object of terror to the beholders in the street below. Snatched from the perilous delight of this bad eminence, I was (again, I think, rather like the Arabian prince) forthwith plunged into the cellar; where I curled myself up on the upper step, close to the heavy door that had been locked upon me, partly for the comfort of the crack of light that squeezed itself through it, and partly, I suppose, from some vague idea that there was no bottom to the steps, derived from my own terror rather than from any precise historical knowledge of oubliettes and donjons, with the execrable treachery of stairs suddenly ending in mid-darkness over an abyss. I suppose I suffered a martyrdom of fear, for I remember upwards of thirty years afterwards having this very cellar, and my misery in it, brought before my mind suddenly, with intense vividness, while reading, in Victor Hugo's Notre Dame, poor Esmeralda's piteous entreaties for deliverance from her underground prison: 'Oh laissez moi sortir! j'ai froid! j'ai peur! et des betes me montent le long du corps.' The latter hideous detail certainly completes the exquisite misery of the picture. Less justifiable than banishment to lonely garrets, whence egress was to be found only by the roof, or dark incarceration in cellars whence was no egress at all, was another device, adopted to impress me with the evil of my ways, and one which seems to me so foolish in its cruelty, that the only amazement is, how anybody entrusted with the care of children could dream of any good result from such a method of impressing a little girl not eight years old. There was to be an execution in the town of some wretched malefactor, who was condemned to be guillotined, and I was told that I should be taken to see this supreme act of legal retribution, in order that I might know to what end evil courses conducted people. We all remember the impressive fable of 'Don't Care',[5] who came to be hanged, but I much doubt if any of the thousands of young Britons whose bosoms have been made to thrill with salutary terror at his untimely end were ever taken by their parents and guardians to see a hanging, by way of enforcing the lesson. Whether it was ever intended that I should witness the ghastly spectacle of this execution, or whether it was expressly contrived that I should come too late, I know not; it is to be hoped that my doing so was not accidental, but mercifully intentional. Certain it is, that when I was taken to the Grande Place the slaughter was over; but I saw the guillotine, and certain gutters running red with what I was told (whether truly or not) was blood, and a sad-looking man, busied about the terrible machine, who, it was said, was the executioner's son; all which lugubrious objects, no doubt, had their due effect upon my poor childish imagination and nervous system, with a benefit to my moral nature which I should think highly problematical.

The experiments tried upon the minds and souls of children by those who undertake to train them, are certainly among the most mysterious of Heaven-permitted evils. The coarse and cruel handling of these wonderfully complex and delicate machines by ignorant servants, ignorant teachers, and ignorant parents, fills one with pity and with amazement that the results of such processes should not be even more disastrous than they are.

In the nature of many children exists a capacity of terror equalled in its intensity only by the reticence which conceals it. The fear of ridicule is strong in these sensitive small souls, but even that is inadequate to account for the silent agony with which they hug the secret of their fear. Nursery and schoolroom authorities, fonder of power than of principle, find their account in both these tendencies, and it is marvellous to what a point tyranny may be exercised by means of their double influence over children, the sufferers never having recourse to the higher parental authority by which they would be delivered from the nightmare of silent terror imposed upon them.

The objects that excite the fears of children are often as curious and unaccountable as their secret intensity. A child four years of age, who was accustomed to be put to bed in her mother's room, and near her nursery, and was left to go to sleep alone, from a desire that she should not be watched and lighted to sleep (or in fact kept awake, after a very common nursery practice), endured this discipline without remonstrance, and only years afterwards informed her mother that she never was so left in her little bed, alone in the darkness, without a full conviction that a large black dog was lying under it, which terrible imagination she never so much as hinted at, or besought for light or companionship to dispel. Miss Martineau[6] told me once, that a special object of horror to her, when she was a child, were the colours of the prism, a thing in itself so beautiful, that it is difficult to conceive how any imagination could be painfully impressed by it; but her terror of these magical colours was such, that she used to rush past the room, even when the door was closed, where she had seen them reflected from the chandelier, by the sunlight, on the wall.

The most singular instance I ever knew, however, of unaccountable terror produced in a child's mind by the pure action of its imagination, was that of a little boy who overheard a conversation between his mother and a friend upon the subject of the purchase of some stuff, which she had not bought, 'because', said she, 'it was ell wide'. The words 'ell wide', perfectly incomprehensible to the child, seized upon his fancy, and produced some image of terror by which for a long time his poor little mind was haunted. Certainly this is a powerful instance, among innumerable and striking ones, of the fact that the fears of children are by no means the result of the objects of alarm suggested to them by the ghost-stories, bogeys, etc., of foolish servants and companions; they quite as often select or create their terrors for themselves, from sources so inconceivably strange, that all precaution  proves ineffectual to protect them from this innate tendency of the imaginative faculty. This 'ell wide' horror is like something in a German story. The strange aversion, coupled with a sort of mysterious terror, for beautiful and agreeable or even quite commonplace objects, is one of the secrets of the profound impression which the German writers of fiction produce. It belongs peculiarly to their national genius, some of whose most striking and thrilling conceptions are pervaded with this peculiar form of the sentiment of fear. Hoffman [sic] and Tieck[7] are especially powerful in their use of it, and contrive to give a character of vague mystery to simple details of prosaic events and objects, to be found in no other works of fiction. The terrible conception of the Doppelganger, which exists in a modified form as the wraith of Scottish legendary superstition, is rendered infinitely more appalling by being taken out of its misty highland half-light of visionary indefiniteness, and produced in frock-coat and trousers, in all the shocking distinctness of commonplace, everyday, contemporary life. The Germans are the only people whose imaginative folly can cope with the homeliest forms of reality, and infuse into them vagueness, that element of terror most alien from familiar things. That they may be tragic enough we know, but that they have in them a mysterious element of terror of quite indefinite depth, German writers alone know how to make us feel.

I do not think that in my own instance the natural cowardice with which I was femininely endowed was unusually or unduly cultivated in childhood; but with a highly susceptible and excitable nervous temperament and ill-regulated imagination, I have suffered from every conceivable form of terror; and though, for some inexplicable reason, I have always had the reputation of being fearless, have really, all my life, been extremely deficient in courage.

Very impetuous, and liable to be carried away by any strong emotion, my entire want of self-control and prudence, I suppose, conveyed the impression that I was equally without fear; but the truth is that, as a wise friend once said to me, I have always been 'as rash and as cowardly as a child'; and none of my sex ever had a better right to apply to herself Shakespeare's line –

A woman, naturally born to fears.[8]

The only agreeable impression I retain of my schooldays at Boulogne is that of the long half-holiday walks we were allowed to indulge in. Not the two-and-two, dull, dreary, daily procession round the ramparts, but the disbanded freedom of the sunny afternoon, spent in gathering wild-flowers along the pretty, secluded valley of the Liane, through which no iron road then bore its thundering freight. Or, better still, clambering, straying, playing hide-and-seek, or sitting telling and hearing fairy tales among the great carved blocks of stone, which lay, in ignominious purposelessness, around the site on the high, grassy cliff where Napoleon the First – the Only – had decreed that his triumphal pillar should point its finger of scorn at our conquered, 'pale-faced shores'. Best of all, however, was the distant wandering, far out along the sandy dunes, to what used to be called 'La Garenne'; I suppose because of the wild rabbits that haunted it, who – hunted and rummaged from their burrows in the hillocks of coarse grass by a pitiless pack of school-girls – must surely have wondered after our departure, when they came together stealthily, with twitching noses, ears, and tails, what manner of fiendish visitation had suddenly come and gone, scaring their peaceful settlement on the silent, solitary sea-shore.

Before I left Boulogne, the yearly solemnity of the distribution of prizes took place. This was, at Madame Faudier's, as at all French schools of that day, a most exciting event. Special examinations preceded it, for which the pupils prepared themselves with diligent emulation. The prefect, the sub-prefect, the mayor, the bishop, all the principal civil and religious authorities of the place, were invited to honour the ceremony with their presence. The courtyard of the house was partly inclosed, and covered over with scaffoldings, awnings, and draperies, under which a stage was erected, and this, together with the steps that led to it, was carpeted with crimson, and adorned with a profusion of flowers. One of the dignified personages, seated around a table on which the books designed for prizes were exhibited, pronounced a discourse commendatory of past efforts and hortatory to future ones, and the pupils, all en grande toilette, and seated on benches facing the stage, were summoned through the rows of admiring parents, friends, acquaintances, and other invited guests, to receive the prizes awarded for excellence in the various branches of our small curriculum. I was the youngest girl in the school, but I was a quick, clever child, and a lady, a friend of my family, who was present, told me many years after, how well she remembered the frequent summons to the dais received by a small, black-eyed damsel, the cadette of the establishment. I have considerable doubt that any good purpose could be answered by this public appeal to the emulation of a parcel of school-girls; but I have no doubt at all that abundant seeds of vanity, self-love, and love of display were sown by it, which bore their bad harvest many a long year after.

I left Boulogne when I was almost nine years old, and returned home, where I remained upwards of two years before being again sent to school. During this time we lived chiefly at a place called Craven Hill, Bayswater, where we occupied at different periods three different houses.

... I imagine that my education must have been making but little progress during the last year of my residence at Craven Hill. I had no masters, and my aunt Dall[9] could ill supply the want of other teachers; moreover, I was extremely troublesome and unmanageable, and had become a tragically desperate young person, as my determination to poison my sister, in revenge for some punishment which I conceived had been unjustly inflicted upon me, will sufficiently prove. I had been warned not to eat privet berries as they were poisonous, and under the above provocation it occurred to me that if I strewed some on the ground my sister might find and eat them, which would insure her going straight to heaven, and no doubt seriously annoy my father and mother. How much of all this was a lingering desire for the distinction of a public execution by guillotine (the awful glory of which still survived in my memory), how much dregs of 'Gypsy Curse' and 'Mountain Hags', and how much the passionate love of exciting a sensation and producing an effect, common to children, servants, and most uneducated people, I know not. I never did poison my sister, and satisfied my desire of vengeance by myself informing my aunt of my contemplated crime, the fulfilment of which was not, I suppose, much apprehended by my family, as no measures were taken to remove myself, my sister, or the privet bush from each other's neighbourhood.

... A quite unpremeditated inspiration which occurred to me upon being again offended – to run away – probably alarmed my parents more than my sororicidal projects, and I think determined them upon carrying out a plan which had been talked of for some time, of my being sent again to school; which plan ran a narrow risk of being defeated by my own attempted escape from home. One day, when my father and mother were both in London, I had started for a walk with my aunt and sister; when only a few yards from home, I made an impertinent reply to some reproof I received, and my aunt bade me turn back and go home, declining my company for the rest of the walk. She proceeded at a brisk pace on her way with my sister, nothing doubting that, when left alone, I would retrace my steps to our house; but I stood still and watched her out of sight, and then revolved in my own mind the proper course to pursue.

At first it appeared to me that it would be judicious, under such smarting injuries as mine, to throw myself into a certain pond which was in the meadow where I stood (my remedies had always rather an extreme tendency); but it was thickly coated with green slime studded with frogs' heads, and looked uninviting. After contemplating it for a moment, I changed my opinion as to the expediency of getting under that surface, and walked resolutely off towards London; not with any idea of seeking my father and mother, but simply with that goal in view, as the end of my walk.

Half-way thither, however, I became tired, and hot, and hungry, and perhaps a little daunted by my own undertaking. I have said that between Craven Hill and Tyburn turnpike there then was only a stretch of open fields, with a few cottages scattered over them. In one of these lived a poor woman who was sometimes employed to do needlework for us, and who, I was sure, would give me a bit of bread and butter, and let me rest; so I applied to her for this assistance. Great was the worthy woman's amazement when I told her that I was alone, on my way to London; greater still, probably, when I informed her that my intention was to apply for an engagement at one of the theatres, assuring her that nobody with talent need ever want for bread. She very wisely refrained from discussing my projects, but, seeing that I was tired, persuaded me to lie down in her little bedroom and rest before pursuing my way to town. The weather was oppressively hot, and having lain down on her bed, I fell fast asleep. I know not for how long, but I was awakened by the sudden raising of the latch of the house door, and the voice of my aunt Dall inquiring of my friendly hostess if she had seen or heard anything of me.

I sat up breathless on the bed, listening, and looking round the room perceived another door than the one by which I had entered it, which would probably have given me egress to the open fields again, and secured my escape; but before I could slip down from the bed and resume my shoes, and take advantage of this exit, my aunt and poor Mrs. Taylor entered the room, and I was ignominiously captured and taken home; I expiated my offence by a week of bread and water, and daily solitary confinement in a sort of tool-house in the garden, where my only occupation was meditation, the 'clear-obscure' that reigned in my prison admitting of none other.

This was not cheerful, but I endeavoured to make it appear as little the reverse as possible, by invariably singing at the top of my voice whenever I heard footsteps on the gravel walk near my place of confinement.

Finally I was released, and was guilty of no further outrage before my departure for Paris, whither I went with my mother and Mrs. Charles Matthews[10] at the end of the summer.

We travelled in the *malle poste*, and I remember but one incident connected with our journey. Some great nobleman in Paris was about to give a grand banquet, and the conducteur of our vehicle had been prevailed upon to bring up the fish for the occasion in large hampers on our carriage, which was the most rapid public conveyance on the road between the coast and the capital. The heat was intense, and the smell of our 'luggage' intolerable. My mother complained and remonstrated in vain; the name of the important personage who was to entertain his guests with this delectable fish was considered an all-sufficient reply. At length the contents of the baskets began literally to ooze out of them and stream down the sides of the carriage; my mother threatening an appeal to the authorities at the bureau de poste, and finally we got rid of our pestiferous load.

I was now placed at a school in the Rue d'Angouleme, Champs Elysees; a handsome house, formerly somebody's private hotel, with porte cochere, cour d'honneur, a small garden beyond, and large, lofty ground-floor apartments opening with glass doors upon them. The name of the lady at the head of this establishment was Rowden; she had kept a school for several years in Hans Place, London, and among her former pupils had had the charge of Miss Mary Russell Mitford,[11] and that clever but most eccentric personage, Lady Caroline Lamb. The former I knew slightly, years after, when she came to London and was often in friendly communication with my father, then manager of Covent Garden, upon the subject of the introduction on the stage of her tragedy of the '*Foscari*'.

... Our Saturday sewing class was a capital institution, which made most of us expert needle-women, developed in some the peculiarly lady-like accomplishment of working exquisitely , and gave to all the useful knowledge of how to make and mend our own clothes. When I left school I could make my own dresses, and was a proficient in marking and darning.

My school-fellows were almost all English, and, I suppose, with one exception, were young girls of average character and capacity. Elizabeth P—, a young person from the west of England, was the only remarkable one among them.

... Meantime, the poetical studies, or rather indulgencies of home, had ceased. No sonorous sounds of Milton's mighty music ever delighted my ears, and for my almost daily bread of Scott's romantic epics I hungered and thirsted in vain, with such intense desire, that I at length undertook to write out *The Lay of the last Minstrel* and *Marmion* from memory, so as not absolutely to lose my possession of them. This task I achieved to a very considerable extent, and found the stirring, chivalrous stories, and spirited, picturesque verse, a treasure of refreshment, when all my poetical diet consisted of *L'Anthologie francaise a l'Usage des Desmoiselles*, and Voltaire's *Henriade*,[12] which I was compelled to learn by heart, and with the opening lines of which I more than once started the whole dormitory at midnight, sitting suddenly up in my bed, and from the midst of perpetual slumbers loudly proclaiming –

> Je chante ce heros qui regna sur la France,
> Et par droit de conquete, et par droit de naissance.

More exciting reading was Madame Cottin's *Mathilde*,[13] of which I now got hold for the first time, and devoured with delight, finishing it one evening just before we were called to prayers, so that I wept bitterly during my devotions, partly from remorse at my own sinfulness in not being able to banish them from my thoughts while on my knees and saying my prayers.

But, to be sure, that baptism in the desert, with the only drop of water they had to drink, seemed to me the very acme of religious fervour and sacred self-sacrifice. I wonder what I should think of the book were I to read it now, which Heaven forfend! The really powerful impression made upon my imagination and feelings at this period, however, was by my first reading of Lord Byron's poetry. The day on which I received that revelation of the power of thought and language remained memorable to me for many a day after.

I had occasionally received invitations from Mrs. Rowden to take tea in the drawing-room with the lady parlour boarders, when my week's report for 'bonne conduite' had been tolerably satisfactory. One evening when I had received this honourable distinction, and was sitting in sleepy solemnity on the sofa, opposite my uncle John's[14] black figure in Coriolanus, which seemed to grow alternately smaller and larger as my eyelids slowly drew themselves together and suddenly opened wide, with a startled consciousness of unworthy drowsiness, Miss H—, who was sitting beside me, reading, leaned back and put her book before my face, pointing with her finger to the lines –

> It is the hour when from the boughs
> The nightingale's high note is heard.[15]

It would be impossible to describe the emotion I experienced. I was instantly wide awake, and, quivering with excitement, fastened a grip like steel upon the book, imploring to be allowed to read on. The fear, probably, of some altercation loud enough to excite attention to the subject of her studies (which I rather think would not have been approved of, even for a 'parlour boarder') prevented Miss H— from making the resistance she should have made to my entreaties, and I was allowed to leave the room, carrying with me the dangerous prize, which, however, I did not profit by.

It was bedtime, and the dormitory light burned but while we performed our night toilet, under supervision. The under teacher and the lamp departed together, and I confided to the companion whose bed was next to mine that I had a volume of Lord Byron under my pillow. The emphatic whispered warnings of terror and dismay with which she received this information, her horror at the wickedness of the book (of which of course she knew nothing), her dread of the result of detection for me, and her entreaties, enforced with tears, that I would not keep the terrible volume where it was, at length, combined with my own nervous excitement about it, affected me with such a sympathy of fear that I jumped out of bed and thrust the fatal poems into the bowels of a straw paillasse on an empty bed, and returned to my own to remain awake nearly all night. My study of Byron went no further then: the next morning I found it impossible to rescue the book unobserved from its hiding-place, and Miss H—, to whom I confided the secret of it, I suppose took her own time for withdrawing it, and so I then read no more of that wonderful poetry, which, in my after days of familiar acquaintance with it, always affected me like an evil potion taken into my blood. The small, sweet draught which I sipped in that sleepy school-salon atmosphere remained indelibly impressed upon my memory, insomuch that when, during the last year of my stay in Paris, the news of my uncle John's death at Lausanne, and that of Lord Byron at Missolonghi, was communicated to me, my passionate regret was for the great poet, of whose writings I knew but twenty lines, and not for my own celebrated relation, of whom, indeed, I knew but little.

It was undoubtedly well that this dangerous source of excitement should be sealed to me as long as possible; but I do not think that the works of imagination to which I was allowed free access were of a specially wholesome or even harmless tendency. The false morality and attitudinizing sentiment of such books as *Les Contes à ma Fille*, and Madame de Genlis' *Veillees du Chateau*, and *Adèle et Theodore*, were rubbish, if not poison.[16] ...

One great intellectual good fortune befell me at this time, and that was reading *Guy Mannering*; the first of Walter Scott's novels that I ever read – the *dearest*, therefore. I use the word advisedly, for I know no other than one of affection to apply to those enchanting and admirable works, that deserve nothing less than love in return for the healthful delight they have bestowed. To all who ever read them, the first must surely be the best; the beginning of what a series of pure enjoyments, what a prolonged, various, exquisite succession of intellectual surprises and pleasures, amounting for the time almost to happiness ...

It was not long before all this imaginative stimulus bore its legitimate fruit in a premature harvest of crude compositions which I dignified with the name of poetry. Rhymes I wrote without stint or stopping, – a perfect deluge of doggerel; what became of it all I know not, but I have an idea that a manuscript volume was sent to my poor parents, as a sample of the poetical promise supposed to be contained in these unripe productions.

*Source*: Frances Anne Kemble, *Record of a Girlhood*, 3 vols (London: Richard Bentley and Son, 1878).


**Notes**

1.  The Muse of Tragedy, and Mrs Siddons's nickname.
2.  Slave girl from Harriet Beecher Stowe's *Uncle Tom's Cabin* (1852), whose catchphrase is 'I's so awful wicked there can't nobody do nothin' with me' (ch. 20).
3.  Charles Mayne Young (1777–1856), actor who began his career in comedy and then became a leading tragedian; described by the *Dictionary of National Biography* as 'perhaps the most distinguished member of the Kemble school' (vol. LXIII, p. 367).
4.  John Philip Kemble (1757–1823), another actor, and her father's older brother.
5.  Don't Care: from the traditional rhyme: 'Don't Care was *made* to care, / Don't Care was hung, / Don't Care was put in a pot / And boiled till he was done.'
6.  Harriet Martineau (1802–76) recounts this reaction to prisms on p. 119 of this anthology.
7.  Ernst Theodor Amadeus (ETA) Hoffmann (1776–1822), German writer known for his supernatural and sinister stories; Johann Ludwig Tieck (1773–1853), Romantic writer and critic who wrote plays and stories based on fairy tales, of which the best known is *Der Blonde Eckbert* (1797).
8.  Spoken by Constance in *King John* 3.1.15.
9.  Her aunt Dall was her mother's sister, Adelaide De Camp, who had wanted to marry the Robert Arkwright whom the other Fanny Kemble married (see note 10 to Anna Jameson). Instead, she was the companion-helper of her sister Therese's household.
10. Anne Jackson was the second wife of actor Charles Matthews (1776–1835). She published her *Memoirs* in 1838–39.
11. Mary Russell Mitford (1787–1855), best known for *Our Village* (1824–32). Charles Kemble, Fanny's father, acted in her play *Foscari* (1826).
12. *La Henriade* (1728), epic poem by Voltaire (1694–1778) on the life of Henri of Navarre (Henri IV of France).
13. *Mathilde* (1805) by Madame 'Sophie' Cottin (née Marie Ristaud) (1770–1807) was a tale of the Crusades, combining the sensational with the sentimental and moral.
14. John Philip Kemble again.
15. The opening lines of Byron's erotic poem, *Parisina* (1816).
16. *Contes à ma Fille* (1817) is by Jean Nicolas Bouilly; Stephanie-Felicite du Crest de Saint-Aubin, Comtesse de Genlis (1746–1830), French writer of educational stories such as *Les Veillées du Chateau* (1784), a collection of tales, and *Adèle et Theodore* (3 vols, 1782).

# 13

# Elizabeth Sewell

Elizabeth Missing Sewell (1815–1906) was born in Newport on the Isle of Wight, one of twelve children of a solicitor, Thomas Sewell (d. 1842), and his wife, Jane Edwards. Her *Autobiography* (1907), which she says was written at her mother's request to continue a history of the family Jane Sewell had begun, is dominated by allusions to her brothers, who were distinguished, but troublesome, involving their unmarried sisters in care of their motherless children. The death of one sister-in-law, Lucy, in 1844, brought one such group of children on to their hands. Her brother, William Sewell (1804–74), Warden of New College, Oxford, and founder of Radley College, turned out to be a bad businessman, like his father, who left the family in debt. Edwards, Warden of New College, once claimed: 'My sister Elizabeth is not remarkable in any way'. In fact, she was a successful High Church novelist, whose career was launched with *Amy Herbert* (1844), and pursued with *Laneton Parsonage* (1846–48) and *The Experience of Life* (1853), based on her own childhood: 'Sarah's troubled mind was a record of my own personal feelings', she comments on her heroine (*Autobiography*, p. 115). Sewell never married, but established a girls' school at Ventnor in 1866. Much of the childhood section of her *Autobiography* is concerned with her own school experiences.

I can just recollect dimly what was quite my infancy at home. My father had removed to a larger and more convenient house in the High Street (Newport, Isle of Wight), before I was born. It adjoined Mr. James Clarke's, and had a garden stretching back into Lugley Street. Our nursery was at the top of the house, and commanded a bright view for a town, as we could see beyond our garden to the hill on which the buildings of Parkhurst Barracks now stand. We had a very kind though rather rough-mannered nurse (Sally Pond), who was devoted to us. I was very small for my age – my brothers used to call me Blighted Betty – and Sally taught me my letters by putting me upon a little chair on the table whilst she washed up the tea things. I can remember also a very early religious taste – I really cannot call it more, for it certainly did not influence my life, as I gave way to a very violent temper, and was extremely self-willed. (My mother used to say she had had the three Furies in her family – William, Emma, and myself.) But in feeling I was always open to religious impressions, and would lie in my cot, whilst the nurse was preparing to dress us, and say little prayers and hymns to myself, with a certain sense of comfort and trust.

We were all sent to school very early. It was a day school, but there were also a very few boarders. The school was kept by a Miss Crooke, a friend of my mother's, and the daughter of a post-captain in the navy. Ellen went when she was only three years and a half old. I and my two younger sisters waited till we were four.

Miss Crooke had a very independent mind, and was very clever naturally, though she could never have had much education. In temper she was hasty and capricious; her disposition was generous; but she was not particularly refined. Independence of spirit led her to set the world and its opinions at defiance. She insisted upon certain strict rules of dress, such as not wearing coloured sashes, or lace, or embroidery, and having the hair cut close like boys. She was a Radical in politics, and I have heard of her standing at an open window wearing a bright blue bow on the day of a violently contested election when the town was in an uproar about the Reform Bill; but she was an absolute despot in her own person, and when urged beyond her patience to break her rules, she was heard one day to exclaim, 'Not if the King of England himself were to ask me!' Still she had very noble qualities, strong religious principles, and a love of truth carried even to an extreme. She was unfitted to manage any but very young children, to whom she would sometimes show tenderness, and in after years we suffered much from her peculiarities; but we were too much afraid of her to complain of anything we did not like, and my dear mother never knew, until we were grown up and had left the school, all we endured there.

The contrast between school and home was very great. Home was a paradise of freedom. My mother insisted indeed upon implicit and instantaneous obedience, but she never fretted us, and she entered into all our amusements. There was much variety in our life from the number of persons, connected with my father's business, who came to the house. I can understand now what a charm my mother's ease of manner and exceeding kindness of heart were to every one. She must have been naturally very clever; for, although she had received little or no education, her knowledge of books, and her memory for poetry and apt quotations, were quite remarkable. She often talked to us of her studies as a girl; how she used not only to devour novels, and read Sir Charles Grandison every winter, but how she also taught herself a little French, learned by heart long passages from the great poets, sometimes read history, and especially delighted in Bayley's Dictionary,[1] with its long meanings and rules for pronunciation. The greater part of what may be termed her education was gained, I imagine, from constant intercourse with my father and the young men articled to my great-uncle, Richard Clarke, who was himself a man of literary tastes, and assisted Sir Richard Worsley in writing his *History of the Isle of Wight*.[2]

... As little girls, we were kept in the background when strangers were present; but my mother devoted her evenings to us, helping us in games, etc.; and when we went to bed she would go upstairs with us and read to us whilst we were being undressed, because she did not like us to run the risk of being frightened by ghost stories told by the nursery-maids, as she had been once frightened herself. I can recall now the pleasure with which (taking my turn with my sisters) I used to jump up into her lap and listen whilst she read to us *Anson's Voyages*, or *Lemprier's Tour to Morocco*, or the *History of Montezuma*.[3] When she had finished, we all, kneeling around her, said our prayers and went to bed happy.

Our house in the High Street was a very pleasant one. My father added to it from time to time, and took in a large space of pretty garden at the back. My mother, however, could not bear going to it, she was so fond of the house she left, which had a much larger drawing-room. She told me that she cried the first day they took possession of the house in High Street. I was born in this house, 19th February, 1815, and lived in it for seven and twenty years, till my father's death.

My father was a very different person from my mother. He was irritable and cold-mannered, but most benevolent and really tender-hearted. His kindness of disposition was indeed almost a fault, for it led him into imprudence, and he would sometimes do what might be really an injury to his own family, rather than favour them against the interests of others. We were all afraid of him, though he scarcely ever punished us. Yet one of our chief delights, as we grew up, was to ride with him over the farms which, as agent to many landlords, he was accustomed to visit. He scarcely spoke to us, but we trotted or ambled by his side through the island lanes, and were quite satisfied.

When I look back upon those days the style of our education seems strange almost beyond belief. Now, girls, as a rule, are supposed to learn everything, and be made to understand everything. At Miss Crooke's we were taught to read and spell correctly, to write and cipher; we learned Pinnock's *Catechisms* of History and geography, and parsed sentences grammatically.[4] For religious instruction we read portions of the Old Testament, and the Gospels, and Acts of the Apostles in a class every day, using Mrs Trimmer's *Selections*; and on Sundays we repeated the Collect and learned Watts's hymns, besides going through the Church Catechism. We also had Crossman's *Catechism*[5] given us as an explanation of the

Church Catechism; but this Sunday work refers to an after period of our school life. At home we were only expected to repeat the Catechism as we learned it, by very slow degrees; and with a Noah's Ark to amuse us, and the pleasure of dining in the parlour, and looking at the pictures in a large Bible, Sunday was a happy, bright day though the church services were very dreary. In addition to the English lessons at Miss Crooke's, we were taught music and drawing by very indifferent country masters, and had French lessons from a very courteous old gentleman, the Abbé de Grenthe, who had left his country during the First Revolution and set up a school in Newport. He told us half the words in the lesson we were expected to repeat, and translated one word before us as we read to him, so that we were certain of not making a mistake. We were required to put French into English, but never English into French, and thus had but little difficulty in any way.

This amount of instruction, with the addition of an occasional lesson in the working of problems on the globes, from our chief writing master (the head of the school, which had once been the Abbé de Grenthe's), and, as we grew older, a little very elementary geometry in the holidays from our brother's tutor, was really all the teaching I had till I was thirteen. Now, such limited and mechanical lessons would be scoffed at, yet there was a counter-balancing good. All that we did was done thoroughly. Our short repetitions from Pinnock's Catechisms were made without the smallest hesitation or the change of a single word; and, to this day, my acquaintance with the History of England rests for a foundation upon a remembrance of the particular page in Pinnock in which the events were noted. Then we went over the little books again and again. The *Catechism of English History* I repeated from the time I was seven or eight years old (I should think) till I left school. Of course the facts were indelibly impressed upon my memory, and without confusion. They were few and far between, but they were landmarks which I have been thankful for ever since.

The strictness of the school discipline was extreme. Not a word was spoken in school time; and as for disobedience, it never entered our thoughts as a possibility. Three mistakes, however trivial, in a lesson learned by rote, were punished by another lesson. To begin a word twice, or even to hesitate, was reckoned as a mistake; and to secure our attention, we were required to fix our eyes upon Miss Crooke's nose, rather a prominent object, and so far helpful. If we were absent from school even from illness, all the absent-lessons (as we called them) were required of us before we could receive the usual reward – a card or ticket marked 'merit' in black letters. A certain number of these were exchanged when gained, for a similar ticket with red letters; and for three of the red we received a golden ticket, 'which was a piece of purple or red leather' made into a ticket and marked with gilt letters. Miss Crooke certainly understood the importance of form, and colour, and ceremony in influencing children's minds. The beauty of the golden tickets formed their chief value in our eyes; and although, when we had gained three, we were allowed to exchange them for a half-crown, I really believe no child ever gave them up and received the money instead without considerable regret. These rewards were not very expensive, they were so difficult to obtain. As a rule we could only gain one black ticket in the day, and for that we were required to be perfect in every lesson, and we might for any fault be made to forfeit a ticket. I was at Miss Crooke's from the age of four to thirteen, but I never gained more than one half-crown, though I was always striving after it; yet the hope was something to work for.

Miss Crooke's great error was that her system was unbending, and applied without consideration to all characters, careless or attentive, conscientious or indifferent. She was most ingenious in inventing punishments, and all fared alike when a rule was broken. So far, no doubt, she was on the whole right, but she had no opening for extenuating circumstances. For accidental, equally with deliberate offences, we were often disgraced by having to stand up in a corner of the schoolroom with some mark of ignominy upon us. A ram's horn (picked up on the Downs), a rod, an old green tassel, and (tradition said) an old shoe were converted into instruments of humiliation by being fastened on the offender's head. The shoe was before my time. I have, however, a vivid recollection of the ram's horn, and also of some brown-paper ass's ears.

Upon one point – truth – Miss Crooke was severe even to a fault. The smallest detail, the slightest equivocation, was punished by a month's disgrace. During that period no tickets could be gained, however perfectly the lessons might be learned or the rules observed; and if a child told a lie, she was not allowed any reward for three months, and was obliged to stand up in the schoolroom for several hours with a long black gown on, and a piece of red cloth – cut in the shape of a tongue, and on which the word 'Liar' was worked in white letters – fastened round the neck so as to hang down in front. The awe which fell upon the school when Miss Crooke in a solemn voice said, 'Put on the Gown and the Liar's tongue', was indescribable. I never had them on but once, and that was for a falsehood which I confessed of my own accord, because I was too miserable to bear the burden of a guilty conscience. I had written in a little memorandum book the letters 'O. W.' meaning 'Old Witch', an epithet which some of us had ventured to apply to Miss Crooke. When the little book was called for (I forget why), I was frightened and threw it away, and then said I had lost it. No mercy was shown me, and the wretchedness of feeling which the punishment caused I shall never forget. It seemed as if I were marked for life, the only one of my family who had ever committed such an offence. I can recollect, though, having deceived before; so I suppose my conscience had not always been so tender.

... I have mentioned previously that I had a very bad temper, and I was also extremely alive to praise or blame; even as a very little girl I liked to dream of being noticed. I can remember going to the Newport Fair with my sisters, and watching some dancing on the tight-rope, and then coming home and fastening a string from one post of a summer-house to another, and moving along it as far as I could without danger, whilst in imagination I was displaying my feats before a large party which I had heard had assembled at Lord Yarborough's cottage at St. Lawrence to meet one of the Royal Dukes. But although I could thus be vain in my thoughts, I shrank from being actually brought forward, and did not at all enjoy personal remarks even when they were to my credit. But there was little fear of my being spoilt by praise, I was laughed at because I was easily made to cry, and scolded because I was perverse and troublesome; and I always felt myself rather a black sheep in the family, though I am sure I had longings for something better, and vague dreams of distinction, kept under from the sense of being a girl.

The religious taste, of which I have before spoken, continued to show itself as time went on, though still my conduct was not influenced by it. When I was able to write with tolerable ease I remember composing little sermons for my younger sisters, which doubtless would have been much better applied to myself; and whilst yet in the nursery, I learned the greater portion of the first chapter of the prophecy of Isaiah, and can repeat it at this day. No one told me to do so, or even knew that I had done it. The beauty of the language, the exquisite musical rhythm of the sentences caught my ear, but I had little perception of anything beyond.

I am afraid I was by no means a pleasant child. My quick, irritable feelings were constantly bringing me into trouble, and then I shut myself up in my own thoughts and determined to keep aloof from every one. To be alone was never unpleasant to me. In the nursery my great pleasure was to sit by myself in a dark closet, opening into a room, with a little lanthorn by my side, and read a story, whilst my sisters played about. I enjoyed hearing their voices, but I did not wish to join them. But the self-consciousness which naturally goes with such a disposition was very easily seen; and I was told that I was affected, and this again acted upon my irritable temper, and I grew more really reserved, though I am not aware that my manner showed it. I am alluding, however, rather to what I was as I grew beyond actual childhood. At the time I told the falsehood for which I was so severely punished I was about twelve years old, and had been for some time a boarder at Miss Crooke's school with my sisters.

People now would scarcely believe what Miss Crooke's house was like, especially the wretchedness of the large bedroom which we four sisters and another little girl inhabited; the uncarpeted floor, the two blocked-up windows, with a third which we were forbidden ever to look out of, on pain of paying half a crown; the great worm-eaten four-post bedsteads, without an atom of curtain or drapery; the deal tables for washing-stands, with the jugs holding rain-water, in which wonderful specimens of entomology disported themselves; the two or three old chairs which, with our trunks, were the only seats – it makes me shudder to look back upon it all, for there was nothing to cheer us, all was dreary and hopeless. The touch of the coarse sheets, on the first night of going back to school, and the sight of the large horn lanthorn, put upon the floor in the centre of the room, as our only light whilst undressing, were as chilling and depressing to the mind as to the body. In this large room we used to sit in the winter mornings learning our lessons until we were called down to a breakfast of milk and water, with an allowance of three pieces of thick bread and butter, but – except on rare occasions – no more, however hungry we might be. We were permitted, when the weather was very cold, to stand near the fire for a few minutes to warm ourselves, and then we were sent to our seats to get on as well as we could for the rest of the day. Lessons went on from morning to night with me, as a rule, for I was always in arrears, as regarded what we termed double (or extra) lessons. Those extra lessons were imposed for any and everything, even for speaking ungrammatically in playtime; saying 'come here', instead of 'come hither', being deemed an error. Once I remember having seventy lessons in arrears.

We were expected to accuse ourselves, and my conscience being a fidgety one I was always badly off; and when my regular lessons for the day were over, I used to sit until bed-time with my back to a long table, on which two candles were placed, and learn by heart columns of French idioms, knowing that I was scarcely advanced a step in the payment of my debt, and that I should be sure to increase it the next day. These lessons we said to each other, so Miss Crooke did not know how many were incurred, and when at the last she was told of my amount and my sister Emma's she saw that she had been unwise and wiped them out; but at that time the discipline was so strict, that no one dared to swerve from the exact law laid down as to the perfect correctness of the repetition. At eight o'clock we said our settled form of prayer, kneeling round the fire in the schoolroom, and taking turn week by week to repeat it aloud, and then we were sent to our dreary rooms.

The school itself was curiously mixed in a social sense. There were a few children of the professional class, and many whose parents were farmers and shopkeepers; but we were too young to think about difference of position, and Miss Crooke, who, in some ways, was very wise, avoided anything like undesirable intimacy by obliging us all to use special forms of civility amongst each other. 'Miss' was the one appellation, we never adopted Christian names – yet we played together when the opportunity was given, and, stiff and dull though the life was, there were some pleasures in it; – I doubt if children can exist without pleasure. If we said our lessons particularly well, we were allowed to have tea and sugar instead of milk and water; or (a most singular reward!) we could stand up before dinner began and say, 'If you please, ma'am, I claim gravy'. This implies that as a rule we did not have gravy, which was the fact. Such little extra indulgences made us for the time proud and happy. Now and then, also, if Miss Crooke was in a good humour, she would tell us a story, or give us an amusing book to read; and although it may seem hard that we should have had nothing but trifles to brighten our lives, I have learnt from experience to be grateful for the temper of mind which was thus cultivated, and which has enabled me through my whole life to find amusement and diversion in small things ...

When I was nearly thirteen it was proposed that Ellen and I should leave Miss Crooke's, and go to a school at Bath, for the advantage of masters; this was my mother's doing. The education of girls was but little considered in those days, but my mother, in after years, told us that she had resolved her girls as well as her boys should be well educated, because then they would be prepared for any change of fortune which might meet them in life. Just at this time, after telling the falsehood to which I have before alluded, I had worked myself into a very fidgety self-worrying state of mind, which I daresay was one reason for the change of school. Miss Crooke herself must have been frightened at the mental condition to which her over-strictness had brought me, and she would have had still greater cause for alarm if she had known all that passed in my mind.

I was always given to strange scrupulous fancies, and not long before I had made myself miserable, after reading about Jephthah's vow,[6] because I imagined that every time the thought of making a vow came into my head I had actually made it, and was bound to keep it. I even went so far as to worry myself with the question whether I was not bound to kill my mother, because I thought I had made a vow that I would. And another notion I had was that I must go off to America because I thought I had vowed I would. Of course no one knew about these troubles; I could have borne anything rather than talk to Miss Crooke, and I had never been accustomed to unreserve with my mother; and I bore all, as best I could, in great wretchedness of mind, until at last the fancies reached a point when my own common-sense told me they must be stopped at all hazards, and I determined to cure myself. With this view I accustomed myself, whenever the troublesome thoughts came into my head, deliberately to count six, and then say to myself, 'No, I won't think of it', and thus the thoughts, being constantly kept down, after a time went away.

Of all this inner suffering, Miss Crooke knew nothing; her only idea of my worries arose from what went on after I had confessed to her that I had told a falsehood, and thrown away the paper on which I had marked the letters 'O.W.' for 'Old Witch'.

The day after my grievous punishment for the lie, I became very miserable, from the thought of what Miss Crooke would say if she knew the full extent of my naughtiness. I went to my companions, and warned them that I was going to confess that we had called her names. None of them, I imagine, supposed it possible that I should carry out my threat; but the following afternoon, after going through my usual reading lesson, I turned round to Miss Crooke, and said aloud, so that every one might hear, 'If you please, ma'am, I called you a witch'.

I can scarcely forbear a smile now when I think of the scene; but the moment was one of terrible agony to me then, for I never dreaded any one, and I don't think I ever could dread any one, as I did Miss Crooke, and I knew she would have no mercy upon me.

There was a fearful silence after I had made my confession. Miss Crooke only said, 'Go and sit down in your place', and so I did, and there I remained in a state of dull hopelessness until the day-scholars had gone. Then all the boarders were called up, made to put their hands on their hearts as a sign of sincerity, and a token that they would speak the truth, and were most solemnly commanded to tell all they knew about the wicked proceedings. It was a kind of inquisitorial examination, and the punishment was a species of slow torture, for it went lingering on for weeks. We were all exiled from favour, not allowed to have any rewards for our lessons, and subjected to cold looks, and cold words, until at length we became comparatively callous to them. My conscience, however, went on working; having once begun to confess, the practice became a necessity, and

I begged that I might be allowed to tell every day the things I had done wrong, because I felt so wicked. Miss Crooke at first treated me as a converted penitent, but by degrees she must have become alarmed. My confessions verged on the ludicrous, and the climax must have been reached when having received an order in common with my companions to mention if we saw any black beetles in the schoolroom, I made it a subject of confession that I had seen a black beetle crawl out from under a large bureau, and had not told of it.

The state of mind which led to such a confession must have been incomprehensible to one who for years had not been subject in small matters to any daily human law but her own will. Miss Crooke talked to my mother, and the result was that I was one day told by my mother to leave off all confessions, and not to tell any one but herself my conscience worries. This order set me at rest at once, for my mother was so indulgent that I soon learned not to distress myself about imaginary shortcomings. And thus ended my first great trouble in life. And yet it did not really end, for to this day I can feel its effects. The greatest difficulties that have come in my way since, as regards self-discipline, have arisen from fatal necessity of using in those years my common-sense as a defence against the working of a morbid and over-strained conscience. It laid the foundation of a sophistical habit of mind; and some of the actions of my life for which I most condemn myself can be traced to it. Happily I was by nature true, and though I might for a time satisfy myself in the indulgence of a wrong inclination by reasoning against what I persuaded myself was only the check of my fidgety conscience, yet in the end truth generally gained the victory; not, however, until I had often yielded sufficiently to be heartily ashamed of myself. I am speaking of this temper of mind now without reference to religious principle, which, of course, must be recognised as, through God's grace, the chief means by which we escape the temptations of sophistry.

It is but just to say when writing about Miss Crooke, that, notwithstanding all I suffered from her system of education, I always respected, and have never ceased to respect her. She acted entirely according to her view of what was right and would in the end be good for us; and she was very charitable and strictly honourable. I remember, when at school, a little girl came from London to be a boarder, much to our surprise, for we thought that education in London must be very superior to that which could be obtained in the Isle of Wight. Great care was taken of this child, and she was especially favoured. Years after I learned that she was the child of a London tradesman, to whom Miss Crooke's father had owed some money which he was unable to pay; and this was the only mode by which the obligation could be recognised.

When Miss Crooke gave up her school she had only secured forty pounds a year for all her expenses; but she was so independent in her tone of mind that no one ventured openly to offer her any assistance. The knowledge that she could not have the comforts and the freedom from anxiety which her age required, and for which she had worked for so many years, distressed her friends; and a little plan was formed by which she might be helped without hurting her feelings. It was arranged that a formal letter should be written to her by a lawyer in London, stating that if she would send a certificate of her birth, and baptism to him, he was empowered to forward to her fifty pounds annually. No explanation was given, but the necessity of sending every year, on a fixed day, a certificate that she was alive, was strongly enforced.

In her simplicity and ignorance of business Miss Crooke, though surprised and delighted, made no inquiries. She said that she supposed it was money due to her father which was thus paid to her; and yearly, as the day came round, she was in a state of excitement and anxiety until she had sent her certificate in due form. Thus she was freed from care, and had enough for her small needs; and she died without any knowledge of the source from which the money came. I believe my brother William, who had been taught by Miss Crooke to read and spell, was the chief originator of the innocent deception, and contributed largely towards carrying it out.

Very soon after I had disturbed the school by my confession, Ellen and I were taken away from Miss Crooke's care. It was a rejoicing time. The last night that we all stood up to repeat some lesson – I forget what – and when I had to give up my tickets and say 'Good-bye' to absent-and-disgrace-lessons, I felt proudly ambitious for the future. I was going into a new world, and in that world I was resolved to make my mark.

*Source*: *The Autobiography of Elizabeth M. Sewell*, ed. Eleanor M Sewell (London: Longmans, 1907).

## Notes

1. Pierre Bayle (1647–1706), French philosopher, whose *Dictionnaire historique et critique* (1697) included erudite notes and commentaries on each article.

2. Sir Richard Worsley (1751–1805), MP for Newport, Isle of Wight (1774–84) and author of *The History of the Isle of Wight* (1781).

3. William Lempriere (d. 1834), doctor and travel writer, was detained in Morocco against his will in 1789–90, to provide medical services. He wrote *A Tour from Gibraltar to Tangier ... and thence ... to Morocco* (1791); Montezuma (1466–1520) was the last Aztec Emperor of Mexico.

4. William Pinnock (1782–1843), educational writer, produced eighty-three *Catechisms* (including one on the *History of England*, 1822, and one on *British Geography*, 1827), which imparted knowledge through a question-and-answer system.

5. *An Introduction to the Knowledge of the Christian Religion* (2 parts, 1742) by Henry Crossman.

6. In Judges 11 Jephthah vows to God that if his enemies, the children of Ammon, are delivered into his hands, he will sacrifice whatever comes out of his house to meet him on his return. He is victorious in battle, but his only daughter is the first to greet him, and after two months on the mountains, she is duly sacrificed.

# 14

# Frances Power Cobbe

Frances Power Cobbe was born in Dublin in 1822, the youngest child and only daughter of a magistrate and landowner, Charles Cobbe (d. 1857) and his wife, Frances Conway (d. 1847). Educated initially at home in Ireland, she attended school in Brighton for two years (1836–38), but felt her real education began when she started a serious course of reading at home. Using the money her father left her on his death to travel, Cobbe became known chiefly as a philanthropist, who worked with the 'ragged school' scheme established by Mary Carpenter in Bristol, and then as an active anti-vivisectionist. She also published essays on women's rights, including *Essays on the Pursuits of Women* (1863) and *The Duties of Women* (1881). Cobbe never married, but set up house in Wales with her friend Mary Lloyd in 1884 when she inherited a further legacy. She died in 1904. Her autobiography, the two-volume *Life of Frances Power Cobbe*, from which the following excerpt is taken, was published in 1894.

I was born on the 4th December, 1822, at sunrise in the morning. There had been a memorable storm during the night, and Dublin, where my father had taken a house that my mother might be near her doctor, was strewn with the wrecks of trees and chimney pots. My parents had already four sons, and after the interval of five years since the birth of the youngest, a girl was by no means welcome. I have never had reason, however, to complain of being less cared for or less well treated in every way than my brothers. If I have become in mature years a 'Woman's Rights' Woman' it has not been because in my own person I have been made to feel a Woman's Wrongs. On the contrary, my brothers' kindness and tenderness to me have been unfailing from my infancy. I was their 'little Fa'', their pet and plaything when they came home from their holidays; and rough words not to speak of knocks, – never reached me from any of them or from my many masculine cousins, some of whom, as my father's wards, I hardly distinguished in childhood from brothers.

A few months after my birth my parents moved to a house named Bower Hill Lodge in Melksham, which my father hired, I believe, to be near his boys at school, and I have some dim recollections of the verandah of the house, and also of certain raisins which I appropriated, and of suffering direful punishment at my father's hands for the crime! Before I was four years old we returned to Newbridge, and I was duly installed with my good old Irish nurse, Mary Malone, in the large nursery at the end of the north corridor – the most charming room for a child's abode I have ever seen. It was so distant from the regions inhabited by my parents that I was at full liberty to make any amount of noise I pleased; and from the three windows I possessed a commanding view of the stable yard, wherein there was always visible an enchanting spectacle of dogs, cats, horses, grooms, gardeners, and milkmaids. A grand old courtyard it is; a quadrangle about a rood in size surrounded by stables, coach-houses, kennels, a laundry, a beautiful dairy, a labourer's room, a paint shop, a carpenter's shop, a range of granaries and fruit-lofts with a great clock in the pediment in the centre; and a well in the midst of all. Behind the stables and the kennels appear the tops of walnut and chestnut trees and over the coach-houses on the other side can be seen the beautiful old kitchen garden of six acres with its lichen-covered red brick walls, backed again by trees; and its formal straight terraces and broad grass walks.

In this healthful, delightful nursery, and in walks with my nurse about the lawns and shrubberies, the first years of my happy childhood went by; fed in body with the freshest milk and eggs and fruit, everything best for a child; and in mind supplied only with the simple, sweet lessons of my gentle mother. No unwholesome food, physical or moral, was ever allowed to come in my way till body and soul had almost grown to their full stature. When I compare such a lot as this (the common lot, of course, of English girls of the richer classes, blessed with good fathers and mothers) with the case of the hapless young creatures who are fed from infancy with insufficient and unwholesome food, perhaps dosed with gin and opium from the cradle, and who, even as they acquire language, learn foul words, curses and blasphemies, – when I compare, I say, my happy lot with the miserable one of tens of thousands of my brother men and sister women, I feel appalled to reflect, by how different a standard must they and I be judged by eternal Justice!

In such an infancy the events were few, but I can remember with amusement the great exercise of my little mind concerning a certain mythical being known as 'Peter'. The story affords a droll example of the way in which fetishes are created among child-minded savages. One day, (as my mother long afterwards explained to me), I had been hungrily eating a piece of bread and butter out of doors, when one of the greyhounds, of which my father kept several couples, bounded past me and snatched the bread and butter from my little hands. The outcry which I was preparing to raise on my loss was suddenly stopped by the bystanders judiciously awakening my sympathy in Peter's enjoyment, and I was led up to stroke the big dog and make friends with him. Seeing how successful was this diversion, my nurse thenceforward adopted the practice of seizing everything in the way of food, knives, &c., which it was undesirable I should handle, and also of shutting objectionably open doors and windows, exclaiming 'O! Peter! Peter has got it! Peter has shut it!' – as the case might be. Accustomed to succumb to this unseen Fate under the name of Peter, and soon forgetting the dog, I came to think there was an all-powerful, invisible Being constantly behind the scenes, and had so far pictured him as distinct from the real original Peter that on one occasion when I was taken to visit at some house where there was an odd looking end of a beam jutting out under the ceiling, I asked in awe-struck tones: 'Mama! is that Peter's head?'

My childhood, though a singularly happy, was an unusually lonely one. My dear mother very soon after I was born became lame from a trifling accident to her ankle (ill-treated, unhappily, by the doctors) and she was never once able in all her life to take a walk with me. Of course I was brought to her continually; first to be nursed, – for she fulfilled that sacred duty of motherhood to all her children, believing that she could never be so sure of the healthfulness of any other woman's constitution as of her own. Later, I seem to my own memory to have been often cuddled up close to her on her sofa, or learning my little lessons, mounted on my high chair beside her, or repeating the Lord's Prayer at her knee. All these memories are infinitely sweet to me. Her low, gentle voice, her smile, her soft breast and arms, the atmosphere of dignity which always surrounded her, – the very odour of her clothes and lace, redolent of dried roses, come back to me after three score years with nothing to mar their sweetness. She never once spoke angrily or harshly to me in all her life, much less struck or punished me; and I – it is a comfort to think it – never, so far as I can recall, disobeyed or seriously vexed her. She had regretted my birth, thinking that she could not live to see me grow to womanhood, and shrinking from a renewal of the cares of motherhood with the additional anxiety of a daughter's education. But I believe she soon reconciled herself to my existence, and me, first her pet, and then her companion and even her counsellor. She told me, laughingly, how, when I was four years old, my father happening to be away from home she made me dine with her, and as I sat in great state beside her on my little chair I solemnly remarked: 'Mama, is it not a very *comflin* thing to have a little girl?' an observation which she justly thought went to prove that she had betrayed sufficiently to my infantine perspicacity that she enjoyed my company at least as much as hers was enjoyed by me.

My nurse who had attended all my brothers, was already an elderly woman when recalled to Newbridge to take charge of me; and though a dear, kind old soul and an excellent nurse, she was naturally not much of a playfellow for a little child, and it was very rarely indeed that I had any young visitor in my nursery or was taken to see any of my small neighbours. Thus I was from infancy much thrown on my own resources for play and amusement; and from that time to this I have been rather a solitary mortal, enjoying above all things lonely walks and studies; and always finding my spirits rise in hours and days of isolation. I think I may say I have *never* felt depressed when living alone. As a child I have been told I was a very merry little chick, with a round, fair face and abundance of golden hair; a typical sort of Saxon child. I was subject then and for many years after, to furious fits of anger, and on such occasions I misbehaved myself exceedingly. 'Nanno' was then wont peremptorily to push me out into the long corridor and bolt the nursery door in my face, saying in her vernacular, 'Ah, then! you *bould Puckhawn* (audacious child of Puck)! I'll get *shut* of you!' I think I feel now the hardness of that door against my little toes, as I kicked at it in frenzy. Sometimes, when things were very bad indeed, Nanno conducted me to the end of the corridor at the top of a very long winding stone stair, near the bottom of which my father occasionally passed on his way to the stables. 'Yes, Sir! Yes, Sir! She'll be good immadiently, Sir, you needn't come upstairs. Sir!' Then, *sotto voce*, to me, 'Don't ye hear the Masther? Be quiet now, my darlint, or he'll come up the stairs!' Of course, 'the Masther' seldom or never was really within earshot on these occasions. Had he been so Nanno would have been the last person seriously to invoke his dreaded interference in my discipline. But the alarm usually sufficed to reduce me to submission. I had plenty of toddling about out of doors and sitting in the sweet grass making daisy and dandelion chains, and at home playing with the remnants of my brother's Noah's Ark, and a magnificent old baby-house which stood in one of the bedrooms, and was so large that I can dimly remember climbing up and getting into the doll's drawing-room.

My fifth birthday was the first milestone on Life's road which I can recall. I recollect being brought in the morning into my mother's darkened bedroom (she was already then a confirmed invalid), and how she kissed and blessed me, and gave me childish presents, and also a beautiful emerald ring which I still possess, and pearl bracelets which she fastened on my little arms. No doubt she wished to make sure that whenever she might die these trinkets should be known to be mine. She and my father also gave me a Bible and Prayer Book, which I could read quite well, and  proudly took next Sunday to church for my first attendance, when the solemn occasion was much disturbed by a little girl in a pew below howling for envy of my white beaver bonnet, displayed in the fore-front of the gallery which formed our family seat. 'Why did little Miss Robinson cry?' I was deeply inquisitive on the subject, having then and always during my childhood regarded 'best clothes' with abhorrence.

Two years later my grandmother, having bestowed on me, at Bath, a sky-blue silk pelisse, I managed nefariously to tumble down on purpose into a gutter full of melted snow the first day it was put on, so as to be permitted to resume my little cloth coat.

Now, aged five, I was emancipated from the nursery and allowed to dine thenceforward at my parents' late dinner, while my good nurse was settled for the rest of her days in a pretty ivy-covered cottage with large garden, at the end of the shrubbery. She lived there for several years with an old woman for servant, who I can well remember, but who must have been of great age, for she had been under-dairymaid to my great-grandfather, the Archbishop, and used to tell us stories of 'old times'. This 'old Ally's' great-grandchildren were still living, recently in the family service in the same cottage which poor 'Nanno' occupied. Ally was the last wearer of the real old Irish scarlet cloak in our part of the country; and I can remember admiring it greatly when I used to run by her side and help her to carry her bundle of sticks. Since those days, even the long blue frieze cloak which succeeded universally to the scarlet – a most comfortable, decent, and withal graceful peasant garment, very like the blue cotton one of the Arab fellah-women – has itself nearly or totally disappeared in Fingal.

On the retirement of my nurse, the charge of my little person was committed to my mother's maid and housekeeper, Martha Jones. She came to my mother a blooming girl of eighteen, and she died of old age and sorrow when I left Newbridge at my father's death a half-century afterwards. She was a fine, fair, broad-shouldered woman, with a certain refinement above her class. Her father had been an officer in the army, and she was educated (not very extensively) at some little school in Dublin where her particular friend was Moore's (the poet's) sister.[1] She used to tell us how Moore as a lad was always contriving to get into the school and romping with the girls. The legend has sufficient verisimilitude to need no confirmation!

'Joney' was indulgence itself, and under her mild sway, and with my mother for instructress in my little lessons of spelling and geography, Mrs. Barbauld, Dr. Watts and Jane Taylor, I was as happy a little animal as well might be. One day being allowed as usual to play on the grass before the drawing-room windows I took it into my head that I should dearly like to go and pay a visit to my nurse at her cottage at the end of the shrubbery. 'Joney' had taken me there more than once, but still the mile-long shrubbery, some of it very dark with fir trees and great laurels, complicated with crossing walks, and containing two or three alarming shelter-huts and *tonnelles* (which I long after regarded with awe), was a tremendous pilgrimage to encounter alone. After some hesitation I set off; ran as long as I could, and then with panting chest and beating heart, went on, daring not to look to right or left, till (after ages as it seemed to me) I reached the little window of my nurse's house in the ivy wall; and set up – loud enough no doubt

– a call for 'Nanno!' The good soul could not believe her eyes when she found me alone but hugging me in her arms, brought me back as fast as she could to my distracted mother who had, of course, discovered my evasion. Two years later, when I was seven years old, I was naughty enough to run away again, this time in the streets of Bath, in company with a hoop, and the Town Cryer was engaged to 'cry' me, but I found my way home at last alone. How curiously vividly silly little incidents like these stand out in the misty memory of childhood, like objects suddenly perceived close to us in a fog! I seem now, after sixty years, to see my nurse's little brown figure and white kerchief, as she rushed out and caught her stray 'darlint' in her arms; and also I see a dignified, gouty gentleman leaning on his stick, parading the broad pavement of Bath Crescent, up whose whole person my misguided and muddy hoop went bounding in my second escapade. I ought to apologise perhaps to the reader for narrating such trivial incidents, but they have left a charm in my memory.

At seven I was provided with a nursery governess, and my dear mother's lessons came to an end. So gentle and sweet had they been that I have loved ever since everything she taught me, and have a vivid recollection of the old map book from whence she had herself learned Geography, and of Mrs. Trimmer's Histories, 'Sacred' and 'Profane';[2] not forgetting the almost incredibly bad accompanying volumes of woodcuts with poor Eli a complete smudge and Sesostris driving the nine kings (with their crowns, of course), harnessed to his chariot. Who would have dreamed we should now possess photos of the mummy of the real Sesostris (Rameses II), who seemed then quite as mythical a personage as Polyphemus? To remember the hideous aberrations of Art which then illustrated books for children, and compare them to the exquisite pictures in *Little Folks*,[3] is to realise one of the many changes the world has seen since my childhood. Mrs. Trimmer's books cost, I remember being told, *ten shillings* a-piece! My governess Miss Kinnear's lessons, though not very severe (our old doctor, bless him for it! solemnly advised that I should never be called on to study after twelve o'clock), were far from being as attractive as those of my mother, and as soon as I learned to write, I drew on the gravel walk this, as I conceived, deeply touching and impressive sentence: '*Lessons! Thou tyrant of the mind!*' I could not at all understand my mother's hilarity over this inscription, which proved so convincingly my need, at all events of those particular lessons of which Lindley Murray was the author.[4] I envied the peacock who could sit all day in the sun, and who ate bowls-full of the griddlebread of which I was so fond; and never was expected to learn anything!

... Some years later, my antipathy to lessons having not at all diminished, I read a book which had just appeared, and of which all the elders of the house were talking, Keith's *Signs of the Times*.[5] In this work, as I remember, it was set forth that a 'Vial' was shortly to be emptied into or near the Euphrates, after which the end of the world was to follow immediately. The writer accordingly warned his readers that they would soon hear startling news from the Euphrates. From that time I persistently inquired of anybody who I saw reading the newspaper (a small sheet which in the Thirties only came three times a week) or who seemed well-informed about public affairs, 'What news was there from the Euphrates?' The singular question at last called forth the inquiry, 'Why I wanted to know?' and I was obliged to confess that I was hoping for the emptying of the 'Vial' which would put an end to my sums and spelling lessons.

My seventh year was spent with my parents at Bath, where we had a house for the winter in James' Square, where brothers and sisters came for the holidays, and in London, where I well remember going with my mother to see the Diorama in the Colosseum in Regent's Park, of St. Peter's, and a Swiss Cottage, and the statues of Tam o'Shanter and his wife (which I had implored her to be allowed to see, having imagined them to be living ogres) and vainly entreating to be taken to see the Siamese Twins. This last longing, however, was gratified just thirty years afterwards. We travelled back to Ireland, posting all the way to Holyhead by the then new high road through Wales and over the Menai Bridge. My chief recollection of the long journey is humiliating. A box of Shrewsbury cakes, exactly like those now sold in the town, was bought for me *in situ*, and I was told to bring it over to Ireland to give to my little cousin Charley. I was pleased to give the cakes to Charley, but then Charley was at the moment far away, and the cakes were always at hand in the carriage; and the road was tedious and the cakes delicious; and so it came to pass somehow that I broke off first a little bit, and then another day a larger bit, till cake after cake vanished, and with sorrow and shame I was obliged to present the empty box to Charley on my arrival. Greediness alas! has been a besetting sin of mine all my life ...

To return to our old life at Newbridge, about 1833 and for many years afterwards, the assembling of my father's brothers, and brothers' wives and children at Christmas was the great event of the year in my almost solitary childhood. Often a party of twenty or more sat down every day for three or four weeks together in the dining-room, and we younger ones naturally spent the short days and long evenings in boyish and girlish sports and play. Certain very noisy and romping games – Blindman's buff, Prisoner's Bass, Giant, and Puss in the Corner and Hunt the Hare – as we played them through the halls below stairs, and the long corridors and rooms above, still appear to me as among the most delightful things in a world which was then all delight. As we grew a little older and my dear, clever brother Tom came home from Oxford and Germany, charades and plays and masquerading and dancing came into fashion. In short our's [sic] was, for the time, like other large country-houses, full of happy young people, with the high spirits common in those old days. The rest of the year, except during the summer vacation, when brothers and cousins mustered again, the place was singularly quiet, and my life strangely solitary for a child. Very early I made a *concordat* with each of my four successive governesses, that when lessons were ended, precisely at twelve, I was free to wander where I pleased about the park and woods, to row the boat on the pond or ride my pony on the sands of the sea-shore two miles from the house. I was not to be expected to have any concern with my instructress outside the doors. The arrangement suited them, of course, perfectly; and my childhood was thus mainly a lonely one. I was so uniformly happy that I was (what I suppose few children are) quite conscious of my own happiness. I remember often thinking whether other children were all as happy as I, and sometimes, especially on a spring morning of the 18th March, – my mother's birthday, when I had a holiday, and used to make coronets of primroses and violets for her, – I can recall walking along the grass walks of that beautiful old garden and feeling as if everything in the world was perfect, and my life complete bliss for which I could never thank God enough.

When the weather was too bad to spend my leisure hours out of doors I plunged into the library at haphazard, often making 'discovery' of books of which I had never been told, but which, thus found for myself, were doubly precious. Never shall I forget thus falling by chance on *Kubla Khan* in its first pamphlet-shape. I also gloated over Southey's *Curse of Kehama*, and *The Cid* and Scott's earlier works. My mother did very wisely, I think, to allow me thus to rove over the shelves at my own will. By degrees a genuine appetite for reading awoke in me, and I became a studious girl, as I shall presently describe. Beside the library, however, I had a play-house of my own for wet days. There were, at that time, two garrets only in the house (the bed-rooms having all lofty coved ceilings) and these two garrets, over the lobbies, were altogether disused. I took possession of them, and kept the keys lest anybody should pry into them, and truly they must have been a remarkable sight! On the sloping roofs I pinned the eyes of my peacock's feathers in the relative positions of the stars of the chief constellations; one of my hobbies being Astronomy. On another wall I fastened a rack full of carpenter's tools, which I could use pretty deftly on the bench beneath. The principal wall was an armoury of old court-swords, and home-made pikes, decorated with green and white flags (I was an Irish patriot at that epoch), sundry javelins, bows and arrows, and a magnificently painted shield with the family arms. On the floor of one room was a collection of shells from the neighbouring shore, and lastly there was a table with pens, ink and paper; implements wherewith I perpetrated, *inter alia*, several poems of which I can just recall one. The *motif* of the story was obviously borrowed from a stanza of Moore's Irish Meolodies. Even now I do not think the verses very bad for 12 or 13 years old.

*[Quotes her poem, 'The Fisherman of Lough Neagh'.]*

I wrote a great deal of this sort of thing then and for a few years afterwards; and of course, like everyone else who has ever been given to waste paper and ink, I tried my hand on a tragedy. I had no real power or originality, only a little Fancy perhaps, and a dangerous facility for flowing versification. After a time my early ambition to become a Poet died out under the terrible hard mental strain and very serious study through which I passed in seeking religious faith. But I have always passionately loved poetry of a certain kind, specially that of Shelley; and perhaps some of my prose writings have been the better for my early efforts to cultivate harmony and for my delight in good similes. This last propensity is even now very strong in me, and whenever I write *con amore*, comparisons and metaphors come tumbling out of my head, till my difficulty is to exclude mixed ones!

My education at this time was of a simple kind. After Miss Kinnear left us to marry, I had another nursery governess, a good creature properly entitled 'Miss Daly', but called by my profane brothers, 'the Daily Nuisance'. After her came a real governess, the daughter of a bankrupt Liverpool merchant who made my life a burden with her strict discipline and her 'I-have-seen-better-days' airs; and who, at last, I detected in a trick which to me appeared one of unparalleled turpitude! She had asked me to let her read something which I had written in a copy-book and I had peremptorily declined to obey her request, and had locked up my papers in my beloved little writing-desk which my dear brother Tom had bought for me out of his school-boy's pocket money. The keys of this desk I kept with other things in one of the old-fashioned pockets which everybody then wore, and which formed a separate article of under clothing. This pocket my maid naturally placed at night on the chair beside my little bed, and the curtains of the bed being drawn, Miss W. no doubt after a time concluded I was asleep and cautiously approached the chair on tiptoe. As it happened I was wide awake, having at that time the habit of repeating certain hymns and other religious things to myself before I went to sleep; and when I perceived through the white curtain the shadow of my governess close outside, and then heard the slight jingle made by my keys as she abstracted them from my pocket, I felt as if I were witness of a crime! Anything so base I had never dreamed as existing outside story books of wicked children. Drawing the curtain I could see that Miss W. had gone with her candle into the inner room (one of the old 'powdering closets' attached to all the rooms in Newbridge) and was busy with the desk which lay on the table therein. Very shortly I heard the desk close again with an angry click, – and no wonder! Poor Miss W., who no doubt fancied she was going to detect her strange pupil in some particular naughtiness, found the MS. in the desk, to consist of solemn religious 'Reflections', in the style of Mrs. Trimmer; and of a poetical description (in round hand) of the *Last Judgment*! My governess replaced the bunch of keys in my pocket and noiselessly withdrew, but it was long before I could sleep for sheer horror; and next day I, of course, confided to my mother the terrible incident. Nothing, I think, was said to Miss W. about it, but she was very shortly afterwards allowed to return to her beloved Liverpool, where, for all I know, she may be living still.

My fourth and last governess was a remarkable woman, a Mdlle. Montriou, a person of considerable force of character, and in many respects an admirable teacher. With her I read a good deal of solid history, beginning with Rollin and going on to Plutarch and Gibbon; also some modern historians. She further taught me systematically a scheme of chronology and royal successions, till I had an amount of knowledge of such things which I afterwards found was not shared by any of my schoolfellows. She had the excellent sense also to allow me to use a considerable part of my lesson hours with a map-book before me, asking her endless questions on all things connected with the various countries; and as she was extremely well and widely informed, this was almost the best part of my instruction. I became really interested in these studies, and also in the great poets, French and English, to whom she introduced me. Of course my governess taught me music, including what was then called *Thorough Bass*, and now *Harmony*; but very little of the practical part of performance could I learn then or at any time. Independently of her, I read every book on Astronomy which I could lay hold of, and I well remember the excitement wherewith I waited for years for the appearance of the Comet of 1835, which one of these books foretold. At last a report reached me that the village tailor had seen the comet the previous night. Of course I scanned the sky with renewed ardour, and thought I had discovered the desired object in a misty-looking star of which my planisphere gave no notice. My father however pooh-poohed this bold hypothesis, and I was fain to wait till the next night. Then, as soon as it was dark, I ran up to a window whence I could command the constellation wherein the comet was bound to show itself. A small hazy star – and a *long train of light from it* – greeted my enchanted eyes! My limbs could hardly bear me as I tore downstairs into the drawing-room, nor my voice publish the triumphant intelligence, 'It *is* the comet!' 'It *has* a tail!' Everybody (in far too leisurely a way as I considered) went up and saw it, and confessed that the comet it certainly must be, with that appendage of the tail! Few events in my long life have caused me such delightful excitement. This was in 1835.

... when it came to my turn to receive education, it was not in London but in Brighton that the ladies' schools most in estimation were to be found. There were even then (about 1836) not less than a hundred such establishments in the town, but that at No. 32, Brunswick Terrace, of which Miss Runciman and Miss Roberts were mistresses, and which had been founded some time before by a celebrated Miss Poggi, was supposed to be *nec pluribus impar.*[6] It was, at all events, the most outrageously expensive, the nominal tariff of £120 or £130 per annum representing scarcely a fourth of the charges for 'extras' which actually appeared in the bills of many of the pupils. My own, I know, amounted to £1,000 for two years' schooling.

I shall write of this school quite frankly, since the two poor ladies, well meaning but very unwise, to whom it belonged have been dead for nearly thirty years, and it can hurt nobody to record my conviction that a better system than theirs could scarcely have been devised had it been designed to attain the maximum cost and labour and the minimum of solid results. It was the typical Higher Education of the period, carried out to the extreme of expenditure and high pressure.

Profane persons were apt to describe our school as a Convent, and to refer to the back door of our garden, whence we issued on our dismal diurnal walks, as the 'postern'. If we in any degree resembled nuns, however, it was assuredly not those of either a Contemplative or Silent Order. The din of our large double schoolrooms was something frightful. Sitting in either of them, four pianos might be heard going at once in rooms above and around us, while at numerous tables scattered about the rooms there were girls reading aloud to the governesses and reciting lessons in English, French, German, and Italian. This hideous clatter continued the entire day till we went to bed at night, there being no time whatever allowed for recreation, unless the dreary hour of walking with our teachers (when we recited our verbs), could so be described by a fantastic imagination. In the midst of the uproar we were obliged to write our exercises, to compose our themes, and to commit to memory whole pages of prose. On Saturday afternoons, instead of play, there was a terrible ordeal generally known as the 'Judgment Day'. The two school-mistresses sat side by side, solemn and stern, at the head of the long table. Behind them sat all the governesses as Assessors. On the table were the books wherein our evil deeds of the week were recorded; and round the room against the wall, seated on stools of penitential discomfort, we sat, five-and-twenty 'damosels', anything but 'Blessed', expecting our sentences according to our ill-deserts. It must be explained that the fiendish ingenuity of some teacher had invented for our torment a system of imaginary 'cards', which we were supposed to 'lose' (though we never gained any) whenever we had not finished all our various lessons and practisings every night before bed-time, or whenever we had been given the mark for 'stooping', or had been impertinent, or had been 'turned' in our lessons, or had been marked 'P' by the music master, or had been convicted of 'disorder' (*e.g.*, having our long shoe-strings untied), or, lastly, had told lies! Any one crime in this heterogeneous list entailed the same penalty, namely the sentence, 'You have lost your card, Miss So-and-so, for such and such a thing'; and when Saturday came round, if three cards had been lost in the week, the law wreaked its justice on the unhappy sinner's head! Her confession having been wrung from her at the awful judgment-seat above described, and the books having been consulted, she was solemnly scolded and told to sit in the corner for the rest of the evening! Anything more ridiculous than the scene which followed can hardly be conceived. I have seen (after a week in which a sort of feminine barring-out had taken place) no less than nine young ladies obliged to sit for hours in the angles of the three rooms, like naughty babies, with their faces to the wall; half of them being quite of marriageable age, and all dressed, as was *de rigeur* with us every day, in full evening attire of silk or muslin, with gloves and kid slippers. Naturally, Saturday evenings, instead of affording some relief to the incessant overstrain of the week, were looked upon with terror as the worst time of all. Those who escaped the fell destiny of the corner were allowed, if they chose to write to their parents, but our letters were perforce committed at night to the schoolmistress to seal, and were not as may be imagined, exactly the natural outpouring of our sentiments as regarded those ladies and their school.

Our household was a large one. It consisted of the two schoolmistresses and joint proprietors, of the sister of one of them and another English governess; of a French, an Italian, and a German lady teacher; of a considerable staff of respectable servants; and finally of twenty-five or twenty-six pupils, varying in age from nine to nineteen. All the pupils were daughters of men of some standing, mostly country gentlemen, members of Parliament, and offshoots of the peerage. There were several heiresses amongst us, and one girl whom we all liked and recognised as the beauty of the school, the daughter of Horace Smith, author of

*Rejected Addresses*.[7] On the whole, looking back after the long interval, it seems to me that the young creatures there assembled were full of capabilities for widely extended usefulness and influence. Many were decidedly clever and nearly all were well disposed. There was very little malice or any other vicious ideas or feelings, and no worldliness at all amongst us. I make this last remark because the novel of *Rose, Blanche and Violet*, by the late Mr. G. H. Lewes, is evidently intended in sundry details to describe this particular school, and yet most falsely represents the girls as thinking a great deal of each other's wealth or comparative poverty.[8] Nothing was further from the fact. One of our heiresses, I well remember, and another damsel of high degree, the granddaughter of a duke, were our constant butts for their ignorance and stupidity, rather than the objects of any preferential flattery. Of vulgarity of feeling of the kind imagined by Mr. Lewes, I cannot recall a trace.

But all this fine human material was deplorably wasted. Nobody dreamed that any one of us could in later life be more or less than an 'Ornament of Society'. That a pupil in that school should ever become an artist, or authoress, would have been looked upon by both Miss Runciman and Miss Roberts as a deplorable dereliction. Not that which was good in itself or useful to the community, or even that which would be delightful to ourselves, but that which would make us admired in society, was the *raison d'etre* of each requirement. Everything was taught us in the inverse ratio of its true importance. At the bottom of the scale were Morals and Religion, and at the top were Music and Dancing; miserably poor music, too, of the Italian school then in vogue, and generally performed in a showy and tasteless manner on harp or piano. I can recall an amusing instance in which the order of precedence above described was naively betrayed by one of our schoolmistresses when she was admonishing one of the girls who had been detected in a lie. 'Don't you know, you naughty girl,' said Miss R. impressively, before the whole school: 'don't you know we had *almost* rather find you have a P—' (the mark of Pretty Well) 'in your music, than tell such falsehoods?'

It mattered nothing whether we had any 'music in our souls' or any voices in our throats, equally we were driven through the dreary course of practising daily for a couple of hours under a German teacher, and then receiving lessons twice or three times a week from a music master (Griesbach by name) and a singing master. Many of us, myself in particular, in addition to these had a harp master, a Frenchman named Labarre, who gave us lessons at a guinea apiece, while we could only play with one hand at a time. Lastly there were a few young ladies who took instructions in the new instruments, the concertina and the accordion!

The waste of money involved in all this, the piles of useless music, and songs never to be sung, for which our parents had to pay, and the loss of priceless time for ourselves, were truly deplorable; and the result of course in many cases (as in my own) complete failure. One day I said to the good little German teacher, who nourished a hopeless attachment for Schiller's Marquis Posa,[9] and was altogether a sympathetic person, 'My dear Fraulein, I mean to practise this piece of Beethoven's till I conquer it.' 'My dear', responded the honest Fraulein, 'you do practise that piece for seex hours a day, and you do live till you are seexty, at the end you will *not* play it!' Yet so hopeless a pupil was compelled to learn for years, not only the piano, but the harp and singing!

Next to music in importance in our curriculum came dancing. The famous old Madame Michand and her husband both attended us constantly, and we danced to their direction in our large play-room (*lucus a non lucendo*),[10] till we had learned not only all the dances in use in England in that anti-polka epoch, but almost every national dance in Europe, the Minuet, the Gavotte, the Cachucha, the Bolero, the Mazurka, and the Tarantella. To see the stout old lady in her heavy green velvet dress, with furbelow a foot deep of sable, going through the latter cheerful performance for our ensample [sic], was a sight not to be forgotten. Beside the dancing we had 'calisthenic' lessons every week from a 'Capitaine' Somebody, who put us through manifold exercises with poles and dumbbells. How much better a few good country scrambles would have been than all these calisthenics it is needless to say, but our dismal walks were confined to parading the esplanade and neighbouring terraces. Our parties never exceeded six, a governess being one of the number, and we looked down from an immeasurable height of superiority on the processions of twenty and thirty girls belonging to other schools. The governess who accompanied us had enough to do with her small party, for it was her duty to utilise these brief hours of bodily exercise by hearing us repeat our French, Italian or German verse, according to her own nationality.

Next to Music and Dancing and Deportment, came Drawing, but that was not a sufficiently *voyant* accomplishment, and no great attention was paid to it; the instruction also being of a second-rate kind, except that it included lessons in perspective which have been useful to me ever since. Then followed Modern Languages. No Greek or Latin were heard of at the school, but French, Italian and German were chattered all day long, our tongues being only set at liberty at six o'clock to speak English. *Such* French, such Italian, and such German as we actually spoke may be more easily imagined than described. We had bad 'Marks' for speaking wrong languages, *e.g.*, French when we [were] bound to speak Italian or German, and a dreadful mark for bad French, which was transferred from one to another all day long, and was a fertile source of tears and quarrels, involving as it did a heavy lesson out of Noel et Chapsal's *Grammar* on the last holder at night. We also read in each language every day to the French, Italian and German ladies, recited lessons to them, and wrote exercises for the respective masters who attended every week ...

Naturally after (a very long way after) foreign languages came the study of English. We had a writing and arithmetic master (whom we unanimously abhorred and despised, though one and all of us grievously needed his instructions) and an 'English master', who taught us to write 'themes', and to whom I, for one, feel that I owe, perhaps, more than to any other teacher in that school, few as were the hours which we were permitted to waste on so insignificant an art as composition in our native tongue!

Beyond all this, our English studies embraced one long, awful lesson each week to be repeated to the schoolmistress herself by a class, in history one week, in geography the week following. Our first class, I remember, had once to commit to memory – Heaven knows how – no less than thirteen pages of Woodhouselee's *Universal History*![11]

Lastly, as I have said, in point of importance, came our religious instruction. Our well-meaning schoolmistresses thought it was obligatory on them to teach us something of the kind, but, being very obviously altogether worldly women themselves, they were puzzled how to carry out their intentions. They marched us to church every Sunday when it did not rain, and they made us on Sunday mornings repeat the Collect and Catechism; but beyond these exercises of body and mind, it was hard for them to see what to do for our spiritual welfare. One Ash-Wednesday, I remember, they provided us with a dish of salt-fish, and when this was removed to make room for the roast mutton, they addressed us in a short discourse, setting forth the merits of fasting, and ending by the remark that they left us free to take meat or not as we pleased, but that they hoped we should fast; 'it would be good for our souls AND OUR FIGURES!'

Each morning we were bound publicly to repeat a text out of certain little books, called *Daily Bread*, left in our bedrooms, and always scanned in frantic haste while 'doing-up' our hair at the glass, or gabbled aloud by one damsel so occupied while her room-fellow (there were never more than two in each bed-chamber) was splashing about behind the screen in her bath. Down, when the prayer-bell rang, both were obliged to hurry and breathlessly to await the chance of being called on first to repeat the text of the day, the penalty for oblivion being the loss of a 'card'. Then came a chapter of the Bible, read verse by verse amongst us, and then our books were shut and a solemn question was asked. On one occasion I remember it was: 'What have you just been reading, Miss S—?' Miss S— (now a lady of high rank and fashion, whose small wits had been wool-gathering) peeped surreptitiously into her Bible again, and then responded with just confidence, 'The first Epistle, Ma'am, of *General Peter*.'

It is almost needless to add, in concluding these reminiscences, that the heterogeneous studies pursued in this helter-skelter fashion were of the smallest possible utility in later life; each acquirement being of the shallowest and most imperfect kind, and all real education worthy of the name having to be begun on our return home, after we had been pronounced 'finished'. Meanwhile the strain on our mental powers of getting through daily, for six months at a time, this mass of ill-arranged and miscellaneous lessons, was extremely great and trying.

One droll reminiscence must not be forgotten. The pupils of Miss Runciman's and Miss Roberts' were all supposed to have obtained the fullest instruction in Science by attending a course of Nine Lectures delivered by a gentleman named Walker in a public room in Brighton. The course comprised one Lecture on Electricity, another on Galvanism, another on Optics, others I think, on Hydrostatics, Mechanics, and Pneumatics, and finally three, which gave me infinite satisfaction, on Astronomy.

If true education be the instilling into the mind, not so much Knowledge, as the desire for Knowledge, mine at school certainly proved a notable failure. I was brought home (no girl could travel in those days alone) from Brighton by a coach called the *Red Rover*, which performed, as a species of miracle, in one day the journey to Bristol, from whence I embarked for Ireland. My convoy-brother naturally mounted the box, and left me to enjoy the interior all day by myself; and the reflections of those solitary hours of first emancipation remain with me as lively as if they had taken place yesterday. 'What a delightful thing it is,' so ran my thoughts 'to have done with study! Now I may really enjoy myself! I know as much as any girl in our school, and since it is the best school in England, I *must* know all that it can ever be necessary for a lady to know. I will not trouble my head ever again with learning anything; but read novels and amuse myself for the rest of my life.'

This noble resolve lasted I fancy a few months, and then, depth below depth of my ignorance revealed itself very unpleasantly! I tried to supply first one deficiency and then another, till after a year or two, I began to educate myself in earnest. The reader need not be troubled with a long story. I spent four years in the study of History – constructing while I did so some Tables of Royal Successions on a plan of my own which enabled me to see at a glance the descent, succession and date of each reigning sovereign of every country, ancient and modern, possessing any History of which I could find a trace. These Tables I still have by me, and they certainly testify to considerable industry. Then the parson of our parish, who had been a tutor in Dublin College, came up three times a week for several years, and taught me a little Greek (enough to read the Gospels and to stumble through Plato's *Krito*), and rather more geometry, to which science I took an immense fancy, and in which he carried me over Euclid and Conic Sections, and through two most delightful books of Archimedes' spherics. I tried Algebra, but had as much disinclination for that form of mental labour as I had enjoyment in the reasoning required by Geometry. My tutor told me he was able to teach me in one lesson as many propositions as he habitually taught the undergraduates of Dublin College in two. I have ever since strongly recommended this study to women as specially fitted to counteract our habits of hasty judgement and slovenly statement, and to impress upon us the nature of real demonstration.

I also read at this time, by myself, as many of the great books of the world as I could reach; making it a rule always (whether bored or not) to go on to the end of each, and also following generally Gibbon's advice, viz, to rehearse in one's mind in a walk before beginning a great book all that one knows of the subject, and then, having finished it, to take another walk, and register how much has been added to our store of ideas. In these ways I read all the *Faery Queen*, all Milton's poetry, and the *Divina Commedia* and *Gerusalemme Liberata* in the originals. Also (in translations) I read through the Iliad, Odyssey, Aeneid, Pharsalia, and all or nearly all, Aeschylus, Sophocles, Euripides, Ovid, Tacitus, Xenophon, Herodotus, Thucydides, &c. There was a fairly good library at Newbridge, and I could also go when I pleased, and read in Archbishop Marsh's old library in

Dublin, where there were splendid old books, though none I think more recent than a hundred and fifty years before my time. My mother possessed a small collection of classics – Dryden, Pope, Milton, Horace, &c., which she gave me, and I bought for myself such other books as I needed out of my liberal pin-money. Happily, I had at that time a really good memory for literature, being able to carry away almost the words of passages which much interested me in prose or verse, and to bring them into use when required, though I had, oddly enough, at the same period so imperfect a recollection of persons and daily events that, being very anxious to do justice to our servants, I was obliged to keep a book of memoranda of the characters and circumstances of all who left us, that I might give accurate and truthful recommendations.

By degrees these discursive studies – I took up various hobbies from time to time – Astronomy, Architecture, Heraldry, and many others – centred more and more on the answers which have been made through the ages by philosophers and prophets to the great questions of the human soul...Having always a passion for Synopses, I constructed, somewhere about 1840, a Table, big enough to cover a sheet of double-elephant paper, wherein the principal Greek philosophers were ranged, – their lives, ethics, cosmogonies and special doctrines, – in separate columns. After this I made a similar Table of the early Gnostics and other heresiarchs, with the aid of Mosheim, Sozomen, and Eusebius.[12]

Does the reader smile to find these studies recorded as the principal concern of the life of a young lady from 16 to 20, and in fact to 35 years of age? It was even so! They *were* (beside Religion, of which I shall speak elsewhere)[13] my supreme interest. As I have said in the beginning, I had neither cares of love, or cares of money to occupy my mind or my heart. My parents wished me to go a little into society when I was about 18, and I was, for the moment, pleased and interested in the few balls and drawing-rooms (in Dublin) to which my father and afterwards my uncle, General George Cobbe, conducted me. But I was rather bored than amused by my dancing partners, and my dear mother, already in declining years, and completely an invalid, could never accompany me, and I pined for her motherly presence and guidance, the loss of which was only half compensated for by her comments on the long reports of all I had said and done, as I sat on her bed, on my return home. By degrees also, my thoughts came to be so gravely employed by efforts to find my way to religious truth, that the whole glamour of social pleasures disappeared and became a weariness; and by the time I was 19 I begged to be allowed to stay at home and only seen to receive our own guests, and attend the occasional dinners in our neighbourhood. With some regret my parents yielded the point, and except for a visit every two or three years to London for a few weeks of sightseeing, and one or two trips in Ireland to houses of our relations, my life, for a long time, was perfectly secluded.

*Source*: Frances Power Cobbe, *Life of Frances Power Cobbe*, 2 vols (London: Richard Bentley and Son Ltd, 1894).

## Notes

1. Thomas Moore (1779–1852), best known for his *Irish Melodies* (1808), *Lalla Rookh* (1817) and *The Letters and Journals of Lord Byron* (1830).

2. Sarah Trimmer (1741–1810), author of *Sacred History, Selected from the Scriptures* (1782–84).

3. *Little Folks*, a children's magazine running from 1871–1932. Some of its illustrations were by Kate Greenaway.

4. Lindley Murray (1745–1826), author of several grammar and spelling books, including his *English Grammar* (1795), widely used in schools. Mrs Garth uses Lindley Murray in George Eliot's *Middlemarch* (1871–72) to teach her children.

5. *Signs of the Times, illustrated by the Fulfilment of Historical Predictions* (1832) by Alexander Keith (1791–1880), a writer on prophecy.

6. No unequal match for several.

7. Horace (Horatio) Smith (1779–1849), poet and author of *Rejected Addresses* (1812), parodies of popular poets purporting to have been written for a competition to celebrate the reopening of the Drury Lane Theatre.

8. *Rose, Blanche and Violet* (1848), novel by George Henry Lewes (1817–1878), critic best known for his partnership with George Eliot.

9. Rodrigo, Marquis of Posa, is Don Carlos's friend in Schiller's tragedy *Don Carlos* (1787).

10. The grove is so named from its not shining: in other words, the playroom is used for anything but playing.

11. *Plan and Outline of a Course of Lectures on Universal History, Ancient and Modern* (1783) by Alexander Fraser (1747–1813), Lord Woodhouselee, and Professor of Universal History at Edinburgh.

12. Johann Lorenz von Mosheim (1694–1755), German Lutheran theologian who founded the pragmatic school of objective church history; Sozomen (c. 400–450), Christian lawyer and church historian in Constantinople, noted for his classical literary style; and Eusebius of Caesarea (4th century), whose *Ecclesiastical History* (about the first four centuries of Christianity) was a landmark of Christian historiography.

13. She does this in the next chapter of her autobiography.

# 15

# Charlotte M. Yonge

Charlotte Mary Yonge (1823–1901) one of the nineteenth-century's most popular children's fiction writers, was born in Otterbourne, near Winchester, the only daughter of William Crawley Yonge (1795–1854) and Frances Mary Bargus (d. 1868). She had one brother, Julian Bargus (1830–92). Her father, a former army officer who had fought at Waterloo and in the Peninsular War, left the army in order to marry Yonge's mother, whose family objected to military men. He became a magistrate and took an active interest in church matters, which his daughter shared, beginning a long career of Sunday-school teaching when she was only seven. Educated by her father, Charlotte learned Latin and Greek; later she looked to John Keble, a leader of the Oxford Movement, who lived nearby, for advice on her writing. Her family decided she should publish only on condition that the profits of her writing were devoted to good works (mainly missionary projects).Yonge's best-known works were *The Heir of Redclyffe* (1853) and *The Daisy Chain* (1856). She never married, and  travelled abroad only once, to France. Yonge's lifespan almost paralleled Queen Victoria's: both dying in 1901. Her conservative, densely detailed novels about large families and their problems upheld the values of the Oxford Movement, her most popular heroine being fifteen-year-old Ethel May of *The Daisy Chain*, who competes with her brother at classical languages, but is ordered to stop and help her widowed father take care of his large family.

Yonge's autobiography, written in 1877, is unfinished, and concentrates solely on her childhood years. It was included in Christabel Coleridge's *Charlotte Mary Yonge: Her Life and Letters* (1903). Extensive family genealogies and anecdotes have been omitted from the following extract.

I was born at Otterbourne on the 11th of August 1823, and my christening was somewhat hurried to let my father return to my grandfather, who was ill. My sponsors were my eldest uncle, Duke Yonge, my father's favourite sister, Charlotte (Mrs George Crawley), and my mother's friend Fanny Eyre, recently married to Mr Bolton, nephew and heir to Lord Nelson. Her little Horatio was a week my elder, and I have heard of the way the two young mothers walked up and own the room comparing their babies and their dexterity in holding them ...

I do not recollect so far back as some people do. I have a hazy remembrance of a green spelling-book, and the room where I read a bit of it to some unaccustomed person. It must have been while I was very young, for I could read to myself at four years old, and I perfectly recollect the pleasure of finding I could do so, kneeling by a chair on which was spread a beautiful quarto edition of *Robinson Crusoe*, whose pictures I was looking at while grandmamma read the newspaper aloud to my mother. I know the page, in the midst of the shipwreck narrative, where to my joy I found myself making out the sense.

Otherwise I can hardly date my earlier recollections. Mine was too happy and too uneventful a childhood to have many epochs, and it has only one sharp line of era in it, namely, my brother's birth when I was six and a half. I can remember best by what happened before, and what happened after.

Young parents of much ability and strong sense of duty were sure to read and think much of the education of an only child, as I was for so long. The Edgeworth system (as I now know) chiefly influenced them, though modified by religion and good sense. It was not spoiling. There was nothing to make me think myself important; I was repressed when I was troublesome, made to be obedient or to suffer for it, and was allowed few mere indulgences in eating and drinking, and no holidays. And yet I say it deliberately, that except for my occasional longings for a sister, no one ever had a happier or more joyous childhood than mine. I have since had reason to know that I was a very pretty and clever child, or at any rate that my mother thought me so, but I really never knew whether I was not ugly. I know I thought myself so, and I was haunted occasionally by doubts whether I were not deficient, till I was nearly grown up. My mother said afterwards that I once asked her if I was pretty, and she replied that all young creatures were, *i.e.* the little pigs. Once when some one praised my chestnut curls, I set every one laughing by replying indignantly, 'You flatter me', having my head full of the flattering lady in Miss Edgeworth's *Frank.*[1] Great hazel eyes, and thick, rich, curling hair, cut rather short, were my best points, for my skin was always brown, and never had much colour.

My nature was eager, excitable, and at that time passionate. The worst passions I remember were excited by a housemaid named Sarah, who used to sit at work in the nursery, and beg my nurse Mason to repeat 'the last dying speech and confession of poor Puss', in *Original Poems* [2] because I could not bear that doleful ditty, and used to stamp and roll on the floor to put a stop to it. Sarah was very good-natured though, she gave me a doll, and when I made a flight of steps to jump down – a chest of drawers, a chair, and a stool – she followed my lead, and jumped with such effect that all the legs of the stool spread out flat on the floor. I think it was found out that she was not a safe companion for me, for she did not stay long.

My nursery would frighten a modern mother. It was like a little passage room, at the back of the house, with a birch-tree just before the window, a wooden crib for me, and a turn-up press bed for my nurse; and it also answered the purpose of work-room for the maids. But I did not live much in it. I was one of the family breakfast party, and dined at luncheon so early that I cannot remember when I began, and never ate in the nursery except my supper. Breakfast and supper were alike dry bread and milk. I so much disliked the hot bowl of boiled milk and cubes of bread that I was allowed to have mine separately, but butter was thought unwholesome, and I believe it would have been so, for I never have been able to eat it regularly. As to eggs, ham, jam, and all the rest, no one dreamt of giving them to children. Indeed my mother made a great point of never letting me think that it was any hardship to see other people eating what I did not partake, and I have been grateful for the habits she gave me ever since.

I remember my indignation when a good-natured housemaid, who thought me cruelly treated, brought me a plateful of slices with the buttered side turned downwards. With conscious pride and honour, I denounced the deceit. I wonder whether the strict obedience edified her, or whether she thought me a horrid little ungrateful tell-tale.

... My great world was indoors with my dolls, who were my children and my sisters; out of doors with an imaginary family of ten boys and eleven girls who lived in an arbour. My chief doll, a big wooden one, Miss Eliza by name, was a prize for hemming my first handkerchief. The said handkerchief had on it the trial of Queen Caroline, weeping profusely in a hat and feathers, and was presented to my contemporary cousin Duke, at Puslinch, where it survived for many years as a bag.

There were about sixteen dolls, large wooden, small wax, and tiny Dutch, who used to be set on chairs along the nursery, and do their lessons when I had finished mine. They did not come downstairs except by special permission, and when left about in the drawing-room were put into what was called the pillory, a place boarded between the balusters at the turn of the staircase, whence they were not released till the next morning.

The two ungratified wishes of those days were for a large wax doll, and a china doll's service. I was seriously told the cost, and that it was not right to spend so much money on a toy when so many were in need of food and clothes.

It was absolutely true that my father and mother had very little ready money, and that they did spend as much as they possibly could on the many needs of the poor. No doubt this gave the lesson reality, for it has always served me as a warning against selfish personal expenditure.

My only real trouble was terrors just like what other solitary or imaginative children have – horrors of darkness, fancies of wolves, one most gratuitous alarm recurring every night of being smothered like the Princes in the Tower, or blown up with gunpowder. In the daylight I knew it was nonsense, I would have spoken of it to no one, but the fears at night always came back.

I knew nothing of ghosts, no one ever mentioned them to me, but the nervous fright could not have been more even if I had been nurtured on them. But I am an arrant coward by nature, both physically and morally, and confess myself to have been always one of those who 'die a thousand deaths' in imagination, and suffer all manner of anticipations of evil for self and friends.

A certain Lord Boringdon, son of Lord Morley, was killed by a beard of barley getting into his throat. I was told of this as a warning when I was biting bits of grass, and for many years *really* thought my uvula was such a bit of grass and would be the death of me.

I will just copy here the notes I find in an old agenda of my mother's on my studies and progress in this period.

*Jan. 7*, 1828. – Charlotte began Fabulous Histories (*i.e.* Mrs Trimmer's *Robin, Dicky, Flapsy, and Pecksy.* I loved them, though the book is one of the former generation – pale, long s's, ct joined together. I have it still).[3]

*Jan. 27.* – 'Why did Pharaoh think his dreams were alike when one was about cattle, and the other about cows?' C. 'Because the fat ate up the lean of both.' 'Was there anything else in which they were alike?' C. 'Oh why, mamma, seven and seven.'

*July 5.* – Charlotte said, 'Mamma, how do the men that write the newspaper know of all the things that occur?' (*N. B.* – I had a passion for fine words.)

*Aug. 3.* – Ch. began *Sandford and Merton.* (This means for lessons.)[4]

*Sept. 11.* – Charlotte saw a picture of the Fire King some time ago at the Southampton Gallery, and to-day she said she thought if he rode in a wax chariot he would be melted.

*Dec. 19.* – C. began Rollin's *Ancient History* (It lasted me *years*, but it was excellent for me; I am very glad I read so real a book.)

*Dec. 28.* – Sunday. C. began Trimmer's *Sacred History.*

*March 20.* – It is noted that C. has done since the 1st of August 1016 lessons; 537 very well, 442 well, 37 badly. Reading, spelling, poetry, one hour every day; geography, arithmetic, grammar, twice a week; history and catechism, once.

Steady work this for a mother to have gone through in six months. The computation was from a card on which a mark was put for each lesson; I had prizes accordingly. Writing was deferred from a theory that it would cramp my hand to begin so soon.

The real zest and joy of existence to me was, however, in the yearly visit to Devonshire. I was happy at home, but it was with calm, solitary happiness; there no one but myself was a native of the land of childhood. The dear home people gave me all they could, but they could not be children themselves, and oh, the bliss of that cousinland to me!

We used to go every autumn, all but grandmamma, in the chariot with post-horses, sleeping either one or two nights on the road. The chariot was yellow, sulphur yellow, lined with dark blue, with yellow blinds and horrid blue and yellow lace. I was always giddy, often sick, in a close carriage, and the very sight of that blue and yellow lace made me worse, but it was willingly endured for the joys beyond. And there were delights. Papa read me the *Perambulations of a Mouse*[5] on one of those journeys. Then there was a game in which each counted the animals at the windows on each side, and the first to reach 100 was the winner, or the game was gained by the sight of a cat looking out of the window. In the sword-case we carried our provision of hard eggs, biscuits, and, as it was called from a mistake of mine, 'spotted meat'. We used to eat this in the middle of the day, and have a mutton-chop tea generally at Honiton. Then what interest there was in rattling up to an inn-door and having our tired horses led off, while we watched for the next pair ridden by a spruce post-boy, either in a blue or a yellow jacket, white hat, corduroys, and top boots.

At last we turned down Sheepstor hill, and, while dragging down the steepest part, over the low wall came the square house in sight if we came by day, or if late, the lights glancing in the windows. Mamma used to tell of my shriek of ecstasy at the sight, and even now, at the very thought, my heart swells as if it *must* bound at the sight, though so many of those who made it glad are passed away.

> I feel the gales that from thee blow,
> A momentary bliss bestow.[6]

There, when the tall front door had once opened, was all I longed for at home – the cousins who have been all my life more than cousins, almost brothers and sisters to me.

I have said nothing of Uncle and Aunt Yonge (as I was taught to call them) since their marriage. They had devoted themselves to their parish and their children. Uncle Yonge refused all the squire side of life, and lived as a hard-working clergyman, far in advance of his neighbours' notions of duty. Aunt Yonge was of homely tastes, and almost ascetic nature as to gaiety or ornament. But how happy a home it was; how thoroughly good principles and deep religious feeling were infused; how bright it was![7] Some of the other cousins called Uncle Yonge 'the father of fun', and no one enjoyed seeing their innocent happiness more.

Their full number of children was ten: John, the eldest, died at four years old; Alethea, a bright-complexioned, dear, joyous creature, born in 1815, used to seem to me at an awful distance. James was a kind, special patron of mine; we used to call one another Jemmy Jummy, and Charlotte Shummy. It was related that immediately after our arrival once I was seen exalted on a locker, with my uncle's bands on, preaching. Each mother was shocked at her sister's permitting such irreverence, but thought she would not begin by blame the first moment, then found out that it was an access of mischief which had seized us in the excitement of meeting. I suppose we were rather wild, for we broke a window together.

Mary, a stout, strong, helpful girl, seemed to me one of the far-off elders. Jane – dear little neat-handed Jenny – was more on my horizon, but was so quiet, and removed from all roughness as to be almost an elder. Then came Johnnie, fair, aquiline-nosed like the Bargus's [sic], the family pickle, audacious, mischievous, and unmanageable. He it was who, when tied to the great four-post bed in the nursery, dragged it across the room. He it was who said to the little under-nurse, 'I don't like Kitty's black bonnet', and threw it into the fire. He it was who was the author of all daring mischief. He had a sullen, rather whiny temper too, and his mother treated him with unwearied patience. My father once asked my uncle whether it was not vain wasting of my aunt's strength to sit quietly enduring the endless whine and dawdle of Johnnie over his lessons. Uncle Yonge answered that it had been the same with Alethea, and that her mother's patience had so perfectly succeeded that he had always resolved not to interfere.

Duke, two months older than I, was a pretty boy with dark soft eyes and lashes. I have a dim remembrance of those two in nankeen frocks, and a more distinct one of them in 'monkey suits', with jacket and waistcoat all in one, and trousers fastened over, and white frilled collars – very hideous dress. Poor Duke, always gentle and timid, had had an inflammation on the lungs, and was too delicate to be turned loose among us little tyrants. I am afraid I joined with Johnnie in teasing him, and so did even the younger Anne. My dear, dear Anne, whom I loved always with all my heart! She was born on Alethea's birthday, the 28th of March, with exactly ten years between them, and was Alethea's special child. She was square and strong, though at six weeks old she had nearly died of the whooping-cough – in fact, was all but dead, when Dr. Yonge opened a vein in her foot which relieved her. She had a wonderful pair of hazel eyes, and was full of spirit and enterprise, which made her the *mauvais sujet* of the nursery, on whom everybody's faults were laid, while she had plenty of her own.

These four were the special world of Puslinch to me; Edmund Charles, born on my birthday in 1827, and Frances Elizabeth two years later, were not yet come to the age of companionship. Indeed what I first recollect was babyish enough. There was one wet Sunday when all we children were left in the house alone together all day, all downwards from Mary, and with the addition of Uncle Duke's daughter, Alethea.[8] The elder ones made a tower with chairs shutting off the recessed dining-room windows – Anne and I coupled together in one house. They shut the shutters when it was to be night, and opened them for day, and went about distributing provisions in the morning. Another sport of those days was making shops in the recesses of the study, when Mary, hanging up a triangular pincushion, uttered the splendid impromptu –

> Hang it up to make a show,
> And cut off every one's great toe,

which was considered such an effort of genius that it became a by-word. I remember too kneeling in the moonlight from the great windows and pretending to gather it into our bosoms, the only poetical thing we ever did.

Our next stage after Puslinch was Plymouth. There 'grandmamma with a stick' lived with Aunt Anne at Mount Pleasant, whence one long garden ran down to Uncle James's house in the Crescent. In this house there were three children – James, a few months older than myself, Eleanora, and Edward, the last born in 1827. Jemmy was, it seems to me, my greatest cousin friend; we used to play in the garden, walk together on the Hoe and on the slip of beach below that then was fit for children to enjoy, and confide to each other our views of life. Then on Sundays we went to church at St Andrew's Chapel, a wonderful building. It was a parallelogram, with such windows and ornaments in the Greek honeysuckle pattern sticking up like ears at the top! The pews in the central block were deal, painted white, narrow beyond belief, up to the neck of even grown up people, and provided with ingenious sloping traps to prevent any one from kneeling down. In one of these suffocating pews I – a little creature of five or six – once fainted, or nearly so, and my father made me a stool to stand on so as to bring my head within reach of air, and left it to Jemmy when we went away. There was evening service there, and once I went to it in a sedan-chair with grandmamma, who always went thus at night, though I think by day she walked with an arm.

From Plymouth we always went on to Antony, Uncle Duke's home, on the other side of the Torpoint ferry across the Tamar. There was no steam ferry in those days, one went in an open boat. There was a big ferry-boat to take horses, and in this grandmamma used to cross, not getting out of her carriage because of her lameness, but my mother did not like the crossing with the horses, so we always went in another boat. I remember our rowing once under the *San Josef*, one of the Trafalgar prizes, and looking up as it rose, like a mighty castle above us.

But there was one crossing rather late on an autumn day, when the water was rough, and a lady with us cried out, 'We shall all be upset', when I shrieked out gleefully, 'Oh then we shall catch a fish.' It is odd that I cannot in the least recollect this, though I do remember how, having been sent on with the maids to walk while my father and mother waited for the carriage, we were overtaken in the dark, and picked up, and I made every one laugh again by saying 'I'm as wet as a shag.'

I was not as happy at Antony as at Puslinch or Plymouth. The cousins were all much older except Arthur, who was only two or three years above me, and teasing was the family fashion. Cordelia, the eldest daughter, was really grown up, and the other, Alethea, then called Missy, a very handsome, dark, high-spirited creature, seven years older than I, appropriated me as a plaything, domineered over me, and dragged me about till I felt like the ploughman whom the giant's daughter stole for her toy. Jane, of Puslinch, coming here for part of our stay, did something to protect me, being more used to small children than Missy, but it must have been great discomfort, for I remember some time after we had been at home again mamma explaining forgiveness, as what I ought to feel as to Missy's teasing of me.

There were dark cupboards too, and a mysterious door where something was supposed to live, and cracks which Arthur used to tell me betokened that the house would fall. And in the distance was seen a tower called Trematon Castle, where wedged into some narrow place the skeleton of a cat had been found with the skeleton of a mouse in her mouth. Somehow my flesh crept at Antony, and I was in terror both of body and mind.

Still there were charms. The nursery was papered from ceiling to floor with pictures cut out of nursery-books. The nurse, Jane Blackler, had some purple and gold plates which we thought the *ne plus ultra* of beauty, and above all there was Whitsand Bay about a mile and a half off. It was then a really solitary bit of waste, a cliff descending from a field. There was a rough path leading to an exquisite beach of white sand, over which curled and dashed waves from the Atlantic, bringing in razor shells, tellinas of a delicate pink, cockles, and mactras. It was the most delicious place that I ever knew, and to this hour a windy night will make me dream of the roll and dash of its waves and the delight of those sands.

Then 'Uncle and Aunt Duke' were very kind, merry, engaging people, who loved to promote happiness, and lived such an easy-going scrambling life that they were said to be found dining at any hour from eleven to eight o'clock.

Antony was our farthest point, thence we worked back to Puslinch, the happiest place of all, and the most free from all teasing or quarreling. Such teasing as there was was very mild. It consisted in exasperating me by calling Otterbourne Hoberton, which I received as an insult, and in terrifying me by rattling the shot belts in the study. Also in tormenting Duke by calling him 'Sweet Honey', because he particularly disliked it.

The visit of 1829 ended in a dinner-party, of which my personal share was following Johnnie in a raid on the sweet things when they came out of the dining-room.

In the morning came the half-understood tidings that my aunt had become very unwell in the course of the evening, and had been found to have the measles. My mother had never had them, so she and I were instantly sent off without seeing another person in the house to Yealmpton, where lived my Uncle Yonge's mother, old Mrs. Yonge of Puslinch, with her daughter, Marianne, and son, Edmund, the sailor. She was very deaf, and I used to call her 'grandmamma with the trumpet', and think I had three grandmammas.

Their house on a steep sloping hill-side was little more than a cottage, with a terrace and a delightful garden running down into an orchard, and then to a green gate opening into a meadow, with the Yealm running through it. But kind as Aunt Marianne was, it was a banishment, and we were only released from quarantine to go home as soon as it was certain we had no disease about us.

Meantime my aunt had barely recovered before her youngest child sickened. All the nine had it one by one, and the fire was not out in her bedroom for six weeks, while she nursed them all there. They all recovered, though I fancy there was some permanent harm done to Frances, but my aunt never did shake off the effects; I don't know the exact nature of her illness, but I think it was some affection of spine or brain, for she never was well again, lay on her bed for a year, and was thought to be relieved by constantly having an issue in her back. Still she was the wise, efficient, all-ruling mother. Her eldest daughter, Alethea, became her father's out-of-doors companion and active manager. Mary, at twelve or thirteen, developed her wonderful powers as a nurse, soon took the nurse Harvey's place in the daily dressing of the back, and began that precious ministry in which her life has been spent, yet without losing the spirits of her age.

On the 31st of January 1830 came the greatest event of my life: my only brother was born. He came with rather short notice, and I remember the being left in the dark in my crib and the puzzled day that ensued. I believe my mother would not have me know the fact till she could see me herself, and soon after breakfast my father took me out to walk across the down to Twyford. There was a deep snow, I had not been properly equipped to encounter it, and though he carried me part of the way I arrived with bitterly cold hands, and when brought to the fire first knew the sensation of aching with cold.

The fire was at the Rev. Charles Shipley's. He had just come to live in a house of his own with his charming wife, and his children about my own age. Anna Maria and Conway Shipley were the first friends I had besides my cousins, so that in every way that cold day was an era.

When I came home, well wrapped up by kind Mrs. Shipley, I was allowed to hear of my brother, and to see him. I wished him to be called Alexander Xenophon, but was not allowed to hear his name till his christening, when it proved to be Julian Bargus, the first of which had been chosen from the Duke pedigree, when it was brought out to suggest a name for Edmund Charles.

It may mark the ebb-tide of church-like customs that Mr. Shuckburgh had just found out that christenings ought to be after the Second Lesson, and wanted to begin with him; but Mr. Shuckburgh was so uncertain and queer that there was no certainty that he would ever have done the same again, and it was feared that it would be thought a showing off of 'the young squire', as the poor women called him. So he was christened on a week-day, with Mr. and Mrs. Shipley and my father representing his sponsors, the uncle and aunt at Puslinch and Richard Bogue. Both he and I were christened by Mr. Westcombe, who was so afraid of forgetting the sex of the child that he compromised matters by calling both sexes 'it'.

The regular lesson life soon began again, the chief novelty being that my father undertook to teach me to write, thinking that a free hand would be of great service in drawing. He made me write, not pot-hooks, but huge S S S in chalk on a slate, without resting finger, wrist, or even arm. Between incapacity and carelessness I shed many tears over the process, but I gained much ease from it, and even now I feel the benefit in the manner of holding pen and hand, which saves me much cramping and fatigue. From that time he began to teach me some part of my studies. He was the most exact of teachers, and required immense attention and accuracy, growing rather hot and loud when he did not meet with it, but rewarding real pains with an approval that was always to me the sweetest of pleasures. Being an innate sloven and full of lazy inaccuracy I provoked him often, and often was sternly spoken to, and cried heartily, but I had a Jack-in-the box temper, and was up again in a moment, and always and never feared my work with him. So we rubbed on with increasing comfort in working together, well deserved by his wonderful patience and perseverance ... [9]

That summer was further diversified by the measles. My father had no confidence in the Winchester apothecaries, and doctored us through it himself alone – yes, and nursed too. I remember his sleeping on the floor in my little room and rising up to give me draughts. He was the best nurse I ever came under, with his tenderness and strength. He read me the *Pilgrim's Progress* out of Southey's edition when I was recovering, and on many Sundays – and how I loved it.

Then grandmamma brought me from Winchester a doll of a sort then new with leathern bodies and papier-mache heads. It was the largest and best doll I had ever had, and as I lay in bed with my hand over my treasure, my mother made it clothes. I can recall the pattern of those frocks now. 'Anna' was more the doll of my heart than any other, and she came when the old establishment had been routed, the big wooden Eliza having been thought dangerous to the baby ...

In the autumn we went into Devon, and there were much better times to me on the road, for the nurse, Maria Mason, went inside with mamma and the baby, and I was exalted to the box in company with my father. Oh, the felicity of sitting there with him! How he explained some things and made fun of others; how he told me stories, of which I above all remember 'Bel and the Dragon', and the history of his old magpie who was cured of sucking eggs by having one filled with mustard! When my incessant chatter may have grown beyond bearing he changed places with Mason, and then the fun was to play at games, and especially Button, made by the mouth pursed up till the incitements of the other party forced it gradually to expand into a laughing buttonhole.

In the course of this year little Eleanor and Edward at the Crescent had both died on the same day. Only Jemmy was left, and it was the last time I saw him. In the winter he fell into an atrophy, and wasted away. He begged for the Holy Communion before his death, and it was sad not to grant it to him, but he was thought *then* to understand his Catechism *too* literally. He had talked of me, and of some curiosities he had to show me when I came. His poor mother put them aside for me, but never could bear to part with them till long after, when I was grown up. Poor thing, she gave way entirely to her grief, she wore mourning for life, never went anywhere but to church, shut herself up from everybody, and could not bear the sight of a child. I, as Jemmy's playfellow, was specially dreaded, and never saw her again till I was grown too old to be a painful reminder.

It was very sad for my uncle. He was too good a man to be alienated, but the effects of the great grief, and the dreariness and desolation at home, showed themselves in the short sharp hurried manner that grew on him, and his rapidity of speech ...

We were in Devonshire when the great agricultural riots took place. Mrs. Bargus was alone at Otterbourne, and nothing was done to alarm her. In this part of the country, the labourers paraded in gangs and asked for money at the great houses, but were easily dispersed or turned aside, and offered no violence. The

Heathcote children remembered being shut up in a strong-room while the parley went on, but nothing came of it ...

One visit to our Devon kindred had sundry charms for which it is still remembered. James had gone from Ottery to Winchester, and John was the head of the 'playing party'. Aunt Yonge lay on the sofa in her room, Alethea sat at the head of the table, and there was a daily governess in the school-room, and plenty of liberty out of it.

Then it was that we made an enormous spider's web with pack-thread tied across from the rail of the balusters of the landing-place to the locks of the doors, intersected by cross lines so as to make a large octagon in the middle where John abode, while we lesser ones had cornerwise abodes all round in which we were just settled when all the owners of the rooms came marching up to dress, and acted the part of housemaid's broom to our web.

That too was the year when we took to 'playing the fool', namely, dancing wildly about the hall in any fantastic garb we could manage to lay hold of. My uncle, to his horror, caught me skating about the stone hall in a pair of wooden pattens with tall iron rings.

'Charlotte,' he said, 'how can you be so foolish?'

'But, Uncle Yonge, I *am* a fool', I squeaked out, as if he had been paying a great compliment.

I was the noisiest of all, being very excitable, shrill-voiced, and with a great capacity of screaming. There was one game called 'Cats and Mice' which I have really forgotten how to play, for we made such a riot that the children were always told beforehand not to play at it when I was there. There was an attempt too at hockey in the hall, summarily squashed by Mary coming down and gathering all the sticks up in her hand.

But riotous as were those days, the great love of all our lives was getting to be conscious. Anne and I were always together. We wanted to walk about with our arms round each other's waists, but our mothers held this to be silly, and we were told we could be just as fond of one another without 'pawing'. I still think this was hard, and that tenderness would have done no harm. But I do remember a long walk with the nurses and little ones round Kitley Point, with the sea sparkling on one side and woods sloping up filled with blue-bells. We gathered them in the ecstasy of childhood among flowers, exchanged our finest clustering stems of blue, and felt our hearts go out to one another. At least I did, so entirely that the Kitley slope – yes, and a white blue-bell – still brings to me that dear Anne and that old love. It was cemented further by our passion for long words when we could utter them without being laughed at for affectation. Poor Anne, when ill with a bad cold, knew she should be called an affected little pussy-cat if she said she had a pain in her side, therefore she said 'it pricked her when she breathed'. She was derided for vanity if she looked at herself in the glass, but found consolation in the brass handles of the locks of the doors. She was very enterprising and would taste whatever came in her way, even to a poultice.

The next time we went, 1832, my aunt had recovered the degree of health that she was to enjoy for the next twelve years or so. She moved about the house and garden with her hands on her sides as if walking were an effort, but she always sat in the school-room in the morning, taking some of the lessons; she managed everything in the house, gardened, and as she could not in general bear the motion of a carriage, used to go to Newton on a donkey, with the whole flock of children round her. Her fine complexion was gone, her colour was dead white, and she was a Puritan as to dress and ornament. She comes before me in a hideous blue cotton in large shaded checks and a perfectly plain white net cap, with very little ribbon about it, and she kept her daughters as simply dressed as possible, their hair cut bowl-dish fashion while little, and in straight bands when older. Alethea and Jane had a grace and an air that nothing could disguise, but Mary and Anne would have looked much better if better dressed.

I was afraid of Aunt Yonge. I always was getting reproofs from her, richly deserved I doubt not, but reproofs from uncles and aunts have a sting that those from one's lawful owners have not. The only scolding that ever made me more angry than Aunt Yonge's was Mrs. Shipley's, when I did not like to eat orange juice out of a pewter spoon.

However, this summer of 1832 had a delightful episode. My father and mother, with my uncle and his brother Edmund, Alethea, James, and Mary, went for 'the inside of a week' to see the North of Devon. How they all packed I cannot conceive, considering that two of the party were men not much under six feet high, but they had post-horses, and a box and dickey to the Puslinch chariot.

We were left at Puslinch, and Aunt Yonge really set herself to give us treats and make us happy – and now one thinks of it, how easy it was to produce that surpassing felicity, which certainly has been a 'joy for ever'. There was one day when we walked to Newton and came back in the boat up the lovely tide river; another when we had our tea in the plantation in Parson's Meadow above the house, and were exquisitely happy in a certain 'lost bower' till a boy friend came and marred our bliss by cruelty to the hornet moths; and another evening we drank tea at the clergyman's at Yealmpton, Mr. Des Brisay, and Johnnie found a garden syringe and played some outrageous tricks with it.

Then we built shops all over the garden, and sold wonderful commodities, made of flowers, beans, and seeds; and down Undercliff, that is on the bank of the tide river, were two heaps of sand, where we searched for tiny sea-shells. We, who considered ourselves reasonable, Jane, Johnnie, Duke, Anne, and myself had our regular divisions of the larger, the smaller was abandoned to the little ones, and called the Spuddler's portion, but Charles would make inroads on us, which I much resented, though Jane connived at them. The great prizes were mussel shells, and our object was to polish these so as to bring out their exquisite blue tinting as one may see them in shops. We did not know that acid was needed, and in the small part of our time we spent indoors we were scrubbing them vehemently with bits of pumice-stone, or else down on our hands and knees polishing them on the library carpet, and feeling how hot the friction would make them. We always came in at ten for lessons, but I believe this really made us all the happier, as we had the sense of duty, and were kept still.

... Aunt Yonge was wonderfully kind that summer, and I suppose it must have been much against the will of the nurses, for after that time we were always told that we could be just as happy playing out of doors, and drinking tea in, which I beg to observe is contrary to all child experience.

In the midst of the pleasant journey our parents met the tidings that the cholera was in England. This was the first visitation of cholera, when it came like the plague, and its causes and treatment had not been discovered. It had come in at Sunderland,[10] and had made its terrible way gradually westwards and southwards, and an attack of it was almost certain death. It was an anxious thing to have a brother a physician in a town nearly certain to be visited by it.

My grandmother no longer lived in Plymouth. Her daughter Anne had become attached to the surgeon who attended her after her accident, and after some delay they were married, and grandmamma lived with them at Plympton. But my other grandmother had been too long alone, and my mother took us children home, escorted by Captain Edmund Yonge, who was going to Portsmouth; for my father had further business, and came home by coach a little later. I *think* the cholera had nearly spent its force before it came to Plymouth, and it never appeared at all in Hampshire that time.

I believe that was my last visit, for when we went next into Devon, my Aunt Catharina (Mrs. Charles Crawley), with her daughter Kate, and her son George, came to meet us, and after being with us at Plympton, went on to Antony, my father alone accompanying them. Kate was a grown-up young lady beyond my horizon, but George and I got on excellently. We used together to scramble about the old green mound on which the Keep of Plympton Castle stands, and when I had to go to bed while the elders were reading *Peter Simple*[11] aloud, he used to tell me the next morning what I had missed.

... My home life had all this time had much less to mark it than the Devon visits. I remember little but great regularity in lessons. The house was added to enough to provide a schoolroom, where my mother taught me from ten till one, and my brother for part of the time. Afternoon lessons there were none, and I was out of doors, either in the garden with my mother, or the nurse and Julian, or taking walks with these last; playing at ball on the attic stairs on wet days, loving my dolls and the dogs, and being very happy on the whole, though with a dull yearning at times for something to look forward to. There were occasional meetings with the Shipleys, but they were the only children I knew, and they were not perfect playmates, for they called all 'pretending games' falsehood. I read a great many little books over and over again, and tried to garden, but was never tidy or persevering enough to succeed, and, as Julian grew older, we used to play on sandheaps, scrape chalk and brick dust for magnesia and rhubarb, and call ourselves Dr. C. and Dr. J.

Mamma took me to her Sunday School. The children used to take places, and after three Sundays went into the first class. I began in the second and soon got into the first, where there was one companion of my subsequent life, Harriet Spratt. Very unlike the attainments of their grandchildren of the present day were those of the big girls with whom I found myself, for at seven years old, in six weeks, I took the head of the class for knowing 'Who were they of the Circumcision?' I kept my place for three Sundays, and then was made a teacher.[12] It was a mistake, for I had not moral balance enough to be impartial, and I must have been terribly ignorant. This led to the worst falsehood I know myself to have ever uttered. A new girl, Lucy Knight, had just come into the class; I admired and favoured her, and took the first opportunity of prompting her so as to get her to the head of the class. My mother, seeing her there, asked me if she was there fairly. 'Yes', said I. The misery of that lie rankled how long I do not know, it seems to me for months, but at last, with my finger on a pane of glass in the schoolroom, I remember the confession of the falsehood and the forgiveness.

I do not believe I ever told an untruth knowingly after that, but I equivocated – when I do not know, but I remember my father's telling me it was worse than a falsehood, because it pretended to be the truth.

In religious knowledge I was forward. We always said the Catechism every Sunday, and we had a great Dutch Bible History, with two engravings on every other page, which kept up in our minds the Bible histories, besides the daily reading with my father. Still I was not at all devoutly minded, I always wished everything of the kind, except teaching the school children, to be over as fast as possible. I think I had a little sense of love and upbreathing devotion when I was by myself out of doors among the daffodils, or under a pink-blossomed double crab. The beauty uplifted me. But all the rest was fear, and I so dreaded the end of the world that, having understood 'Watch lest He cometh' to mean that He would come when no one was awake, I used to try to keep awake by means of pulling hairs out of my mattress. All the little Sunday books in those days were Mrs. Sherwood's, Mrs. Cameron's,[13] and Charlotte Elizabeth's, and little did my mother guess how much Calvinism one could suck out of them, even while diligently reading the story and avoiding the lesson.

When James, my eldest boy cousin, came into Commoners at Winchester, a fresh delight began. Every Saint's day he had leave out to us, and the day of his arrival was always spent with us. What parcels used to come! Anne and I only wrote to one another by him, our letters not being worth elevenpence postage. And the oddest little gifts! – for it was a law in the two families that no presents except of our own manufacture should pass between us. Nor did I have an allowance, but I had certain hens of my own, and Grandmamma Bargus paid me two shillings and sixpence for each couple of their chickens, also she gave me a half-sovereign on my birthday, and I think my money was rationally spent, though with shame I confess that no diligent training, and diligent it was, ever succeeded in making me keep regular accounts.

It seems to me that 1834, the year when I was between ten and eleven, was like a new era, both from the friends we then first made and the events that happened.

First, our strange curate, Mr. Shuckburgh, went away. A Fellow of New College was to succeed him, but sent a substitute, another Fellow, for six weeks. It ended in the said substitute staying thirty-seven years! He was the Rev. William Henry Walter Bigg-Wither, to give his full name, though he only signed the first; for when first he went to Winchester, one of the masters took up a book with the whole inscribed, and exclaimed, 'What, sir, do you thus proclaim the folly of your godfathers and godmothers?'

... He set to work on the parish as no one else had done. From his first coming, Holy Week and Ascension Day began to be observed, and christenings were after the Second Lesson. There were only twelve communicants, of whom at least half must have been in our house. Communion only took place three times a year, and his first step was to make it four times, and then repeat it the Sunday after a festival to give opportunities to those left at home.

... That year brought another intimate. A young physician, John Harris, a Plymouth man, was intending to practise at Winchester, and was placed under a sort of care of my father by Dr. Yonge. He was a small man with a Jewish face and a nervous sensitive manner. The first day he called he found Julian on the floor playing with his wooden bricks. Before he said a single word to any one, he popped the child into the basket belonging to the bricks, and hoisted him on his knee, Julian quietly remarking, 'I don't like it.' It was all rampant embarrassment; the next moment he was likening the boy to Uncle James's Jemmy. He was a very curious character, full of enthusiasm and paradox, and he used to come to us as to a home to pour it all out, and be argued with seriously or laughed at. Wordsworth was his chief delight, and he strove hard to infuse his admiration into my father, who cared for an entirely different school, and turned 'Peter Bell' and 'The Pet Lamb' into ridicule. He had a hard struggle. Two old-fashioned general practitioners who believed in calomel had possession of the neighbourhood, and his adventures were so like those in *Middlemarch* that I am sure the picture was a true one. For eight or ten years he was the constant familiar of our house, enlivening us with his never-ending fancies and schemes, and even, poor man, by his occasional depression, when he used to complain of the 'everlasting everything'.

... I have described our visit of 1834 to Devon. Alethea was to come home with us, we all first going to spend Commemoration week at Oxford, at Exeter College, to see the installation of the Duke of Wellington, Dr. Jones[14] being Vice-Chancellor at the time. Mrs Mudge's[15] death, however, prevented Alethea from going to such gaiety, and she was met by her brother James at Andover and taken to Otterbourne to grandmamma, while we went on to Oxford. The Chancellor is always lodged at Christ Church, but the Bishop of Exeter with Mrs. Phillpotts and two daughters, and Sir Hussey and Lady Vivian with a young cousin of ours, Elizabeth Daubeny, were our fellow-guests; also her grandfather and my great-uncle, the Rev. Charles Crawley of Stowe, more than eighty, but full of life and energy.

We children were taken out walking in Christchurch Meadows, and there saw the great Duke walking between two gentlemen. When I came in at dessert, as little girls then did, I reported having seen the Duke, and being examined as to what he was like, said he was a man with a nose like the Duke of Bedford, *i.e.* the brother of Henry V., in Vertue's heads – which was considered satisfactory evidence.[16]

They took me to the theatre, and I am very glad of it, for I was astonished when some thirty-five years later I saw the installation of the Marquis of Salisbury to find how complete my recollection was, and it was a great thing to have seen.

I remember the hawk-like profile in the black and golden robe, the centre of the grand semi-circle of scarlet doctors, among them the Bishops who were still wigged ... The Duke made his speech, which I believe was in Latin as characteristically Wellingtonian and to the point as the French of his letters. The prize poems were declaimed from the rostrum; Lord Maidstone had the Newdigate, which was on the Duke himself. So in came the line –

We have one hero, and that one is here.

Out went his white gloved hand towards the one hero, and thunders of applause burst from every one.

... The prime event of all to us was the last day, when the Duke came round to call on the heads of houses to thank them for his reception. We were all in the room to see him. My mother, in a sudden impulse, led Julian forward, saying, 'Will your Grace shake hands with a soldier's little boy?'

He kissed Julian, and shook hands with me.

'I did not think you had been so impudent', said my father afterwards.

We gloried in the kiss, but the boy himself was desperately shy about it, and if his cousins wanted to tease him it was by asking him to 'show the place where the Duke bit him'.

That visit was further memorable as the last sight of the good Aunt Charlotte, the godmother who was always held up as my model. She gave me a *Bishop Wilson*[17] then, in case she should not live to see me confirmed. I have it still.

We came home, and found Alethea with grandmamma. She stayed till her brothers' holidays (for John Bargus Yonge had now joined James at Winchester).

But in the next half-year, in the autumn of 1834, death for the first time was in our house. James, then eighteen, suffered from headache and nose-bleeding. He was sent out to Otterbourne for rest and change of air, and for a week was our playfellow as usual. We loved him very much, and it was held as remarkable that Julian, learning Watts's hymn on dress,[18] saying

This is the raiment Angels wear,

paused and observed, 'I think James has that clothing.'

Indeed he had, and well it was. In a week other symptoms came on that caused his father to be summoned. The next night he was unconscious, and never was fully himself again. He died on the Sunday. It was the first experience of an illness since too well known in his family, which has left (1889) only three of the joyous band of nine.

Uncle Yonge's calmness and patience were beautiful. Never can I read the verse,

> The father who his vigil keeps
> By the sad couch whence hope has flown, etc.[19]

without recollecting him.

His wife, who could not come, was patient and resolute, showing such self-command that she would not send for his letters by the second post in the evening, that her girls might not have bad news before they went to bed. I remember her writing, 'It was on the 2nd of November that our little John died.' It was on the 2nd of November, twenty years later, that James was taken. They buried him in our churchyard.

To me the time was a dull dreary dream. I thought of it with much awe, but I was a frivolous creature of untamed spirits, and I was in much disgrace for being unfeeling. I could not cry, and I was ready for any distraction. It was a great satisfaction to run down the kitchen garden, and recollect the cats must be fed whatever happened! Yet I think I carried something away. Reverence for James I know I did, and for my uncle a veneration only expressed by the verse I quoted before. I have no very distinctive recollection of 1835, except that when Julian was five, and I eleven, we began Latin; my father teaching us, and I, who of course went on the fastest, having to help him to learn. I think too that it was then that my father took my arithmetic in hand. He used to call me at six or half-past, and I worked with him for an hour before breakfast. It was in a degree like the writing lessons. He required a diligence and accuracy that were utterly alien to me. He thundered at me so that nobody could bear to hear it, and often reduced me to tears, but his approbation was so delightful that it was a delicious stimulus, and I must have won it oftener than it used to seem to me, for at the end of the first winter, my watch, the watch of my life, was given to me as a reward, to my great surprise. I believe, in spite of all breezes over my innate slovenliness, it would have broken our hearts to leave off working together. And we went on till I was some years past twenty, and had worked up to the point of such Greek, Euclid, and Algebra as had furnished forth the Etonian and soldier of sixteen, till his eyes were troubled by Homer and Algebra, and his time too fully occupied. Of course the serious breezes had long been over, and the study together had become very great pleasure. He did hear me read French for a little while, but a capital French master came into the neighbourhood.

... My master was named De Normanville. He was an old man, with white hair powdered, and a huge French nose, and hemless ears. He said he had left

France in the early days of the Revolution, crossing the border to Spain, and had been unable to save any property. He had since been in the West Indies ... From the French letters I was bidden to write rose my first beginning of composition – an endless story, in which Emilie, Rosalie, Henriette and Pauline Melville had endless adventures. I did not write easily enough even then to write *out* of lesson times the stories that filled my brain.

M. de Normanville was my only master, except a dancing master from Southampton, a lugubrious man, so pious that he gave us tracts, and said going to balls was contrary to his profession. How we hated his lessons!

My brother and I began Latin together, as has been said, when he was five years old, with my father. Of course, at eleven, I got to learn the quickest, so for some years longer I had to teach him his work in preparation for my father. So we worked through Latin Grammar with the old 'Propria quae maribus' and 'As in praesenti', and through Phaedrus and Cornelius Nepos. (Our old copy of Phaedrus has served me again with one of his boys.) Then I went on to Virgil, and selections from Horace, but all this work was spread over a good many years.

... The appointment of Mr. Coleridge[20] as a Judge brought us for the first time the great pleasure of having his wife and children with us for the Assize week at Winchester, when he went on the Western Circuit. It was ecstasy to May and Alley to be in the country, and the going into Court and seeing trials was a great pleasure to me. And the play, the jokes, the romancings, the debatings – whether Napoleon was courageous; whether St. Louis was 'henpecked by his mother', as May called it; our horror at the age of a hero of Madame de Genlis, 'Lord Arthur Selby', who married at the venerable age of twenty-six; an exclusive preference for imaginary heroes with 'pokers in their backbones' – all this childish, harmless fun, frolic and aspiration, was like a fairyland of imagination to us.

People used to tell us then, as we say to children now, that we had too many books to care for them, but I am sure we did heartily care for our favourites, Scott above all. I think I was allowed a chapter a day of the Waverley novels, provided I first read twenty pages of Goldsmith's *Rome* or some equally solid book.

As to new books, in those days circulating libraries consisted generally of third-rate novels, very dirty, very smoky, and with remarks plentifully pencilled on the margins. It was thought foolish and below par to subscribe to them, and book-clubs were formed in which each family might either ask for or order a book, which was covered with white cartridge paper with the list of subscribers pasted on one side. After going the round of the society, the books were disposed of either at half price or by auction, any book that no one would bid for being necessarily purchased by its orderer. Thus every one was responsible to all the rest, and though people grumbled sometimes, the plan prevented an immense amount of mischievous reading. People mostly dined at 5.30 or 6, and in the long evening that ensued the books from the club used to be read aloud to the assembled family, and the effect was a guiding power on the parents' part, and a community of interest in the subject before them that scarcely exists now ...

I think I look on the finishing era of my childhood as a visit to Devon in 1836, when, Julia Davys being left with Mrs. Bargus, we went to Puslinch earlier in the year than usual. It was a time of rare fun and highly developed games, and they seem to me to have culminated on the 21st of June, Duke's thirteenth birthday. There was an ordinance against our active spirits disturbing the house at an outrageously early hour in the morning, and we sent in a petition the night before that we might rise soon enough to finish our purse, our birthday present, before breakfast. Our ecstasy was unspeakable when Uncle Yonge answered us in verse. Here are a few lines:–

> No doubt when the music has ceased in your nose,
> You will rush to the room where the Graces repose,
> Miss Mary, Miss Jane, and Miss Prate-Apace Anne,
> To make them get up as fast as they can
> To put on the tags and the tassels so gay
> On the purse you have made by night as by day.
> Take heed lest my nest you disturb with your racket,
> And force me to rise and to put on my jacket,
> Then you'll say, 'Oh I wish that my restless young head
> Had known wisdom enough to lie longer in bed.'

How very delightful it was ! We not only finished our purse, but we walked to Yealmpton and purchased by subscription a hen canary (I can see her now, she was of a very pale complexion). I do not think we had holidays on birthdays, but in the afternoon we went down Undercliff. The tide was out and we wanted to catch materials for the feast which was to take place at home. The two maids were intent over one of Joseph Mason's Australian letters, and we were left to our own devices, which resulted in my plunging ankle deep in the mud, Anne with me, the little ones following. We were hauled out by the boys, and the maids made up for their negligence by scolding us. Harvey, the Puslinch nurse, 'Now, Miss Anne, you don't care, and there's Miss Charlotte sorry, she's crying!' Mason, 'Now, Miss Charlotte, don't be crying. It's all pretence. I'd rather you were like Miss Anne, who doesn't care.'

Our mothers met us, and laughed so much at the maids' wrath that they forgave us on the spot, and we had our feast. One captured winkle was bestowed on me, as the visitor, and being extracted with a pin disgusted me extremely! The evening concluded with 'Dicky's Ground', till Duke, always conscientious, decided that he ought to go in and learn his lessons.

Thus brilliantly ended childhood's wild delights. We did not go into Devon again for five years *en famille*. Partly I think it was because my grandmother was growing too old to be left, and partly that all that my father could spare of money, and much of his time, was devoted to the new church ... This was to us a time of making friendships. The Kebles[21] had come to Hursley Vicarage, and as this parish was then joined to Hursley, our intercourse was doubly close, over church-building matters, parish affairs, and one especial blessing of my life, that Mr.

Keble prepared me for Confirmation, when I was fifteen ... The fatherly kindness and the delightful sympathy I received then never failed, through all the years of happy intercourse between our two houses. My master he was in every way, and there was no one like Mrs. Keble for bright tender kindness. In her transparency of complexion and clear, dark, hazel eyes, she was like a delicate flower.

*Source*: 'Autobiography', in *Charlotte Mary Yonge: Her Life and Letters*, ed. Christabel Coleridge (London: Macmillan, 1903).

## Notes

1. Frank appears in Maria Edgeworth's *Early Lessons* (1801), stories aimed at educating young children about the world they lived in.
2. *Original Poems for Infant Minds by Several Young Persons* [Ann, Jane and Isaac Taylor], (1804).
3. *Fabulous Histories* (1786), subtitled *The History of the Robins* by Sarah Trimmer was about the relationship of a group of children with a family of robins and other animals.
4. *Sandford and Merton* (1783) by Thomas Day tells the story of Tommy Merton, the spoilt son of wealthy parents, and Harry Sandford, the active, good-humoured son of a 'plain, honest farmer'.
5. *Life and Perambulations of a Mouse* (c. 1780–90) by Dorothy Kilner.
6. From Thomas Gray (1716–71), 'On a Distant Prospect of Eton College'.
7. 'Uncle Yonge' was her father's first cousin. 'Aunt Yonge' was Alethea Bargus, her mother's half-sister. [*Footnote by Christabel Coleridge.*]
8. Duke Yonge of Antony in Cornwall. [*Christabel Coleridge's note.*]
9. The impression produced on onlookers was of great sternness and severity. [*Original footnote.*]
10. Note by Christabel Coleridge: 'The cholera came to Sunderland in 1831, to Edinburgh in 1832. I do not think Miss Yonge distinguishes very clearly between these annual visits to Puslinch. She gives the general impression.'
11. A novel by Frederick Marryat, published in 1834. It tells the story of Peter who eventually proves to be a successful and courageous sailor.
12. She was a teacher for seventy-one years. [*Christabel Coleridge's footnote.*]
13. Mrs Cameron was Mrs Sherwood's younger sister, Lucy Littleton Cameron (née Butt) (1781–1858), whose children's books included *The Two Lambs* (1821).
14. John Collier Jones (1770–1838), the Rector of Exeter College, was married to Yonge's Aunt Charlotte.
15. A sister of old Mrs Yonge of Puslinch, and wife of Admiral Mudge, who lived near Plympton.
16. George Vertue (1684–1756) was an engraver, known for his portraits and book illustrations.
17. Probably a reference to Thomas Wilson (1663–1755), Bishop of Sodor and Man, author of *Principles and Duties of Christianity* (1707). Keble wrote a biography of him (1863).

18. 'Against Pride in Clothes', from *Divine Songs for Children* (1715) by Isaac Watts (1674–1748), hymn-writer.

19. From 'Nineteenth Sunday after Trinity' in John Keble's *The Christian Year* (1827).

20. Sir John Taylor Coleridge (1790–1876), a nephew of the poet. Besides being a judge, he was a reviewer and wrote a life of Keble (1869).

21. John Keble (1792–1866), author of *The Christian Year* (1827), and leading figure in the Oxford Movement. He came to Hursley in 1836, with his wife, Charlotte (née Clarke).

# 16

# Annie Besant

Annie Besant (1847–1933) was born in London, the only daughter of William Wood and Emily Roche Morris, who also had two sons, Henry and Alfred. Her father, who had trained as a medical student at Trinity College, Dublin, subsequently became a businessman. Educated privately by Ellen Marryat, an Evangelical sister of the novelist Captain Frederick Marryat, she made a disastrous marriage to a clergyman, Frank Besant, in 1867, from whom she was legally separated in 1873, having had two children, Digby and Mabel. Besant was involved for much of her life in controversial social campaigns, such as that for birth control. She worked closely with Charles Bradlaugh, who was denied his seat in Parliament because he was an atheist; together, they were prosecuted for publishing Charles Knowlton's *The Fruits of Philosophy* (1875), a birth-control manual, and she lost custody of her daughter. Organizer of the London matchgirls' strike at Bryant and May's in 1888, Besant converted to Theosophy after reading Helena Blavatsky's *The Secret Doctrine* in 1889. She became International President of the Theosophical Society in 1907. Finally, she converted to Hinduism on believing that she had been an Indian in most of her previous incarnations. The final phase of her active political life was with the Indian nationalist movement, culminating in her election as President of the Indian National Congress.

Besant's *Autobiography*, from which the following extract is taken, was published in 1893.

My earliest personal recollections are of a house and garden that we lived in when I was three and four years of age, situated in Grove Road, St. John's Wood. I can remember my mother hovering round the dinner-table to see that all was bright for the home-coming husband; my brother – two years older than myself – and I watching 'for papa'; the loving welcome, the game of romps that always preceded the dinner of the elder folks. I can remember on the 1st of October, 1851, jumping up in my little cot, and shouting out triumphantly: 'Papa! mamma! I am four years old!' and the grave demand of my brother, conscious of superior age, at dinner-time: 'May not Annie have a knife to-day, as she is four years old?'

It was a sore grievance during that same year, 1851, that I was not judged old enough to go to the Great Exhibition, and I have a faint memory of my brother consolingly bringing me home one of those folding pictured strips that are sold in the streets, on which were imaged glories that I longed only the more to see. Far-away, dusky, trivial memories, these. What a pity it is that a baby cannot notice, cannot observe, cannot remember, and so throw light on the fashion of the dawning of the external world on the human consciousness. If only we could remember how things looked when they were first imaged on the retinae; what we felt when first we became conscious of the outer world; what the feeling was as faces of father and mother grew out of the surrounding chaos and became familiar things, greeted with a smile, lost with a cry; if only memory would not become a mist when in later years we strive to throw our glances backward into the darkness of our infancy, what lessons we might learn to help our stumbling psychology, how many questions might be solved whose answers we are groping for in the West in vain.

The next scene that stands out clearly against the background of the past is that of my father's death-bed. The events which led to his death I know from my dear mother. He had never lost his fondness for the profession for which he had been trained, and having many medical friends, he would now and then accompany them on their hospital rounds, or share with them the labours of the dissecting-room. It chanced that during the dissection of the body of a person who had died of rapid consumption, my father cut his finger against the edge of the breast-bone. The cut did not heal easily, and the finger became swollen and inflamed. 'I would have that finger off, Wood, if I were you', said one of the surgeons, a day or two afterwards, on seeing the state of the wound. But the others laughed at the suggestion, and my father, at first inclined to submit to the amputation, was persuaded to 'leave Nature alone'.

About the middle of August, 1852, he got wet through, riding on the top of an omnibus, and the wetting resulted in a severe cold, which 'settled on his chest'. One of the most eminent doctors of the day, as able as he was rough in manner, was called to see him. He examined him carefully, sounded his lungs, and left the room followed by my mother. 'Well?' she asked, scarcely anxious as to the answer, save as it might worry her husband to be kept idly at home. 'You must keep up his spirits', was the thoughtless answer. 'He is in a galloping consumption; you will not have him with you six weeks longer.' The wife staggered back, and fell like a stone on the floor. But love triumphed over agony, and half an hour later she was again at her husband's side, never to leave it again for ten minutes at a time, night or day, till he was lying with closed eyes asleep in death.

I was lifted on to the bed to 'say good-bye to dear papa' on the day before his death, and I remember being frightened at his eyes which looked so large, and his voice which sounded so strange, as he made me promise always to be 'a very good girl to darling mamma, as papa was going right away'. I remember insisting that 'papa should kiss Cherry', a doll given me on my birthday, three days before, by his direction, and being removed, crying and struggling, from the room. He died on the following day, October 5th, and I do not think that my elder brother and I – who were staying at our maternal grandfather's – went to the house again until the day of the funeral. With the death, my mother broke down, and when all was over they carried her senseless from the room. I remember hearing afterwards how, when she recovered her senses, she passionately insisted on being left alone, and locked herself into her room for the night; and how on the following morning her mother, at last persuading her to open the door, started back at the face she saw with the cry: 'Good God, Emily! Your hair is white!' It was even so; her hair, black, glossy and abundant, which, contrasting with her large grey eyes, had made her face so strangely attractive, had turned grey in that night of agony, and to me my mother's face is ever framed in exquisite silver bands of hair as white as the driven unsullied snow.

I have heard that the love between my father and mother was a very beautiful thing, and it most certainly stamped her character for life. He was keenly intellectual and splendidly educated; a mathematician and a good classical scholar, thoroughly master of French, German, Italian, Spanish and Portuguese, with a smattering of Hebrew and Gaelic, the treasures of ancient and modern literature were his daily household delight. Nothing pleased him so well as to sit with his wife, reading aloud to her while she worked; now translating from some foreign poet, now rolling forth melodiously the exquisite cadences of *Queen Mab*. Student of philosophy as he was, he was deeply and steadily sceptical; and a very religious relative has told me that he often drove her from the room by his light, playful mockery of the tenets of the Christian faith. His mother and sister were strict Roman Catholics, and near the end forced a priest into his room, but the priest was promptly ejected by the wrath of the dying man, and by the almost fierce resolve of the wife that no messenger of the creed he detested should trouble her darling at the last.

Deeply read in philosophy, he had outgrown the orthodox beliefs of his day, and his wife, who loved him too much to criticise, was wont to reconcile her own piety and his scepticism by holding that 'women ought to be religious', while men had a right to read everything and think as they would, provided that they were upright and honourable in their lives. But the result of his liberal and unorthodox thought was to insensibly modify and partially rationalise her own beliefs, and she put on one side as errors the doctrines of eternal punishment, the vicarious atonement, the infallibility of the Bible, the equality of the Son with the Father in the Trinity, and other orthodox beliefs, and rejoiced in her later years in the writings of such men as Jowett, Colenso, and Stanley ...[1]

To me, who took my religion in strenuous fashion, this dainty and well-bred piety seemed perilously like Laodicean lukewarmness, while my headlong vigour of conviction and practice often jarred on her as alien from the delicate balance and absence of extremes that should characterise the gentlewoman. She was of the old *regime*; I of the stuff from which fanatics are made: and I have often thought, in looking back, that she must have had on her lips many a time unspoken a phrase that dropped from them when she lay a-dying: 'My little one, you have never made me sad or sorry except for your own sake; you have always been too religious.' And then she murmured to herself: 'Yes, it has been darling Annie's only fault; she has always been too religious.' Methinks that, as the world judges, the dying voice spake truly, and the dying eyes saw with a real insight. For though I was then kneeling beside her bed, heretic and outcast, the heart of me was religious in its very fervour of repudiation of a religion, and in its rebellious uprising against dogmas that crushed the reason and did not satisfy the soul. I went out into the darkness alone, not because religion was too good for me, but because it was not good enough; it was too meagre, too commonplace, too little exacting, too bound up with earthly interests, too calculating in its accommodations to social conventionalities. The Roman Catholic Church, had it captured me, as it nearly did, would have sent me on some mission of danger and sacrifice and utilised me as a martyr; the Church established by law transformed me into an unbeliever and an antagonist.

For as a child I was mystical and imaginative, religious to the very finger-tips, and with a certain faculty for seeing visions and dreaming dreams ... To me in my childhood, elves and fairies of all sorts were very real things, and my dolls were as really children as I was myself a child. Punch and Judy were living entities, and the tragedy in which they bore part cost me many an agony of tears; to this day I can remember running away when I heard the squawk of the coming Punch, and burying my head in the pillows that I might shut out the sound of the blows and the cry of the ill-used baby. All the objects about me were to me alive, the flowers that I kissed as much as the kitten I petted, and I used to have a splendid time 'making believe' and living out all sorts of lovely stories among my treasured and so-called inanimate playthings. But there was a more serious side to this dreamful fancy when it joined hands with religion.

And now began my mother's time of struggle and of anxiety. Hitherto, since her marriage, she had known no money troubles, for her husband was earning a good income; he was apparently vigorous and well: no thought of anxiety clouded their future. When he died, he believed that he left his wife and children safe, at least, from pecuniary distress. It was not so. I know nothing of the details, but the outcome of all was that nothing was left for the widow and children, save a trifle of ready money. The resolve to which my mother came was characteristic. Two of her husband's relatives, Western and Sir William Wood, offered to educate her son at a good city school, and to start him in commercial life, using their great city influence to push him forward. But the young lad's father and mother had talked of a different future for their eldest boy; he was to go to a public school, and then to the University, and was to enter one of the 'learned professions' – to take orders, the mother wished; to go to the Bar, the father hoped. On his death-bed there was nothing more earnestly urged by my father than that Harry should receive the best possible education, and the widow was resolute to fulfil that last wish. In her eyes, a city school was not 'the best possible education', and the Irish pride rebelled against the idea of her son not being 'a University man'. Many were the lectures poured out on the young widow's head about her 'foolish pride', especially by the female members of the Wood family; and her persistence in her own way caused a considerable alienation between herself and them. But Western and William, though half-disapproving, remained her friends, and lent many a helping hand to her in her first difficult struggles. After much cogitation, she resolved that the boy should be educated at Harrow, where the fees are comparatively low to lads living in the town, and that he should go thence to Cambridge or to Oxford, as his tastes should direct. A bold scheme for a penniless widow, but carried out to the letter; for never dwelt in a delicate body a more resolute mind and will than that of my dear mother ...

After about a year my mother found a house which she thought would suit her scheme, namely, to obtain permission from Dr. Vaughan,[2] the then head-master of Harrow, to take some boys into her house, and so gain means of education for her own son ... Into this house we moved on my eighth birthday, and for eleven years it was 'home' to me, left always with regret, returned to always with joy.

Almost immediately afterwards I left my mother for the first time; for one day, visiting a family who lived close by, I found a stranger sitting in the drawing-room, a lame lady with a strong face, which softened marvellously as she smiled at the child who came dancing in; she called me to her presently, and took me on her lap and talked to me, and on the following day our friend came to see my mother, to ask if she would let me go away and be educated with this lady's niece, coming home for the holidays regularly, but leaving my education in her hands. At first my mother would not hear of it, for she and I scarcely ever left each other; my love for her was idolatry, hers for me a devotion ... But it was urged upon her that the advantages of education offered were such as no money could purchase for me; that it would be a disadvantage for me to grow up in a houseful of boys – and, in truth, I was as good a cricketer and climber as the best of them – that my mother would soon be obliged to send me to school, unless she accepted an offer which gave me every advantage of school without its disadvantages. At last she yielded, and it was decided that Miss Marryat, on returning home, should take me with her.

Miss Marryat – the favourite sister of Captain Marryat, the famous novelist – was a maiden lady of large means. She had nursed her brother through the illness that ended in his death, and had been living with her mother at Wimbledon Park. On her mother's death she looked round for work which would make her useful in the world, and finding that one of her brothers had a large family of girls, she offered to take charge of one of them, and to educate her thoroughly. Chancing to come to Harrow, my good fortune threw me in her way, and she took a fancy to me and thought she would like to teach two little girls rather than one. Hence her offer to my mother.

Miss Marryat had a perfect genius for teaching, and took in it the greatest delight. From time to time she added another child to our party, sometimes a boy, sometimes a girl. At first, with Amy Marryat and myself, there was a little boy, Walter Powys, son of a clergyman with a large family, and him she trained for some years, and then sent him on to school admirably prepared. She chose 'her children' – as she loved to call us – in very definite fashion. Each must be gently born and gently trained, but in such position that the education freely given should be a relief and aid to a slender parental purse. It was her delight to seek out and aid those on whom poverty presses most heavily, when the need for education for the children weighs on the proud and the poor. 'Auntie' we all called her, for she thought 'Miss Marryat' seemed too cold and stiff. She taught us everything herself except music, and for this she had a master, practising us in composition, in recitation, in reading aloud English and French, and later, German, devoting herself to training us in the soundest, most thorough fashion. No words of mine can tell how much I owe her, not only of knowledge, but of that love of knowledge which has remained with me ever since as a constant spur to study.

Her method of teaching may be of interest to some, who desire to train children with least pain, and the most enjoyment to the little ones themselves. First, we never used a spelling-book – that torment of the small child – nor an English grammar. But we wrote letters, telling of the things we had seen in our walks, or told again some story we had read; these childish compositions she would read over with us, correcting all faults of spelling, of grammar, of style, of cadence; a clumsy sentence would be read aloud, that we might hear how unmusical it sounded, an error in observation or expression pointed out. Then, as the letters recorded what we had seen the day before, the faculty of observation was drawn out and trained. 'Oh, dear! I have nothing to say!' would come from a small child, hanging over a slate. 'Did you not go out for a walk yesterday?' Auntie would question. 'Yes,' would be sighed out; 'but there's nothing to say about it.' 'Nothing to say! And you walked in the lanes for an hour and saw nothing, little No-eyes? You must use your eyes better to-day.' Then there was a very favourite 'lesson', which proved an excellent way of teaching spelling. We used to write out lists of all the words we could think of which sounded the same but were differently spelt. Thus: 'key, quay', 'knight, night', and so on, and great was the glory of the child who found the largest number. Our French lessons – as the German later – included reading from the very first. On the day on which we began German we began reading Schiller's *Wilhelm Tell*, and the verbs given to us to copy out were those that had occurred in the reading. We learned much by heart, but always things that in themselves were worthy to be learned. We were never given the dry questions and answers which lazy teachers so much affect. We were taught history by one reading aloud while the others worked – the boys as well as the girls learning the use of the needle. 'It's like a girl to sew', said a little fellow, indignantly, one day. 'It is like a baby to have to run after a girl if you want a button sewn on,' quoth Auntie. Geography was learned by painting skeleton maps – an exercise much delighted in by small fingers – and by putting together puzzle maps, in which countries in the map of a continent, or counties in the map of a country, were always cut out in their proper shapes. I liked big empires in those days; there was a solid satisfaction in putting down Russia, and seeing what a large part of the map was filled up thereby.

The only grammar that we ever learned as grammar was the Latin, and that not until composition had made us familiar with the use of the rules therein given. Auntie had a great horror of children learning by rote things they did not understand, and then fancying they knew them. 'What do you mean by that expression, Annie?' she would ask me. After feeble attempts to explain, I would answer: 'Indeed, Auntie, I know in my own head, but I can't explain.' 'Then, indeed, Annie, you do not know in your own head, or you could explain, so that I might know in my own head.' And so a healthy habit was fostered of clearness of thought and expression. The Latin grammar was used because it was more perfect than the modern grammars, and served as a solid foundation for modern languages ...

How or when I learned to read, I do not know, for I cannot remember the time when a book was not a delight. At five years of age I must have read easily, for I remember being often unswathed from a delightful curtain, in which I used to roll myself with a book, and told to 'go and play', while I was still a five-years'-old dot. And I had a habit of losing myself so completely in the book that my name might be called in the room where I was, and I never hear it, so that I used to be blamed for wilfully hiding myself, when I had simply been away in fairyland, or lying trembling beneath some friendly cabbage-leaf as a giant went by.

I was between seven and eight years of age when I first came across some children's allegories of a religious kind, and a very little later came across *Pilgrim's Progress*, and Milton's *Paradise Lost*. Thenceforth my busy fancies carried me ever into the fascinating world where boy-soldiers kept some outpost for their absent Prince, bearing a shield with his sign of a red cross on it; where devils shaped as dragons came swooping down on the pilgrim, but were driven away defeated after hard struggle; where angels came and talked with little children, and gave them some talisman which warned them of coming danger, and lost its light if they were leaving the right path. What a dull, tiresome world it was that I had to live in, I used to think to myself, when I was told to be a good child, and not to lose my temper, and to be tidy, and not mess my pinafore at dinner. How much easier to be a Christian if one could have a red-cross shield and a white banner, and have a real devil to fight with, and a beautiful Divine Prince to smile at you when the battle was over. How much more exciting to struggle with a winged and clawed dragon that you knew meant mischief, than to look after your temper, that you never remembered you ought to keep until you had lost it. If I had been Eve in the garden, that old serpent would never have got the better of me; but how was a little girl to know that she might not pick out the rosiest, prettiest apple from a tree that had no serpent to show it was a forbidden one? And as I grew older the dreams and fancies grew less fantastic, but more tinged with real enthusiasm. I read tales of the early Christian martyrs, and passionately regretted I was born so late when no suffering for religion was practicable; I would spend many an hour in daydreams, in which I stood before Roman judges, before Dominican Inquisitors, was flung to lions, tortured on the rack, burned at the stake; one day I saw myself preaching some great new faith to a vast crowd of people, and they listened and were converted, and I became a great religious leader. But always, with a shock, I was brought back to earth, where there were no heroic deeds to do, no lions to face, no judges to defy, but only some dull duty to be performed. And I used to fret that I was born so late, when all the grand things had been done, and when there was no chance of preaching and suffering for a new religion.

From the age of eight my education accented the religious side of my character. Under Miss Marryat's training my religious feeling received a strongly Evangelical bent, but it was a subject of some distress to me that I could never look back to an hour of 'conversion'; when others gave their experiences, and spoke of the sudden change they had felt, I used to be sadly conscious that no such change had occurred in me, and I felt that my dreamy longings were very poor things compared with the vigorous 'sense of sin' spoken of by the preachers, and used dolefully to wonder if I were 'saved'. Then I had an uneasy sense that I was often praised for my piety when emulation and vanity were more to the front than religion; as when I learned by heart the Epistle of James, far more to distinguish myself for my good memory than from any love of the text itself; the sonorous cadences of many parts of the Old and New Testaments pleased my ear, and I took a dreamy pleasure in repeating them aloud, just as I would recite for my own amusement hundreds of lines of Milton's *Paradise Lost*, as I sat swinging on some branch of a tree, lying back often on some swaying bough and gazing into the unfathomable blue of the sky, till I lost myself in an ecstasy of sound and colour, half chanting the melodious sentences and peopling all the blue with misty forms. This facility of learning by heart, and the habit of dreamy recitation, made me very familiar with the Bible and very apt with its phrases. This stood me in good stead at the prayer-meetings dear to the Evangelical, in which we all took part; in turn we were called on to pray aloud – a terrible ordeal to me, for I was painfully shy when attention was called to me; I used to suffer agonies while I waited for the dreaded words, 'Now, Annie, dear, will you speak to our Lord.'

But when my trembling lips had forced themselves into speech, all the nervousness used to vanish and I was swept away by an enthusiasm that readily clothed itself in balanced sentences, and alack! at the end, I too often hoped that God and Auntie had noticed that I prayed very nicely – a vanity certainly not intended to be fostered by the pious exercise. On the whole, the somewhat Calvinistic teaching tended, I think, to make me a little morbid, especially as I always fretted silently after my mother. I remember she was surprised on one of my home-comings, when Miss Marryat noted 'cheerfulness' as a want in my character, for at home I was ever the blithest of children, despite my love of solitude; but away, there was always an aching for home, and the stern religion cast somewhat of a shadow over me, though, strangely enough, hell never came into my dreamings except in the interesting shape it took in *Paradise Lost*. After reading that, the devil was to me no horned and hoofed horror, but the beautiful shadowed archangel, and I always hoped that Jesus, my ideal Prince, would save him in the end. The things that really frightened me were vague, misty presences that I felt were near, but could not see; they were so real that I knew just where they were in the room, and the peculiar terror they excited lay largely in the feeling that I was just going to see them. If by chance I came across a ghost story it haunted me for months, for I saw whatever unpleasant spectre was described; and there was one horrid old woman in a tale by Sir Walter Scott, who glided up to the foot of your bed and sprang on it in some eerie fashion and glared at you, and who made my going to bed a terror to me for many weeks. I can still recall the feeling so vividly that it almost frightens me now!

In the spring of 1861 Miss Marryat announced her intention of going abroad, and asked my dear mother to let me accompany her. A little nephew whom she had adopted was suffering from cataract, and she desired to place him under the care of the famous Dusseldorf oculist. Amy Marryat had been recalled home soon after the death of her mother, who had died in giving birth to the child adopted by Miss Marryat, and named at her desire after her favourite brother Frederick (Captain Marryat). Her place had been taken by a girl a few months older than myself, Emma Mann, one of the daughters of a clergyman, who had married Miss Stanley, closely related, indeed, if I remember rightly, a sister of the Miss Mary Stanley who did such noble work in nursing in the Crimea.[3]

For some months we had been diligently studying German, for Miss Marryat thought it wise that we should know a language fairly well before we visited the country of which it was the native tongue. We had been trained also to talk French daily during dinner, so we were not quite 'helpless foreigners' when we steamed away from St. Catherine's Docks, and found ourselves on the following day in Antwerp, amid what seemed to us a very Babel of conflicting tongues. Alas for our carefully spoken French, articulated laboriously! We were lost in that swirl of disputing luggage-porters, and could not understand a word! But Miss Marryat was quite equal to the occasion, being by no means new to travelling, and her French stood the test triumphantly, and steered us safely to a hotel. On the morrow we started again through Aix-la-Chapelle to Bonn, the town which lies on the borders of the exquisite scenery of which the Siebengebirge and Rolandsdeck serve as the magic portal. Our experiences in Bonn were not wholly satisfactory. Dear Auntie was a maiden lady, looking on all young men as wolves to be kept far from her growing lambs. Bonn was a university town, and there was a mania just then prevailing there for all things English. Emma was a plump, rosy, fair-haired typical English maiden, full of frolic and harmless fun; I a very slight, pale, black-haired girl, alternating between wild fun and extreme pensiveness. In the boarding-house to which we went at first – the 'Chateau du Rhin', a beautiful place overhanging the broad, blue Rhine – there chanced to be staying the two sons of the late Duke of Hamilton, the Marquis of Douglas and Lord Charles, with their tutor.[4] They had the whole drawing-room floor: we a sitting-room on the ground floor and bedrooms above. The lads discovered that Miss Marryat did not like her 'children' to be on speaking terms with any of the 'male sect'. Here was a fine source of amusement. They would make their horses caracole on the gravel in front of our window; they would be just starting for their ride as we went for a walk or drive, and would salute us with doffed hat and low bow; they would waylay us on our way downstairs with demure 'Good morning'; they would go to church and post themselves so that they could survey our pew, and Lord Charles – who possessed the power of moving at will the whole skin of the scalp – would wriggle his hair up and down till we were choking with laughter, to our own imminent risk. After a month of this Auntie was literally driven out of the pretty chateau, and took refuge in a girls' school, much to our disgust; but still she was not allowed to be at rest. Mischievous students would pursue us wherever we went; sentimental Germans, with gashed cheeks, would whisper complimentary phrases as we passed; mere boyish nonsense of most harmless kind, but the rather stern English lady thought it 'not proper', and after three months of Bonn we were sent home for the holidays, somewhat in disgrace. But we had some lovely excursions during those months; such clambering up mountains, such rows on the swift-flowing Rhine, such wanderings in exquisite valleys. I have a long picture-gallery to retire into when I want to think of something fair, in recalling the moon as it silvered the Rhine at the foot of Drachenfels, or the soft, mist-veiled island where dwelt the lady who is consecrated for ever by Roland's love.[5]

A couple of months later we rejoined Miss Marryat in Paris, where we spent seven happy, workful months. On Wednesdays and Saturdays we were free from lessons, and many a long afternoon was passed in the galleries of the Louvre, till we became familiar with the masterpieces of art gathered there from all lands ... In the spring of 1862 it chanced that the Bishop of Ohio visited Paris, and Mr. Forbes, then English chaplain at the Church of the Rue d'Aguesseau, arranged to have a confirmation. As said above, I was under deep 'religious impressions', and, in fact, with the exception of that little aberration in Germany, I was decidedly a pious girl. I looked on theatres (never having been to one) as traps set by Satan for the destruction of foolish souls; I was determined never to go to a ball, and was prepared to 'suffer for conscience' sake' – little prig that I was – if I was desired to go to one. I was consequently quite prepared to take upon myself the vows made in my name at my baptism, and to renounce the world, the flesh, and the devil, with a heartiness and sincerity only equalled by my profound ignorance of the things I so readily resigned. That confirmation was to me a very solemn matter; the careful preparation, the prolonged prayers, the wondering awe as to the 'seven-fold gifts of the Spirit', which were to be given by 'the laying on of hands', all tended to excitement. I could scarcely control myself as I knelt at the altar rails, and felt as though the gentle touch of the aged bishop, which fluttered for an instant on my bowed head, were the very touch of the wing of that 'Holy Spirit, heavenly Dove', whose presence had been so earnestly invoked. Is there anything easier, I wonder, than to make a young and sensitive girl 'intensely religious'?

This stay in Paris roused into activity an aspect of my religious nature that had hitherto been latent. I discovered the sensuous enjoyment that lay in introducing colour and fragrance into religious services, so that the gratification of the aesthetic emotions became dignified with the garb of piety. The picture-galleries of the Louvre, crowded with Madonnas and saints, the Roman Catholic churches with their incense-laden air and exquisite music, brought a new joy into my life, a more vivid colour to my dreams. Insensibly, the colder, cruder Evangelicalism that I had never thoroughly assimilated, grew warmer and more brilliant, and the ideal Divine Prince of my childhood took on the more pathetic lineaments of the Man of Sorrows, the deeper attractiveness of the suffering Saviour of Men. Keble's *Christian Year* took the place of *Paradise Lost*, and as my girlhood began to bud towards womanhood, all its deeper currents set in the direction of religious devotion. My mother did not allow me to read love stories, and my daydreams of the future were scarcely touched by any of the ordinary hopes and fears of a girl lifting her eyes towards the world she is shortly to enter. They were filled with broodings over the days when girl-martyrs were blessed with visions of the King of Martyrs, when sweet St. Agnes saw her celestial Bridegroom, and angels stooped to whisper melodies in St. Cecilia's raptured ear. 'Why then and not now?' my heart would question, and I would lose myself in these fancies, never happier than when alone.

The summer of 1862 was spent with Miss Marryat at Sidmouth, and, wise woman that she was, she now carefully directed our studies with a view to our coming enfranchisement from the 'schoolroom'. More and more were we trained to work alone; our leading-strings were slackened, so that we never felt them save when we blundered; and I remember that when I once complained, in loving fashion, that she was 'teaching me so little', she told me that I was getting old enough to be trusted to work by myself, and that I must not expect to 'have Auntie for a crutch all through life'. And I venture to say that this gentle withdrawal of constant supervision and teaching was one of the wisest and kindest things that this noble-hearted woman ever did for us. It is the usual custom to keep girls in the schoolroom until they 'come out'; then, suddenly, they are left to their own devices, and bewildered by their unaccustomed freedom, they waste time that might be priceless for their intellectual growth. Lately, the opening of universities to women has removed this danger for the more ambitious; but at the time of which I am writing no one dreamed of the changes soon to be made in the direction of the 'higher education of women'.

During the winter of 1862–63 Miss Marryat was in London, and for a few months I remained there with her, attending the admirable French classes of M. Roche. In the spring I returned home to Harrow, going up each week to the classes; and when these were over, Auntie told me that she thought all she could usefully do was done, and that it was time that I should try my wings alone. So well, however, had she succeeded in her aims, that my emancipation from the schoolroom was but the starting-point of more eager study, though now the study turned into the lines of thought towards which my personal tendencies most attracted me. German I continued to read with a master, and music, under the marvellously able teaching of Mr. John Farmer, musical director of Harrow School, took up much of my time. My dear mother had a passion for music, and Beethoven and Bach were her favourite composers. There was scarcely a sonata of Beethoven's that I did not learn, scarcely a fugue of Bach's that I did not master. Mendelssohn's *Lieder* gave a lighter recreation, and many a happy evening did we spend, my mother and I, over the stately strains of the blind Titan, and the sweet melodies of the German wordless orator. Musical 'At Homes', too, were favourite amusements at Harrow, and at these my facile fingers made me a welcome guest.

Thus set free from the schoolroom at 16 ½, an only daughter, I could do with my time as I would, save for the couple of hours a day given to music, for the satisfaction of my mother. From then till I became engaged, just before I was 19, my life flowed on smoothly, one current visible to all and dancing in the sunlight, the other running underground, but full and deep and strong ... So guarded and shielded had been my childhood and youth from every touch of pain and anxiety that love could bear for me, that I never dreamed that life might be a heavy burden, save as I saw it in the poor I was sent to help; all the joy of those happy years I took, not ungratefully I hope, but certainly with as glad unconsciousness of anything rare in it as I took the sunlight. Passionate love, indeed, I gave to my darling, but I never knew all I owed her till I passed out of her tender guardianship, till I left my mother's home. Is such training wise? I am not sure. It makes the ordinary roughnesses of life come with so stunning a shock, when one goes out into the world, that one is apt to question whether some earlier initiation into life's sterner mysteries would not be wiser for the young. Yet it is a fair thing to have that joyous youth to look back upon, and at least it is a treasury of memory that no thief can steal in the struggles of later life. 'Sunshine' they called me in those bright days of merry play and earnest study. But that study showed the bent of my thought and linked itself to the hidden life; for the Fathers of the early Christian Church now became my chief companions, and I pored over the Shepherd of Hermas, the Epistles of Polycarp, Barnabas, Ignatus, and Clement, the commentaries of Chrysostom,[6] the confessions of Augustine. With these I studied the writings of Pusey, Liddon, and Keble,[7] with many another smaller light, joying in the great conception of a Catholic Church, lasting through the centuries, built on the foundations of apostles and of martyrs, stretching from the days of Christ Himself down to our own – 'One Lord, one Faith, one Baptism', and I myself a child of that Holy Church. The hidden life grew stronger, constantly fed by these streams of study; weekly communion became the centre round which my devotional life revolved, with its ecstatic meditation, its growing intensity of conscious contact with the Divine; I fasted, according to the ordinances of the Church; occasionally flagellated myself to see if I could bear physical pain, should I be fortunate enough ever to tread the pathway trodden by the saints; and ever the Christ was the figure round which clustered all my hopes and longings, till I often felt that the very passion of my devotion would draw Him down from His throne in heaven, present visibly in form as I felt Him invisibly in spirit. To serve Him through His Church became more and more a definite ideal in my life, and my thoughts began to turn towards some kind of 'religious life', in which I might prove my love by sacrifice and turn my passionate gratitude into active service.

*Source*: Annie Besant, *An Autobiography* (London: T. Fisher Unwin, 1893).

**Notes**

1. John William Colenso (1814–83), Anglican Bishop of Natal, who doubted the historical accuracy of the Pentateuch. Arthur Penrhyn Stanley (1815–81), Dean of Westminster, and Broad Churchman, defended Colenso, although he disagreed with his views. Benjamin Jowett (1817–1893), Master of Balliol (1870), had been accused of heresy for his contributions to *Essays and Reviews* in 1860.
2. Charles John Vaughan (1816–97), Headmaster of Harrow from 1844 to 1859, whose reforms did much to revitalize the school.
3. Mary Stanley (1813–79), sister of the Dean of Westminster, A.P. Stanley, had visited Scutari and the Crimea in 1861. Her 'Ten Days in the Crimea', introduced by her brother, appeared in *Macmillan's Magazine* in February 1862.
4. William (1845–95), 12th Duke of Hamilton, and his brother Charles (1847–86), sons of William Alexander (1811–63), 11th Duke.
5. Roland's love was Aude, sister of Olivier in the *Chanson de Roland*. She dies of grief at the feet of Charlemagne when she hears that Roland has died in battle against the Saracens.
6. The writers she lists were all early Church Fathers, whose epistles provide information about the Church in the second century. *The Shepherd of Hermas* is a piece of writing which records five visions, in the last of which the Angel of Repentance appears dressed as a shepherd.

7. Edward Pusey (1800–1882), leading figure of the Oxford Movement; Henry Parry Liddon (1829–90), last great popular exponent of traditional Anglican orthodoxy. He nearly completed a Life of Pusey before his death; and John Keble (1792–1866), another leading Tractarian and poet, author of *The Christian Year* (1827). He was also a close neighbour and friend of Charlotte M. Yonge.

# Index